MW01702165

UNITED ARAB EMIRATES
2007

This project is undertaken with support and assistance from the Ministry of Presidential Affairs, United Arab Emirates, and the National Media Council. It is a multimedia publishing programme involving publication of the *UAE Yearbook* in English, French and Arabic printed and electronic editions; management of UAEINTERACT (www.uaeinteract.com), which contains news updates linked to pages of the *Yearbook;* publication of *UAE at a Glance,* which summarises main data on the UAE; and production of a DVD containing films and e-books on the UAE.
The publishers wish to acknowledge and thank the Ministry of Presidential Affairs and the National Media Council for their valuable encouragement and support for this multifaceted project.

Editors:
Ibrahim Al Abed
Paula Vine
Peter Hellyer

Additional Contributors:
Simon Aspinall
Peter Vine
Daniel Potts

English edition design and typesetting: Jane Stark and James Kelly, Trident Press

Published by Trident Press Ltd
175 Piccadilly, Mayfair, London WIJ 9TB
Tel: 020 7491 8770; Fax: 020 7491 8664
E-mail: admin@tridentpress.com
Website: www.tridentpress.com
British Library Cataloguing in Publication Data:
A CIP catalogue record for this book is available from the British Library.

For further information please contact:
National Media Council,
Department of External Information,
Abu Dhabi,
United Arab Emirates.
Tel: 00971 2 4452 922
Fax: 00971 2 4450 458
Email: admin@extinfo.gov.ae or info@extinfo.gov.ae

ISBN 1-905486-14-6 (hardback); 1-905486-15-4 (paperback)

CONTENTS

FOREWORD

THE DYNAMICS OF CHANGE IN THE UAE are such that it is sometimes difficult to stand back from the day-to-day tasks of government to gain a more objective perspective of our progress. The UAE has been blessed by the far-sighted vision of its leaders; first by the late Sheikh Zayed bin Sultan Al Nahyan and Sheikh Rashid bin Said Al Maktoum as President and Vice-President; and also by Sheikh Maktoum bin Rashid Al Maktoum, who succeeded his father and who sadly passed away in 2006. President HH Sheikh Khalifa bin Zayed Al Nahyan and Vice-President HH Sheikh Mohammed bin Rashid Al Maktoum both draw on the rich experience of their family upbringing and the lessons so fluently expressed by their parents.

One of the basic tenets of our culture and indeed of our faith is that we do not take anything for granted. Despite our huge oil reserves we are maximising the efficiency of our oil industry and exploring areas of alternative energy. Although we have a well-proven federal system of government, we are improving this with initiatives such as the first elections for the Federal National Council and a nationwide project to activate e-government. Despite our advanced education and healthcare systems, we are investing further in these in conjunction with the private sector. Indeed, we are promoting a massive privatisation programme in all sectors involving innovative public-private partnership schemes that place a high emphasis on community development and social cohesion. Respecting our past and the impressive endurance and achievements of our forefathers, we have established many museums and heritage centres and are building on this effort, creating some of the finest cultural institutions in the region.

The UAE *Yearbook* provides a comprehensive and valuable review of this progress, focusing in particular on the last twelve months. I hope it will inspire you to join us in our efforts to create a more healthy, peaceful and prosperous world.

Mansour bin Zayed Al Nahyan,
Minister of Presidential Affairs

PREFACE

The United Arab Emirates *Yearbook* for 2007 provides a unique summary of events that have taken place in the UAE during the past 12 months, but it is much more than just this. It is a valuable reference source on the UAE that has gained a well-earned place in many private, corporate and public libraries around the world. Whether one is interested in delving into our past, understanding our administrative model, analysing our economy, unravelling our infrastructure, investigating our social development, participating in our sporting activities, joining our nature activities or attending our exhibitions and events, there is information here that will enhance your experiences of the UAE.

The UAE Government places a high priority on development of the media and has established a National Media Council to foster improvements throughout the media. There has been considerable progress over the last few years and the latest technologies have been employed to improve on all areas of news services, from research, writing and illustration to delivery and presentation. But technology is only a tool in the hands of the dedicated people who are at the centre of news gathering services: the reporters, camera persons, sound recordists, editors, researchers, producers and directors. A great responsibility rests on their shoulders to create honest and balanced reports on current events. It is not an easy task and in certain situations it can be extremely dangerous. I take this opportunity to express my deep appreciation to those who strive to achieve the highest standards in their various fields.

The internet has had a profound impact on the UAE's media and E-media is a rapidly growing ingredient of the country's media-mix. The 2007 UAE *Yearbook* takes full advantage of IT and includes weblinks to e-pages that are updated daily on UAEInteract. I trust that these resources enable you to find all the information that you seek in your quest for knowledge on the United Arab Emirates.

Abdullah bin Zayed Al Nahyan
Chairman, National Media Council

HISTORY & TRADITIONS

'He who does not know his past cannot make the best of his present and future, for it is from the past that we learn.'

Preserving the heritage and traditions of the past is a key focus of Government policy.

HISTORY & TRADITIONS

THE UAE HAS A LONG HISTORY stretching back over 100,000 years, stone tools from the Early Stone Age having been found recently along the edge of the Hajar Mountains. Prior to this the earliest known human occupation for which there is significant evidence dated from the Neolithic period, 5500 BC or 7500 years ago, when the climate was wetter and food resources abundant. Even at this early stage, there is proof of interaction with the outside world, especially with civilisations to the north. These contacts persisted and became wide-ranging, probably motivated by trade in copper from the Hajar Mountains, as the climate became more arid and fortified oasis communities focused on agriculture.

Foreign trade, the recurring motif in the history of this strategic region, seems to have flourished also in later periods, facilitated by domestication of the camel at the end of the second millennium. At the same time, the discovery of new irrigation techniques (*falaj* irrigation) made possible the extensive watering of agricultural areas that resulted in an explosion of settlement in the region.

By the first century AD overland caravan traffic between Syria and cities in southern Iraq, followed by seaborne travel to the important port of Omana (probably present-day Umm al-Qaiwain) and thence to India was an alternative to the Red Sea route used by the Romans. Pearls had been exploited in the area for millennia but at this time the trade reached new heights. Seafaring was also a mainstay and major fairs were held at Dibba bringing merchants from as far afield as China.

The arrival of envoys from the Prophet Muhammad in 630 AD heralded the conversion of the region to Islam with Dibba again featuring, this time as a battleground in the wake of the Prophet's death. By 637 AD Islamic armies were using Julfar (Ra's al-Khaimah) as a staging post for the conquest of Iran. Over many centuries, Julfar became a wealthy port and pearling centre of considerable importance from which great wooden dhows ranged far and wide across the Indian Ocean.

The earliest known inhabitants of the UAE seem to have arrived in the Early Stone Age, over 100,000 years ago. Their stone tools have been found along the edge of the Hajar Mountains.

Many stone tools have been found in the UAE.

www.uaeinteract.com/uaehistory

IMPORTANT DATES

c.5500 BC Evidence of extensive human occupation in UAE.

5500–3000 BC Occupation by skilled groups of herders using finely made stone tools (so-called 'Arabian bifacial tradition').

3000–2500 BC Hafit period – era of earliest collective burials first noted on the lower slopes of Jebel Hafit in the interior of Abu Dhabi.

2500–2000 BC Umm al-Nar period – era of first oasis towns (e.g. at Hili, Tell Abraq, Bidiya, Kalba) dominated by large, circular fortresses; burial of the dead in round communal tombs; wide-ranging trade contact with Mesopotamia, Iran, Indus Valley, Baluchistan, Bactria (Afghanistan); first intensive use of copper resources of Hajar Mountains; area referred to as *Magan* in Mesopotamian sources.

2000–1300 BC Wadi Suq period and Late Bronze Age – an era which is characterised by fewer towns; change in burial customs to long, generally narrow collective tombs; close ties to Dilmun (Bahrain).

1300–300 BC Iron Age – introduction of new irrigation technology in the form of *falaj* (pl. *aflaj*), subterranean galleries which led water from mountain aquifers to lower-lying oases and gardens; explosion of settlement; first use of iron; first writing, using South Arabian alphabet; contacts with Assyrian and Persian empires.

300 BC–0 Mleiha period (or Late Pre-Islamic A–B) – flourishing town at Mleiha; beginnings of local coinage; far-flung imports from Greece (black-glazed pottery), South Arabia (alabaster unguent jars); first use of the horse.

0–250 AD Ed-Dur period (or late Pre-Islamic C–D) – flourishing towns at ed-Dur and Mleiha; extensive trade network along the Gulf linking up the Mediterranean, Syria and Mesopotamia with India; imports include Roman glass, coinage, brass; massive production of coinage by a ruler called Abi'el; first use of Aramaic in inscriptions from ed-Dur and Mleiha.

240 AD Rise of the Sasanian dynasty in south-western Iran, conquest of most of eastern Arabia.

6th/7th cent. AD Introduction of Christianity via contacts with south-western Iran and southern Mesopotamia; establishment of monastery on Sir Bani Yas by Nestorian Christian community; Sasanian garrisons in inner Oman and evidence for contact in the UAE shown by coins and ceramics from Kush (Ra's al-Khaimah), Umm al-Qaiwain and Fujairah.

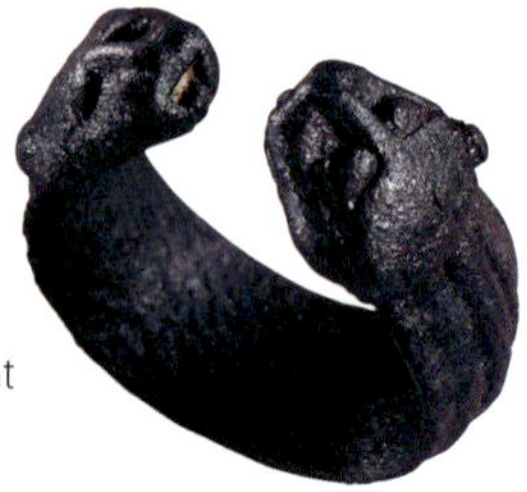

630 AD Arrival of envoys from the Prophet Muhammad; conversion of the people to Islam.

632 AD Death of the Prophet Muhammad; outbreak of the *ridda* movement, a widespread rebellion against the teachings of Islam; dispatch of Hudhayfah b. Mihsan by the Caliph Abu Bakr to quell rebellion of Laqit b. Malik Dhu at-Tag at Dibba; major battle at Dibba, collapse of the rebels.

Julfar used as staging post for Islamic invasion of Iran.	637 AD
Julfar used as staging post for Abbasid invasion of Oman.	892 AD
Buyids (Buwayhids) conquer south-eastern Arabia.	963 AD
Geographer Yaqut mentions Julfar as a fertile town.	c. 1220
Close commercial contact between Northern Emirates and kingdom of Hormuz, based on Jarun island in the Straits of Hormuz.	14th–15th cent.
Portuguese circumnavigation of Cape of Good Hope by Vasco da Gama using Arab navigational information.	1498
Portuguese–Ottoman rivalry in the Gulf.	16th cent.
Venetian traveller Gasparo Balbi's description of coast of UAE from Qatar to Ra's al-Khaimah; mention of Portuguese fortress at Kalba; first mention of Bani Yas in Abu Dhabi.	1580
Description of the East Coast of the UAE by a Dutch mariner sailing in the *Meerkat.*	1666
Growth of English trade in the Gulf; increasing Anglo–Dutch rivalry.	1720s
Sharjah and most of Musandam and the UAE East Coast, all the way to Khor Fakkan, under control of Qawasim according to Carsten Niebuhr, German surveyor working with the King of Denmark's scientific expedition.	1764
Repeated English East India Company attacks on Qawasim navy.	1800–1819
General Treaty of Peace between British Government and sheikhs of Ra's al-Khaimah, Umm al-Qaiwain, Ajman, Sharjah, Dubai and Abu Dhabi.	1820
Survey of the Gulf resulting in the publication of the first accurate charts and maps of the area.	1820–1864
Collapse of the natural pearl market; first agreements signed by rulers of Dubai, Sharjah and Abu Dhabi for oil exploration.	1930s
Oil exploration agreements finalised in Ra's al-Khaimah, Umm al-Qaiwain and Ajman.	1945–1951
First export of oil from Abu Dhabi.	1962
British Government announced its intention to withdraw from the Gulf region; discussions begin on formation of a federation of the emirates.	1968
First export of oil from Dubai.	1969
Agreement reached amongst rulers of the emirates to form a union.	10 July 1971
Formation of the State of the United Arab Emirates.	2 Dec 1971
Sheikh Zayed, 1st President of the UAE died.	2 Nov 2004
Sheikh Khalifa bin Zayed Al Nahyan elected as new President of the UAE.	3 Nov 2004

IBN MAJID

We use 32 rhumbs and we have tirfa, zam and qiyas (measurement of star attitude) but they are not able to do these things nor can they understand the things which we do although we can understand what they do and we can use their knowledge and travel in either ships. They acknowledge that we have the better knowledge of the sea and its sciences and the wisdom of the stars in the high roads of the sea. For we divide the ship in length and breadth according to the compass rose and we have measurements of star altitudes. They have no similar division or any means of dividing them from the prow of the ship to guide themselves; neither do they use star altitude measurements to guide them when they incline to the right or left.

Ibn Majid, the 'Lion of the Sea' and a legendary figure in UAE history, wrote the verse quoted opposite long before Vasco da Gama ever rounded the Cape of Good Hope or set foot in the Arabian lands from which Ibn Majid, his equally skilled father, grandfather and other forebears had been sailing and exploring throughout their working lives. The 'they' of whom he wrote were, of course, Europeans, and it is true to say that the Arabs had sailed into European waters long before the Europeans had mastered the art of crossing the Indian Ocean. Born in Julfar, close to present-day Ra's al-Khaimah, in around 1432–37, Ibn Majid came from a long line of intrepid sailors. His reputation as a navigator is based upon 40 surviving works, 39 of which are in verse. Some are brief, others, such as the 805-verse *al-Sofaliya* describing the sea route from India to Sofala on the Mozambique coast, are considerably longer. One treatise (the *Fawa'id*) is a lengthy opus that not only summarises all of Ibn Majid's own knowledge of navigation, but also draws extensively on the work of early Arab astronomers. His last-known poem was written in 1500 AD and it is believed that he died soon after, at a little over 70 years of age.

A cannon outside the walls of Umm al-Qaiwain Fort

The Portuguese arrival in the Gulf in the sixteenth century had bloody consequences for the Arab residents of Julfar and East Coast ports like Dibba, Bidiya, Khor Fakkan and Kalba. However, while European powers competed for regional supremacy, a local power, the Qawasim, were gathering strength. At the beginning of the nineteenth century they had built up a fleet of over 60 large vessel and could put nearly 20,000 sailors to sea, eventually provoking a British offensive to control the maritime trade routes between the Gulf and India.

Inland, the arc of villages at Liwa were the focus of economic and social activity for the Bani Yas from before the sixteenth century. But by the early 1790s the town of Abu Dhabi had become such an important pearling centre that the political leader of all the Bani Yas groups, the Sheikh of the Al Bu Falah (Al Nahyan family) moved there from the Liwa. Early in the nineteenth century, members of the Al Bu Falasah, a branch of the Bani Yas, settled by the Creek in Dubai and established Maktoum rule in that emirate.

Following the defeat of the Qawasim, the British signed a series of agreements with the sheikhs of the individual emirates that, later augmented with treaties on preserving a maritime truce, resulted in the area becoming known as 'The Trucial States'.

The British offensive was based on a desire to control the maritime trade routes between the Gulf and India.

The pearling industry thrived in the relative calm at sea during the nineteenth and early twentieth centuries, providing both income and employment to the people of the Arabian Gulf coast. Many of the inhabitants were semi-nomadic, pearling in the summer months and tending to their date gardens in the winter. However, their meagre economic resources were soon to be dealt a heavy blow. The First World War impacted severely on the pearl fishery, but it was the economic depression of the late 1920s and early 1930s, coupled with the Japanese invention of the cultured pearl, that damaged it irreparably. The industry eventually faded away just after the Second World War, when the newly independent Government of India imposed heavy taxation on pearls imported from the Gulf. This was catastrophic for the area. Despite their resourcefulness, the population faced considerable hardship with little opportunity for education and no roads or hospitals.

Fortunately oil was on the horizon and in the early 1930s the first oil company teams arrived to carry out preliminary surveys and the first cargo of crude was exported from Abu Dhabi in 1962. With revenues growing as oil production increased, Sheikh Zayed bin Sultan Al Nahyan, who was chosen as Ruler of Abu Dhabi on 6 August 1966, undertook a massive programme of construction of schools, housing, hospitals and roads. When Dubai's oil exports commenced in 1969, Sheikh Rashid bin Saeed Al Maktoum, *de facto* Ruler of Dubai since 1939, was also able to use oil revenues to improve the quality of life of his people.

FEDERATION

At the beginning of 1968, when the British announced their intention of withdrawing from the Arabian Gulf by the end of 1971, Sheikh Zayed acted rapidly to initiate moves towards establishing closer ties with the emirates. Along with Sheikh Rashid, who was to become Vice-President and Prime Minister of the newly formed state, Sheikh Zayed took the lead in calling for a federation that would include not only the seven emirates that together made up the Trucial States, but also Qatar and Bahrain. Following a period of negotiation however, agreement was reached between the rulers of six of the emirates (Abu Dhabi, Dubai, Sharjah, Umm al-Qaiwain, Fujairah and Ajman) and the Federation to be known as the United Arab Emirates (UAE) was formally established on 2 December 1971. The seventh emirate, Ra's al-Khaimah, formally acceded to the new Federation on 10 February 1972.

The United Arab Emirates was formally established on 2 December 1971.

ZAYED AND THE UAE

The prosperity, harmony and modern development that characterises the United Arab Emirates, led today by President HH Sheikh Khalifa bin Zayed Al Nahyan, also the Ruler of the Emirate of Abu Dhabi, and his fellow-members of the Supreme Council of Rulers of the seven emirates, is due to a very great extent to the role played by Sheikh Zayed, both prior to the formation of the Federation and in the nearly 33 years that followed until his death in November 2004. The achievements of

THE DISCOVERY OF OIL

It is now over four decades since oil production first began in the United Arab Emirates. The story of oil, however, goes back much further. In the 1930s, the consortium of what became BP, Shell, Total, ExxonMobil and Partex, operating in Iraq as the Iraq Petroleum Company, turned their eyes to the Lower Gulf. Over the next few years, several concession agreements were signed, of which the most important was that with Abu Dhabi in January 1939. To handle those in the Trucial States, as the UAE was then known, IPC established a subsidiary, Petroleum Development (Trucial Coast), PD(TC), which drilled its first well at Ra's Sadr, north-east of Abu Dhabi, in 1951. Although dry, it was, at the time, the deepest well ever drilled in the Middle East.

PD(TC) drilled several other wells before finding traces of hydrocarbons at Murban, (now known as Bab), south-east of Abu Dhabi, in 1954. With its third well on this structure completed in 1960, PD(TC) declared the field commercially viable and it went into production in 1963. The company was later renamed the Abu Dhabi Petroleum Company (ADPC).

Meanwhile, in 1953, BP had negotiated an offshore concession, assigned to a specially created subsidiary, Abu Dhabi Marine Areas Ltd (ADMA). Surveys were carried out with the assistance of the famous French underwater explorer, Jacques Cousteau. The first well was drilled on a structure called Umm Shaif in 1958, and struck oil in massive quantities. With Das Island as the export terminal, Umm Shaif went into production in 1962.

Since then, many more important fields have been identified, while the Abu Dhabi National Oil Company (ADNOC), established in 1971, has now taken controlling shares in the concessions, with ADMA being replaced as operator by the Abu Dhabi Marine Operating Company (ADMA-OPCO) and ADPC by the Abu Dhabi Company for Onshore Oil Operations (ADCO), although foreign shareholders retain a share.

Memories of the early days of exploration are now fading fast. The results of the efforts of those, both UAE nationals and expatriates, who took part, however, continue to define the economy of the United Arab Emirates today.

Sheikh Zayed believed that all of the country's citizens have a role to play in its development. Both men and women, he believed, should play their part.

Better informed about the character of the country, Sheikh Zayed was naturally more optimistic and the predictions of those early pessimists were shown to be unfounded.

During his years in Al Ain Sheikh Zayed had been able to develop a vision of how the country should progress. Once Ruler of Abu Dhabi, and then President, he had over three and a half decades to devote to making that vision a reality.

One foundation of his philosophy as a leader and statesman was that the resources of the country should be fully used to the benefit of the people. He saw them to be not as a means unto themselves, but as a tool to facilitate the development of what he believed to be the real wealth of the country – its people, and, in particular, the younger generation.

Within this framework, Sheikh Zayed believed that all of the country's citizens have a role to play in its development. Both men and women, he believed, should play their part. Recognising that in the past a lack of education and development had prevented women from playing a full role in much of the activity of society, he took action to ensure that this situation was addressed rapidly and, under his leadership, the country's women came increasingly to play their part in political and economic life.

Sheikh Zayed also believed in encouragement of initiatives designed to conserve the traditional culture of the people, in order to familiarise the younger generation with the ways of their ancestors. In his view, it was of crucial importance that the lessons and heritage of the past were remembered.

He who does not know his past cannot make the best of his present and future, for it is from the past that we learn. We gain experience and we take advantage of the lessons and results [of the past].

If the heritage of the people of the UAE was important to Sheikh Zayed, so too was the conservation of its natural environment. His belief in conservation derived from his own upbringing where a sustainable use of resources required man to live in harmony with nature. This led him to ensure that conservation of the environment was a key part of government policy.

As in other areas of national life, Sheikh Zayed made it clear that conservation is not simply the task of government. He believed firmly that there was also a role for the individual and for non-governmental organisations, both of citizens and expatriates, applying this belief not just to concerns such as environmental conservation, but to other areas of national life as well.

Sheikh Zayed imbibed the principles of Islam in his childhood and they remained the foundation of his beliefs and principles throughout his life. He was a firm and dedicated opponent of those who sought to pervert the message of Islam to justify harsh dogmas, intolerance and terrorism. In Sheikh Zayed's view, however, such an approach was not merely a perversion of the message but is in direct contradiction of it. Extremism, he believed, has no place in Islam. In contrast, he stressed that:

Islam is a civilising religion that gives mankind dignity. A Muslim is he who does not inflict evil upon others. Islam is the religion of tolerance and forgiveness, and not of war, of dialogue and understanding. It is Islamic social justice which has asked every Muslim to respect the other. To treat every person, no matter what his creed or race, as a special soul is a mark of Islam. It is just that point, embodied in the humanitarian tenets of Islam, that makes us so proud of it.

He recognised, however, the necessity not only of eradicating terrorism, but of tackling its fundamental causes. Besides the international campaign against the types of terrorism, there should, he believed, be a strong international alliance that worked, in parallel, to exert real and sincere efforts to bring about a just and lasting solution to the Middle East conflict.

Sheikh Zayed was also an eager advocate of tolerance, discussion and a better understanding between those of different faiths and, in particular, was an ardent advocate of dialogue between Muslims and Christians.

In the realm of the foreign policy of the state, his firmly-held belief in eschewing rhetoric in the search for solutions led the UAE to adopt an approach of seeking to find compromises, and to

Abu Dhabi's 'White Fort' was the seat of regional government and home of previous rulers of the emirate.

Sheikh Zayed recognised the necessity of not only eradicating terrorism but also of tackling its fundamental causes.

avoid, wherever possible, a resort to the use of force, whether in the Arab arena or more widely. Under his leadership, therefore, the country became an important provider of overseas aid, both for the development of infrastructure and for humanitarian relief, whether provided through civilian channels, as in the case of the reconstruction of Iraq following the defeat of the Saddam Hussein government in 2003 or, occasionally, by sending units of the UAE Armed Forces as international peacekeepers, such as to Kosovo in the late 1990s.

At the same time, the UAE, under his leadership, showed its preparedness to fight to defend justice, as was seen by its active participation in the war to liberate Kuwait from occupation in 1990–1991.

ARCHAEOLOGY REVIEW

Since the formal study of the archaeology of the UAE began, nearly 50 years ago, there has been one major query about the results from surveys and excavations that have taken place. Substantial evidence of human occupation in the past has been identified, stretching back into the Neolithic, or Late Stone Age, period, which commenced around 5500 BC, or 7500 years ago. Archaeologists have always considered it likely that ancient man was living in the Emirates long before that, but no sites had been found, and it was thought that any traces of earlier occupation must have been buried beneath the dunes, or under gravel and stones washed out by thousands of years of rainfall.

A decorated red jar from the Umm al-Nar period, found at Tell Abraq.

Over the course of the last year, however, evidence of earlier occupation, in the Palaeolithic period, going back many tens of thousands of years, has finally been found. The discoveries were made at Jebel Faiyah, a rocky outcrop in the east of Sharjah, by a team from Sharjah's Directorate of Antiquities and Germany's University of Tubingen, and were first announced at the annual Symposium on Recent Palaeontological and Archaeological Discoveries in the UAE, organised by the Zayed Centre for History and Heritage.

The site was used during several periods, with evidence of Iron Age occupation near the surface, some Bronze Age material just below that, and then artefacts from the Neolithic period at a depth of between 40 and 70 centimetres under the present surface. The joint Sharjah & Tubingen team then excavated to a total depth of over 2 metres beneath the present surface, finding around a metre of deposits below the Neolithic artefacts in which there was no evidence of occupation at all. Around 170 to 180 centimetres beneath the present surface, however, they found several flint tools that had clearly been worked by Man. Efforts to date the site properly are continuing, and further investigation is planned. But the archaeologists have assigned a provisional date in the early part of the Upper Pleistocene, which began around 125,000 years ago, and ended around 10,000 years ago, when today's era of geological time, known as the Holocene, began. Nothing more is yet known about these early inhabitants of the Emirates, but a search is now under way for further sites of the same period.

While this discovery is the most significant to have been made over the last year in terms of studying the UAE's past, there have been other important finds as well. Going back beyond the Pleistocene, to the Late Miocene period, around 6 to 8 million years ago, another site with fossil bones has been identified at Umm al-Ishtan, in the far west of the country. The bones were first discovered by animal rangers from the Environmental Agency – Abu Dhabi (EAD) who reported them to President HH Sheikh Khalifa bin Zayed Al Nahyan in late 2005. The President promptly ordered an investigation, and a team from the Abu Dhabi Islands Archaeological Survey (ADIAS) paid a visit to discover that the bones were not from camels, as the rangers had thought, but from the primitive elephant *Stegotetrabeladon syrticus*. Several bones have now been excavated and will eventually go on display in Abu Dhabi.

The presence of this ancient elephant in western Abu Dhabi was already known, but the Umm al-Ishtan site is much further inland than any other Late Miocene site, showing, yet again, that there is still much to discover about the UAE's past.

A hoard of coins from the eleventh century AD. This is one of several such hoards found in the UAE. It is on display at Al Ain Museum.

www.uaeinteract.com/archaeology

More work by ADIAS, in association with the Department of Antiquities and Tourism in Al Ain, (now part of the new Abu Dhabi Authority for Culture and Heritage, ADACH), focused on Neolithic sites near Umm az-Zamul, in the south-eastern deserts of Abu Dhabi, where around 3000 individual stone artefacts have now been collected and mapped. One interesting discovery was a possible tomb of a type not previously recorded in the Emirates.

Other work has taken place in Abu Dhabi's eastern city of Al Ain where a team from France's Centre Nationale des Recherches Scientifiques (CNRS), working in association with the Department of Antiquities and Tourism, has undertaken an eighth year of excavations at a pit-grave at Hili that dates to the late Umm al-Nar period, just over 4000 years ago. The many hundreds of skeletons that have been recovered from the grave, as well as other associated material, has provided valuable data on the diet, health and customs of the people.

The Abu Dhabi Authority for Culture and Heritage is planning a unified approach to the study of Abu Dhabi's past.

Although archaeologists have continued to devote attention to particular sites, of varying periods, a major current focus is on trying to understand the landscapes in which they are found, and assessing how these have evolved over thousands of years.

One recent study has been of the bay of Dhayah, in northern Ra's al-Khaimah, which provides a cross-section through the coast, mangroves, palm gardens, gravel fans and mountains. Results show that the area has been occupied since at least the Hafit period (around 3200–2500 BC) onwards, with sites from the Wadi Suq period in the early second millennium BC, the Iron Age and into the Late Islamic period.Further studies of landscapes and their archaeological sites will play a major part in building up a more complete picture of the UAE's history and heritage.

Finally, re-structuring of Abu Dhabi's government during late 2005 and early 2006 saw the creation of the Abu Dhabi Authority for Culture and Heritage (ADACH), which is now planning a unified approach to the study of Abu Dhabi's past, including plans for what will be the capital city's first – and long-awaited – museum. The Authority has absorbed the former Department of Antiquities and Tourism.

Before the Oil Age life in the UAE was ordered by the seasons. Falcons, salukis, camels and horses were integral elements in daily life of the Emirati people.

THE CAMEL

Uniquely adapted to the desert, the camel was the mainstay of the semi-nomadic lifestyle that was practiced by many of the UAE's inhabitants. The largest tribe in the UAE, the Bani Yas, roamed the vast sandy areas that cover almost all of the emirates of Abu Dhabi and Dubai. Other tribes, too, such as the Awamir and Manasir, shared this challenging environment for numerous generations, guarding their valuable knowledge of where to obtain water in the harsh terrain. The camel was both the reason for these lengthy excursions and the means by which they were carried out. Long periods were spent wandering great distances in search of winter grazing provided by dormant vegetation brought to life by intermittent rainfall. Once the arid summer approached, almost all the Bani Yas families, with the exception of fishing groups like the Al Rumaithat, returned to a home in one of the oasis settlements, many to tend and harvest their date gardens. Camel owners who had sufficient summer grazing close to their date palms were particularly fortunate as they could harvest whilst watering their livestock at the wells that supplied the local communities.

The camel was not just a useful mount and means of transporting possessions and goods on long treks across inhospitable terrain; it also provided food, clothing, household items and recreation, and at the end of the day was a primary source of wealth. In many cases camel milk and the products derived from it were the only protein available to *bedu* families for months on end. The camels were capable of surviving for long periods without water, but it was camels' milk that quenched the herders' thirst. Young male camels were slaughtered on special occasions to provide meat for feasts and informal camel races were held during the festivities. Camel hide was used to make bags and other useful utensils, while tents, rugs and items such as fine cloaks (*bisht*) were woven from camel hair.

THE DATE PALM

Over the centuries, *bedu* families that had spent the winter searching for grazing for their camels returned in the summer to the oasis gardens in the hollows of the dunes to harvest the date crop.

The date palm was traditionally propagated from side shoots that grow out from the base of a mature trunk. Today, tissue culture techniques are also used to propagate plants. In each case, the outer branches sprouting at ground level are trimmed every year and as the tree grows these branches are cut higher up, until eventually the trunk is formed. After three or more years, depending on the amount of available water, the date palm will flower in spring; flowers of the female tree must then be hand-pollinated with the panicles from a male tree, of which only very few are planted. Harvesting takes place during the hottest period of the year, between late June and early October, depending on the type of date tree – there are more than 50 varieties in the UAE alone.

Not so long ago, the harvested dates were essential for survival. Ripe dates were lightly boiled and compressed into a congealed substance called *tamr* that can be kept almost indefinitely because the high sugar content acts as a preservative. The dried palm fronds were plaited into containers in which the nourishing, vitamin-rich staple diet could be taken on journeys through the desert, into the mountains, or out to sea. The dates were also stacked in small storerooms with underlying drainage for collecting valuable date syrup. Palm fronds were used to build the walls and roofs of *'arish* houses and as roof matting for the more sturdy coral-block constructions. Trunks supported the roofs of mudbrick and stone castles and towers. Even boats (canoe-like *shashah*) were made from the midrib of the palm frond. The palm trunk was also hollowed out to form a mortar for crushing wheat with the tree stump shaped into a pestle.

PEARLING

Pearling has been an important economic activity in the region since ancient times, but the trade fluctuated throughout the centuries. At the end of the nineteenth century pearling was flourishing yet again, and an increasing number of able-bodied men participated in diving expeditions (*ghaus*) during four months in the summer, those of the Liwa-based subtribes of the Bani Yas migrating 'home' to tend their date gardens further inland in the winter. By the beginning of the twentieth century there were, according to one calculation, over 1200 pearling boats operating out of the area now known as the UAE, each carrying an average crew of 18 men. The pearling fleet leaving harbour must have been a wonderful sight, but this level of participation meant that during the summer more than 22,000 men were absent on the pearl banks. Long periods away from home placed enormous responsibility on the women of the family, both economically and socially.

For the men, conditions on board the pearling boats were tough and the work was arduous. The profits from a good season's harvest made it all worthwhile, but bad seasons were followed by spiralling debt. Many of the Bani Yas men formed cooperatives, all the crew jointly owning a boat and sharing the proceeds of the sale of the pearls according to an established arrangement: the biggest share to the captain (*nakhuda*), a larger share to the divers than the haulers, and some money left aside to finance preparations for the following year. Over several generations, some tribes involved in pearling became tied to particular locations, and coastal towns such as Abu Dhabi, Dubai and Ra's al-Khaimah thrived. All were badly affected by the collapse of pearl markets in the 1940s.

FALCONRY

Falconry, once an important means of supplementing the diet of the UAE's desert inhabitants, is now enjoyed as a traditional pastime. The most popular hunting birds remain the saker falcon and the peregrine falcon. These were traditionally trapped along the coast during their autumn migration, trained, used for hunting, and then released in the spring.

Once the falconers managed to capture one of the highly prized birds, they had only two to three weeks to train it before the migrating houbara bustards started to arrive. This was done by developing a strong bond of trust between a wild captured bird and its handler, a unique skill that commands the respect of falconers worldwide. Ideally, the training of the falcon was completed by the day when the first houbara arrived and the bedouin would hunt the bustards with his falcon throughout the winter months. Although houbara were the favoured quarry, falcons were also used in the past to take stone curlews and hares, and sometimes with salukis to hunt gazelle.

Today, many birds are caught abroad and imported. In fact, most falconry now takes place outside the Emirates, and the UAE is a leader in research into conservation of falcons.

INTERNET LINKS

Abu Dhabi Culture and Heritage Authority:	www.uaeinteract.com/adcha
Abu Dhabi Islands Archaeological Survey:	www.adias-uae.com/
Al Ain Museum:	www.aam.gov.ae/
Archaeology:	www.uaeinteract.com/archaeology
Arts:	www.uaeinteract.com/arts
Culture:	www.uaeinteract.com/uaeculture
Falconry:	www.uaeinteract.com/falconry
Heritage:	www.uaeinteract.com/heritage
History:	www.uaeinteract.com/uaehistory
Monuments:	www.uaeinteract.com/monuments
Museums:	www.uaeinteract.com/museums
Ramadan:	www.uaeinteract.com/ramadan
Salukis:	www.uaeinteract.com/salukis
Theatre:	www.uaeinteract.com/theatre
Traditions:	www.uaeinteract.com/tradition

GOVERNMENT

HH Sheikh Khalifa bin Zayed Al Nahyan was elected President of the United Arab Emirates on 3 November 2004, succeeding his father, the late HH Sheikh Zayed bin Sultan Al Nahyan.

HH Sheikh Mohammed bin Rashid Al Maktoum, Vice-President and Prime Minister of the UAE and Ruler of Dubai

GOVERNMENT

POLITICAL SYSTEM

SINCE THE ESTABLISHMENT OF THE FEDERATION IN 1971, the seven emirates that comprise the United Arab Emirates (UAE) have forged a distinct national identity through consolidation of their federal status and enjoy an enviable degree of political stability. The UAE's political system, a unique combination of the traditional and the modern, has underpinned this political success, enabling the country to develop a modern administrative structure while, at the same time, ensuring that the best of the traditions of the past are maintained, adapted and preserved.

During 2006 major steps forward were made in terms of enhancing public participation in Government, through the introduction of indirect elections to the country's Parliament, the Federal National Council (FNC). The changes were first announced by the country's President, HH Sheikh Khalifa bin Zayed Al Nahyan, in his statement on the occasion of National Day on 2 December 2005. Formerly, the 40 members of the FNC, drawn from each of the seven emirates on the basis of their size and population, were appointed by the rulers but under the new reforms, each ruler is now to select an electoral college whose members should be at least 100 times the number of FNC members for the emirate, (eight each for Abu Dhabi and Dubai, six each for Sharjah and Ra's al-Khaimah, and four each for Fujairah, Ajman and Umm al-Qaiwain). The members of each college will then elect half of the FNC members for their emirate, with the remaining half being appointed by the ruler.

The UAE comprises
seven emirates,
Abu Dhabi
Dubai
Sharjah
Ajman
Umm al-Qaiwain
Ra's al-Khaimah
and Fujairah.

Following the expiry of the term of office of the previous FNC early in the year, the process of introducing the changes got under way in August, with the issuing of a decree by the President that spelt out the new procedures and also established a National Electoral Committee, headed by the Minister of State for FNC Affairs, a post that had been created in a cabinet reshuffle in February.

In a lengthy interview published after the issuing of the decree, the Minister of State for FNC Affairs said that the move to introduce an indirect system of elections reflected the need to reform and to modernise the system of government. The President, he said, had noted in his December 2005 statement, that 'the founders of this nation established a viable federal system that is capable of developing and accommodating the changes of time and modern developments and changes. What we are currently going to embark upon is a national programme that meets this demand and that will be pursued within a framework of gradual transformation . . . It is a gradual process which provides opportunities for assessing the situation, stage by stage.'

The Minister also noted that the introduction of indirect elections was only the first phase of a process designed to enhance the role played by the FNC in the process of government. Other steps, he said, would include a strengthening of the legislative and legal powers of the FNC and the development of more effective and more viable channels of coordination between the FNC and the executive authorities, like the Cabinet.

'The election process is new to our people,' the Minister said, 'so we need to educate the public about the objectives and the mechanics of this national political programme. We are on the threshold of making history in grassroots political participation.'

The UAE flag was first raised on 2 December 1971.

The new process, according to the Minister, is expected to lead to the election of women and young people to FNC membership. An expansion of the number of FNC members is also expected in due course, to reflect the increase in the number of the country's citizens, now many times larger than it was when the UAE was founded in 1971. Elections for the FNC will be held on 16, 18 and 20 December 2006..

The seven member emirates of the UAE, known until 1971 as the Trucial States, which had separate treaty relationships with Britain, together form a federal state officially entitled *Dawlat al Imarat al Arabiyya al Muttahida* (State of the United Arab Emirates).

The philosophy behind the UAE was explained in a statement that was released on 2 December 1971 as the new state was formally established:

The United Arab Emirates has been established as an independent state, possessing sovereignty. It is part of the greater Arab nation. Its aim is to maintain its independence, its sovereignty, its security and its stability, in defence against any attack on its entity or on the entity of any of its member Emirates. It also seeks to protect the freedoms and rights of its people and to achieve trustworthy co-operation between the Emirates for the common good. Among its aims, in addition to the purposes above described, is to work for the sake of the progress of the country in all fields, for the sake of providing a better life for its citizens, to give assistance and support to Arab causes and interests, and to support the charter of the United Nations and international morals.

Each of the component emirates already had its own existing institutions of government prior to 1971 and, to provide for the effective governing of the new state, the rulers agreed to draw up a provisional Constitution specifying the powers that were to be allocated to new federal institutions, all others remaining the prerogative of the individual emirates.

The federal system of government includes a Supreme Council, a Cabinet, or Council of Ministers, a parliamentary body, the Federal National Council, and an independent judiciary, at the apex of which is the Federal Supreme Court.

Areas of responsibility assigned to the federal authorities, under Articles 120 and 121 of the Constitution, were foreign affairs, security and defence, nationality and immigration issues, education, public health, currency, postal, telephone and other communications services, air traffic control and licensing of aircraft, in addition to a number of other topics specifically prescribed, including labour relations, banking, delimitation of territorial waters and extradition of criminals.

The Constitution also stated in Article 116 that 'the Emirates shall exercise all powers not assigned to the Federation by this Constitution'. This was reaffirmed in Article 122, which stated that 'the Emirates shall have jurisdiction in all matters not assigned to the exclusive jurisdiction of the Federation, in accordance with the provision of the preceding two Articles'.

In May 1996, the Federal Supreme Council approved two amendments to the provisional Constitution, making it permanent and naming Abu Dhabi as the capital of the state.

The federal system of government includes a Supreme Council, a Cabinet, or Council of Ministers, a parliamentary body, the Federal

Sheikh Zayed bin Sultan Al Nahyan, first President of the UAE, 1971–2004

National Council, and an independent judiciary, at the apex of which is the Federal Supreme Court.

During their initial discussions on forming a federation, the rulers of the seven emirates agreed that each of them would be a member of a Supreme Council, the top policy-making body in the new state and that they would elect a President and a Vice-President from amongst their number, to serve for a five-year, renewable, term of office. The Ruler of Abu Dhabi, Sheikh Zayed bin Sultan Al Nahyan, was elected as the first President, a post to which he was re-elected at successive five-yearly intervals until his death in November 2004, while the Ruler of Dubai, Sheikh Rashid bin Saeed Al Maktoum, was elected as first Vice-President, a post he continued to hold until his death in 1990. Both were succeeded by their Crown Princes, who became rulers of their emirates and were elected by the members of the Federal Supreme Council to become respectively President, for the Ruler of Abu Dhabi, HH Sheikh Khalifa bin Zayed Al Nahyan, and Vice-President, for the Ruler of Dubai. Sheikh Rashid's successor as Vice-President, Sheikh Maktoum, died in early 2006, and was succeeded as ruler by his younger brother and Crown Prince, Sheikh Mohammed bin Rashid, who was then elected as the UAE's third Vice-President.

The Federal Supreme Council has both legislative and executive powers.

SUPREME COUNCIL MEMBERS

HH President Sheikh Khalifa bin Zayed Al Nahyan, Ruler of Abu Dhabi

HH Vice-President, Prime Minister Sheikh Mohammed bin Rashid Al Maktoum, Ruler of Dubai

HH Dr Sheikh Sultan bin Mohammed Al Qasimi, Ruler of Sharjah

HH Sheikh Saqr bin Mohammed Al Qasimi, Ruler of Ra's al-Khaimah

HH Sheikh Hamad bin Mohammed Al Sharqi, Ruler of Fujairah

HH Sheikh Rashid bin Ahmed Al Mu'alla, Ruler of Umm al-Qaiwain

HH Sheikh Humaid bin Rashid Al Nuaimi, Ruler of Ajman

CROWN PRINCES

General Sheikh Mohammed bin Zayed Al Nahyan, Crown Prince of Abu Dhabi and Deputy Supreme Commander of the UAE

Armed Forces, Chairman of the Executive Council of the Emirate of Abu Dhabi

Sheikh Sultan bin Mohammed Al Qasimi, Crown Prince and Deputy Ruler of Sharjah, Chairman of the Sharjah Executive Council

Sheikh Saud bin Saqr Al Qasimi, Crown Prince and Deputy Ruler of Ra's al-Khaimah

Sheikh Saud bin Rashid Al Mu'alla, Crown Prince of Umm al-Qaiwain

Sheikh Ammar bin Humaid Al Nuaimi, Crown Prince of Ajman

HH Sheikh Khalifa bin Zayed Al Nahyan, second President of the UAE

DEPUTIES OF THE RULERS

Sheikh Hamdan bin Rashid Al Maktoum, Deputy Ruler of Dubai, Minister of Finance and Industry

Sheikh Ahmed bin Sultan Al Qasimi, Deputy Ruler of Sharjah

Sheikh Sultan bin Saqr Al Qasimi, Deputy Ruler of Ra's al-Khaimah

Sheikh Hamad bin Saif Al Sharqi, Deputy Ruler of Fujairah

The Federal Supreme Council has both legislative and executive powers. It ratifies federal laws and decrees, plans general policy, approves the nomination of the Prime Minister and accepts his resignation. It also relieves him of his post on the recommendation of the President.

The Council of Ministers or Cabinet, described in the Constitution as 'the executive authority' for the Federation, includes the usual complement of ministerial portfolios and is headed by a Prime Minister, chosen by the President in consultation with his colleagues on the Supreme Council. The Prime Minister, currently the Vice-President (although this has not always been the case), then selects the ministers, who may be drawn from any of the Federation's component emirates, although, naturally, the more populous emirates have generally provided more members of each Cabinet.

The current 24-member Cabinet was formed on 11 February 2006.

The current 24-member Cabinet was appointed on 11 February 2006, according to the proposal of Vice-President HH Sheikh

Mohammed bin Rashid Al Maktoum, who had been requested to form a new Government following his accession as Ruler of Dubai and election as Vice-President the previous month. The Cabinet has three more members than the previous one, formed in November 2004, as a result of the introduction of new portfolios and the re-structuring of others.

HH Sheikh Mohammed bin Rashid Al Maktoum, Vice-President and Prime Minister of the UAE with UN Secretary General, Kofi Annan

MEMBERS OF THE CABINET

Prime Minister and Minister of Defence: Vice-President HH Sheikh Mohammed bin Rashid Al Maktoum
Deputy Prime Minister: Sheikh Sultan bin Zayed Al Nahyan
Deputy Prime Minister: Sheikh Hamdan bin Zayed Al Nahyan
Minister of Finance and Industry: Sheikh Hamdan bin Rashid Al Maktoum
Minister of Interior: Lt Gen. Sheikh Saif bin Zayed Al Nahyan
Minister of Presidential Affairs: Sheikh Mansour bin Zayed Al Nahyan
Minister of Foreign Affairs: Sheikh Abdullah bin Zayed Al Nahyan
Minister of Higher Education and Scientific Research: Sheikh Nahyan bin Mubarak Al Nahyan
Minister of Public Works: Sheikh Hamdan bin Mubarak Al Nahyan
Minister of Economy: Sheikha Lubna Al Qasimi
Minister of Justice: Mohammed Nukhaira Al Dhahiri
Minister of State for Financial and Industrial Affairs: Dr Mohammed Khalfan bin Kharbash
Minister of Energy: Mohammed bin Dha'en Al Hamili
Minister of Labour: Dr Ali bin Abdullah Al Ka'abi
Minister of Governmental Sector Development: Sultan bin Saeed Al Mansouri
Minister of State for Cabinet Affairs: Mohammed Abdullah Al Gargawi
Minister of State for Foreign Affairs: Mohammed Hussein Al Shaali
Minister of Social Affairs: Mariam Mohammed Khalfan Al Roumi
Minister of Education: Dr Hanif Hassan Ali

Minister of State for Federal National Council Affairs: Dr Anwar Mohammed Gargash
Minister of Health: Humaid Mohammed Obaid Al Qattami
Minister of Environment and Water: Dr Mohammed Saeed Al Kindi
Minister of Culture, Youth and Community Development: Abdul Rahman Mohammed Al Owais

FEDERAL NATIONAL COUNCIL

The Federal National Council (FNC) has 40 members drawn from the emirates on the basis of their population, and is currently in the process of major reforms to introduce greater public participation in the choosing of its membership, as noted above.

Day-to-day operation of the FNC is governed by standing orders based on the provisions of Article 85 of the Constitution, first issued in 1972 and subsequently amended by Federal Decree No. 97 of 1977.

The FNC plays an important role in consolidating the principles of *shura* (consultation) in the country, this being enhanced as a result of the introduction of indirect elections for half of the FNC members. Presided over by a speaker, or either of two deputy speakers, elected from amongst its members, the FNC has both a legislative and supervisory role under the Constitution. It is responsible for examining, and amending, if necessary, all proposed federal legislation, and may summon and question any federal minister regarding ministry performance.

In September 2006 the National Election Committee approved an Electoral College of 6689 members, including 1189 women.

Since its inception the Council has been successively chaired by the following Speakers:

Thani bin Abdulla
Taryam bin Omran Taryam
Hilal bin Ahmed bin Lootah
Al-Haj bin Abdullah Al Muhairbi
Mohammed Khalifa Al Habtoor
Saeed Mohammed Al Kindi (elected 2003)

The FNC is a member of the International Parliamentary Union (IPU) as well as the Arab Parliamentary Union (APU) and participates actively in these bodies.

www.uaeinteract.com/fnc

Total independence of the federal judiciary is guaranteed under the Constitution.

FEDERAL JUDICIARY

The federal judiciary, whose total independence is guaranteed under the Constitution, includes the Federal Supreme Court and Courts of First Instance. The Federal Supreme Court consists of five judges appointed by the Supreme Council of Rulers. The judges decide on the constitutionality of federal laws and arbitrate on inter-emirate disagreements and disputes between the Federal Government and the emirates.

LOCAL GOVERNMENT

Parallel to, and interlocking with, the federal institutions, each of the seven emirates also has its own local government. All have expanded significantly as a result of the country's growth over the last 35 years, though they differ in complexity from emirate to emirate, depending on factors such as population, area, and degree of development.

The largest and most populous emirate, Abu Dhabi, has its own central governing organ, the Executive Council, chaired by the Crown Prince, Sheikh Mohammed bin Zayed Al Nahyan, under which there are a number of separate departments, equivalent to ministries. A number of autonomous agencies, such as the Environmental Agency – Abu Dhabi (EAD) also exist, with clearly specified powers. The emirate is divided into two regions, the Western Region and the Eastern Region, headed by Ruler's Representatives, and there is also a Ruler's Representative on the important oil terminal island of Das. The main cities, Abu Dhabi and Al Ain, are administered by municipalities, each of which has a nominated municipal council, these coming under the Department of Municipalities and Agriculture, while a new municipal authority has been created for the Western Region.

UAE Vice-President and Prime Minister, HH Sheikh Mohammed bin Rashid Al Maktoum with HM King Abdullah of Jordan and Sheikh Mohammed bin Zayed Al Nahyan, Crown Prince of Abu Dhabi and Deputy Supreme Commander of the UAE Armed Forces

Abu Dhabi's National Consultative Council, chaired by a Speaker, and with 60 members selected from among the emirate's main tribes and families, undertakes a role similar to that of the FNC on a country-wide level.

Both Dubai and Sharjah also have an Executive Council, and Sharjah a Consultative Council, to cover the whole emirate, while Sharjah, with three enclaves on the country's East Coast, has also adopted the practice of devolving some authority on a local basis, with branches of the Sharjah Emiri Diwan (Court), headed by deputy chairmen, in both Kalba and Khor Fakkan. A similar pattern of municipalities, departments and autonomous agencies can be found in each of the other emirates.

In smaller or more remote settlements, the ruler of each emirate may choose a local representative, an emir or wali, to act as a conduit through which the concerns of inhabitants may be directed to government. In most cases, these are the leading local tribal figures, whose authority derives both from their fellow tribesmen and from the confidence placed in them by the ruler, an example of the way in which leaders within the traditional system have become involved with, and lend legitimacy to, the new structures of government.

Parallel to, and interlocking with, the federal institutions, each of the seven emirates also has its own local government.

FEDERAL AND LOCAL GOVERNMENT

The powers of the various federal institutions and their relationship with the separate local institutions have evolved and changed since the establishment of the state. Under the terms of the Constitution, rulers may relinquish certain areas of authority to the Federal Government, one significant such decision being that to unify the armed forces in the mid-1970s. The 1971 Constitution also permitted each emirate to retain, or to take up, membership in the Organisation of Petroleum Exporting Countries (OPEC) and the Organisation of Arab Petroleum Exporting Countries (OAPEC), although none have done so; the only emirate to be a member in 1971, Abu Dhabi, having chosen to relinquish its memberships in favour of the Federation.

The relationship between the federal and local systems of government continues to evolve.

In line with the development that has taken place since the foundation of the state, the organs of federal and local government have also developed, and they now affect almost all aspects of life, for both UAE citizens and expatriates.

The relationship between the federal and local systems of government continues to evolve. As the smaller emirates have benefited from significant development in terms of, for example, education, so they have been able to recruit personnel to offer local government services that had once been handled on their behalf by federal institutions. At the same time, in other areas, such as the judiciary, there has been a trend towards a further voluntary relinquishment of local authority to the federal institutions. These new systems of government have not, however, replaced the traditional forms which coexist and evolve alongside them.

TRADITIONAL GOVERNMENT

Majlises continue to play a unique role in providing efficient local government.

Traditionally, the ruler of an emirate, the sheikh, was the leader of the most powerful, though not necessarily the most populous, tribe, while each tribe, and often its sub-sections, also had a chief or sheikh. These maintained their authority only insofar as they were able to retain the support of their people, in essence a form of direct democracy. Part of that process was the unwritten but strong principle that the people should have free access to their sheikh, and that he should hold a frequent and open *majlis*, or council, in which his fellow tribesmen could voice their opinions.

Such a direct democracy, which may be ideally suited to small societies, becomes more difficult to maintain as populations grow, while the increasing sophistication of government administration means that many people now find it more appropriate to deal directly with these institutions on most matters, rather than to seek to meet personally with their ruler or sheikh.

Nevertheless, a fascinating aspect of life in the UAE today, and one that is essential to an understanding of its political system, is the way in which the institution of the *majlis* maintains its relevance. In larger emirates, not only the ruler, but also a number of other senior family members, continue to hold open majlises (or *majalis*), in which participants may raise a wide range of topics, both of personal interest and of broader concern.

In smaller emirates, the *majlis* of the ruler himself, or of the crown prince or deputy ruler, remains the main focus. The Ruler of Fujairah, for example, holds an open *majlis* at least once a week, attended by both citizens and expatriates. To these majlises come traditionally minded tribesmen who may have waited months for the opportunity to discuss with their ruler directly, rather than pursuing their requests or complaints through a modern governmental structure.

Just as the modern institutions have developed in response to public need and demand, however, so the traditional forms of tribal administration have adapted. With many routine matters now being dealt with by the modern institutions, traditional institutions, like the *majlis*, have been able to focus on more complex issues out of which a consensus approach may emerge that is then subsequently reflected in changes in government policy.

Through such means, the well-tested traditional methods of government in the United Arab Emirates have been able to retain both their essential relevance and unique vitality, and they continue to play an important role in the evolution of the state today.

A BALANCED APPROACH

When the rulers of the emirates met 35 years ago to agree on the forms of government for their new federal state, they deliberately chose not simply to copy from others but, instead, to work towards a society that would offer the best of modern administration, while retaining the traditional forms of government that, with their inherent commitment to consensus, discussion and direct democracy, offered the best features of the past.

The UAE is the only federal system in the Arab world to stand the test of time.

With the benefit of hindsight, it is evident that they made the correct choice. For, despite the massive economic growth and the social dislocation caused by an explosion in the population, the state has enjoyed political stability. During the last few decades there have been numerous attempts to create federal states, both in the Arab world and elsewhere. The UAE is the only one in the Arab world to have stood the test of time, proof of that being the smooth transition that occurred, in Government and throughout the country, following the death of the Federation's founder, Sheikh Zayed bin Sultan Al Nahyan.

SHEIKH KHALIFA BIN ZAYED AL NAHYAN

HH Sheikh Khalifa bin Zayed Al Nahyan, Ruler of Abu Dhabi, was elected as the new President of the United Arab Emirates on 3 November 2004, to succeed his father, the late HH Sheikh Zayed bin Sultan Al Nahyan, UAE President from 1971 to 2004, from whom, he has said, he learned 'the need for patience and prudence in all things'.

Since becoming UAE President, HH Sheikh Khalifa has presided over a major re-structuring of both the Federal Government and the government of the Emirate of Abu Dhabi. The appointment of a new Cabinet in February 2006, with Vice-President and Dubai Ruler HH Sheikh Mohammed bin Rashid Al Maktoum as Prime Minister, saw major changes in the portfolios with, crucially, the creation of new ministries devoted to the streamlining and modernising of the business of government, a new focus on community development and, through the new Ministry of Federal National Council (FNC) Affairs, an important step towards reform of the political process with the introduction of indirect elections for half of the FNC's membership.

In his message to the nation on the occasion of the UAE's National Day on 2 December 2005, he noted:

'We shall work to make the Council more capable, more effective and more sensitive to the issues affecting the nation and the people.'

The years ahead require a bigger role for the Federal National Council by empowering it to be an authority that would provide great support and guidance for the executive arm of the government. We shall work to make the Council more capable, more effective and more sensitive to the issues affecting the nation and the people. This would be done by ensuring a more participatory process and the entrenchment of the policy of 'Shura' consultation. And through a gradual, organised course, we have decided to start activating the role of the FNC through electing half of its members through councils for each emirate and appointing the other half. By doing this, we will embark on a march that culminates in more participation and interaction from all the citizens of the country. . . . Today, we stand at a threshold of a new era, whose ultimate objective is to entrench the rule of law and due process, accountability, transparency and equal opportunity.

Sheikh Khalifa has also undertaken extensive tours throughout the UAE to study the needs of the Northern Emirates, during which he has given instructions for the building of a number of projects related to housing, education and the social services.

Sheikh Khalifa has overseen dramatic changes too in the government of Abu Dhabi, where particular attention has been paid to two aspects – improvements in terms of efficiency and cost for services provided to the public and the opening up of

UAE President HH Sheikh Khalifa bin Zayed Al Nahyan with Egyptian President Hosni Mubarak

much of the economy so that greater scope has been provided for direct private investment and for public-private partnerships. During the early years of the Federation, he believes, it was right and appropriate for government to play the leading role, but now, with a burgeoning private sector and with a well-educated population, the time is right for government, both local and federal, to step back and to concentrate on the core areas of government responsibility.

The re-structuring of government, he believes, will only be effective if the people of the UAE take upon themselves the task of contributing effectively. 'We have already begun preparing for the new era by promulgating legislation (and) placing some regulatory measures on the existing departments, institutions, activities and relations,' he said in his December 2005 National Day message. 'This is to tighten up the loose ends, to straighten the curves, put an end to wrongdoings (and) . . . to improve production and services.' He continued:

It is high time for our political, religious, cultural, information, educational and civil society institutions to take up their responsibilities to instil in our society the values of love of work, to change the negative perceptions about vocational work. It is high time to make them understand the true meaning of work – that it

'The time is right for government, both local and federal, to step back and to concentrate on the core areas of government responsibility.'

means responsibility and reflects human, civil and religious values. These institutions also need to work hard to diversify the skills of the national human resources, to raise productivity, encourage investment in human resources development, improve voluntary work and create awareness on this noble work and its significance to individuals and society in general.

While emphasising the need for a re-structuring at home, not just in terms of government, but also in the way in which the UAE's people look upon their own duties towards society, President Sheikh Khalifa has, at the same time, continued to ensure that the country pursues an active foreign policy.

The UAE is a strong supporter of the Gulf Cooperation Council.

He is a strong supporter of the six-member Gulf Cooperation Council (GCC), believing that the success and achievements of this body reflect the depth of understanding reached amongst its leaders. That support was re-affirmed at the 2005 GCC summit conference, held in Abu Dhabi, while he has exchanged numerous visits with the leaders of other GCC states, which have provided him with the opportunity to discuss both ways in which the GCC can continue to develop and other issues of regional and wider importance.

One of the wider issues, of course, has been the continuing turmoil in Iraq, and Sheikh Khalifa has pursued a consistent policy of supporting the efforts by Iraq's elected representatives to restore peace and stability, both through offering diplomatic support and through a wide range of assistance for reconstruction of Iraq's shattered economy. At the same time, he has urged the various communities in Iraq, whether regional or religious, to recognise that their future is best guaranteed by working together and by promoting the unity of both the country and its people.

Another issue seen by Sheikh Khalifa as being of crucial importance is that of the conflict between Israel and the Palestinian people. As has been the case since the creation of the Federation in 1971, the UAE has continued to express its support for the Palestinian people, with Sheikh Khalifa demonstrating his own personal interest by funding a major housing programme, Sheikh Khalifa City, in Rafah in the Gaza Strip.

President of the UAE HH Sheikh Khalifa bin Zayed Al Nahyan with French President, Jacques Chirac

At a political level, the President noted in a speech on the occasion of the International Day of Solidarity with the Palestinian People in November 2005 that the UAE remained committed to work for the restoration of security, peace and stability in the region, saying that this, as well as economic and development cooperation between countries of the region including Israel, 'cannot be achieved while Israeli occupation of the Palestinian and Arab territories continues, but only through compliance with obligations as provided in the Road Map and the Arab peace initiative that calls for justice, ending the Israeli occupation and establishment of an independent Palestinian state with Jerusalem as its capital.'

www.uaeinteract.com/governmentaffairs

Sheikh Khalifa said: 'We have rejoiced over the Israeli military pullout from Gaza Strip and have regarded it as a first legal step which must be followed by other comprehensive and serious withdrawals from all the Palestinian and Arab territories occupied since 1967.'

President Sheikh Khalifa has demonstrated his commitment to continuing to build relations with other countries both by receiving visiting leaders, from countries in Asia and Europe, as well as from other Arab countries, and by paying visits to Central Asian states, with whom he has been an active proponent of closer ties ever since they emerged after the dissolution of the Soviet Union. He has also proved to be a generous donor of emergency assistance at times of natural disaster, responding immediately in sending help after events such as the 2004 Indian Ocean tsunami and the autumn 2005 earthquake that devastated much of northern Pakistan and neighbouring parts of India.

'We have rejoiced over the Israeli military pullout from Gaza Strip and have regarded it as a first legal step which must be followed by other comprehensive and serious withdrawals from all the Palestinian and Arab territories occupied since 1967.'

Sheikh Khalifa assumed his posts as Ruler of Abu Dhabi and President of the United Arab Emirates in 2004 after many decades working closely with his father, Sheikh Zayed bin Sultan Al Nahyan, the founder of the Federation.

Born in the inland oasis-city of Al Ain in 1948, Sheikh Khalifa was educated in the local school. On 18 September 1966, following his father's assumption of the post of Ruler of Abu Dhabi, Sheikh Khalifa was appointed as Ruler's Representative in the Eastern Region of Abu Dhabi and as Head of the Courts Department in Al Ain.

On 1 February 1969 Sheikh Khalifa was nominated as Crown Prince of Abu Dhabi, this being followed on 2 February 1969 by his appointment as the Head of the Abu Dhabi Department of Defence, in which post he oversaw the building up of the Abu Dhabi Defence Force (ADDF), which later became the nucleus of the UAE Armed Forces.

On 1 July 1971, as part of the restructuring of the government of the emirate, Sheikh Khalifa was appointed Prime Minister of Abu Dhabi and Minister of Defence and Finance. On 23 December 1973 Sheikh Khalifa assumed the post of Deputy Prime Minister in the second UAE Federal Cabinet. Shortly afterwards, when the Cabinet of Abu Dhabi Emirate was dissolved, as part of the process of strengthening the institutions of the UAE Federation, Sheikh Khalifa was appointed, on 20 January 1974, as the first Chairman of the Abu Dhabi Executive Council, which replaced the emirate's Cabinet.

Under his direction, and in accordance with the instructions of HH Sheikh Zayed, the Executive Council oversaw the realisation of a wide-ranging development programme in Abu Dhabi, including the construction of housing, water supplies and other essential services, roads and general infrastructure that led to the emergence of the city of Abu Dhabi as the modern city that it is today.

The 'Khalifa Committee' played a crucial role in helping UAE citizens.

Of particular importance in terms of ensuring that citizens were able to benefit from the country's increasing wealth was the establishment by Sheikh Khalifa in 1981 of the Abu Dhabi Department of Social Services and Commercial Buildings, charged with the provision of loans to citizens for construction.

The establishment of the Department, popularly known as the 'Khalifa Committee', followed another decision taken by Sheikh Khalifa in 1979 to alleviate the burden on citizens of the repayment of loans from the commercial banks.

A further step to ensure that citizens were able to build the properties that they needed, both for residential and for investment purposes, came with the creation by Sheikh Khalifa of the Private Loans Authority, early in 1991.

President HH Sheikh Khalifa has also been involved extensively in other areas of the country's development. In May 1976, following the unification of the armed forces of the emirates, Sheikh Khalifa was nominated as Deputy Supreme Commander of the UAE Armed Forces. In this capacity, he devoted much attention to the building up of the country's defensive capability, through the establishment of many military training institutions and through the procurement of the latest military equipment and training.

Sheikh Khalifa has held a number of other top posts in the Abu Dhabi government. Since the late 1980s, for example, he has been Chairman of the Supreme Petroleum Council, responsible for oversight of Abu Dhabi's upstream and downstream oil and gas industries, although he has also actively encouraged diversification of the country's economy away from dependence on its depletable reserves of hydrocarbons.

He is also Chairman of the Abu Dhabi Investment Council (which replaced the Abu Dhabi Investment Authority (ADIA) in mid-2006 and manages the emirate's financial reserves and investments) and Honorary Chairman of the Environment Agency – Abu Dhabi (EAD) and was until 2006 the Chairman of the Abu Dhabi Fund for Development (ADFD), which overseas the country's international development assistance programme.

He has stated that his key objectives as President of the United Arab Emirates will be to continue on the path laid down by his father, whose legacy, he says, 'will continue to be the beacon guiding us into the future, a prosperous future where security and stability will reign.'

FOREIGN AFFAIRS

FOREIGN POLICY

UAE foreign policy is based on justice, non-interference in the internal affairs of other states and on the pursuit of peaceful resolutions of disputes.

The foreign policy of the United Arab Emirates is based upon a set of guiding principles laid down by the country's first President, Sheikh Zayed bin Sultan Al Nahyan. These are based upon a belief in the need for justice in international dealings between states, including the necessity of adhering to the principle of non-interference in the internal affairs of others and the pursuit, wherever possible, of peaceful resolutions of disputes, together with a support for international institutions, such as the United Nations.

Within the Arabian Gulf region, and in the broader Arab world, the UAE has sought to enhance cooperation and to resolve disagreement through dialogue. Thus one of the central features of the country's foreign policy has been the development of closer ties with its neighbours in the Arabian Peninsula. The Arab Gulf Cooperation Council (AGCC), grouping the UAE, Kuwait, Saudi Arabia, Bahrain, Qatar and Oman, was established at a summit conference held in Abu Dhabi in May 1981, and has since become, with strong UAE support, an effective and widely respected grouping.

The annual summit meeting of the AGCC Heads of State was held in Abu Dhabi in December 2005. Called the 'Fahd Summit', after the former King of Saudi Arabia, who had died earlier in the year, the meeting, chaired by President HH Sheikh Khalifa, agreed on a number of steps to further develop collaboration between the member states and to harmonise their economic policies.

President HH Sheikh Khalifa sees the promotion of intra-GCC ties as being a fundamental element in the UAE's foreign policy. 'I strongly believe that the Gulf region is one entity and one area,' he has said. 'Unity is strength. It is my hope that we would be able to forge a greater union or federation, across the Gulf, not just in the UAE, and the success of our federation in the UAE is a cause for hope. Unity is a conviction and a belief.'

Within this framework of a belief in the unity of the Gulf, the UAE has sought through negotiation to resolve issues related to the 1974 provisional and, as yet, unratified, agreement with Saudi Arabia on the border between the two countries, which the UAE believes should be substantially amended.

The UAE continued to provide support to the new Government of Iraq in its efforts to restore stability and security to the country. During talks with Iraq's Prime Minister, Nouri Al Maliki, in July, President HH Sheikh Khalifa stressed the UAE view that all political forces and religious sects in the country should put aside their differences. 'Reason must prevail. The greater interest of Iraq should take precedence over any political differences or animosities which will yield nothing but disunity,' he said.

The UAE has long opposed the presence of nuclear weapons in the region.

With regards to the UAE's Gulf neighbour, Iran, relations have been complicated during the course of the last year because of the apparent determination by the Iranian Government to continue developing a nuclear weapons capacity. While acknowledging the right of all countries to have peaceful nuclear power programmes, the UAE has long opposed the presence of nuclear weapons in the region. There has also been concern about potential accidents, with UAE Foreign Minister Sheikh Abdullah bin Zayed Al Nahyan warning in June of the 'enormous ecological catastrophe' that would occur if there was a leak from Iran's proposed nuclear power plant at Bushehr into the waters of the Arabian Gulf.

www.uaeinteract.com/foreign_policy

The UAE provided aid to Gaza during the Israeli aggression.

The issue was raised by the Foreign Minister with Iran's leaders during a visit to Tehran in July, during which he also raised the issue of the UAE's sovereignty over the three Gulf islands of Abu Musa and Greater and Lesser Tunb, in dispute since 1971. The UAE continues to propose, as it has done for many years, that the issue of the islands should be submitted to the International Court of Justice in The Hague or to impartial arbitration, but Iran has consistently rejected this approach.

During the year, the explosion of conflict between the Palestinians and Israel and the month-long Israeli attack on Lebanon caused major concern. In Gaza, following the capture of an Israeli soldier by a Palestinian militia in May, Israel imposed a complete blockade and launched a major assault that led over the next few months to hundreds of Palestinians being killed and wounded, with extensive economic damage. The UAE strongly criticised Israel's moves, which included the kidnapping of Palestinian Ministers and the destruction of government offices.

The Israeli assault against the Gaza Strip was joined in mid-July by another unexpected conflict between Israel and Lebanon. By mid-August, when UN Security Council resolution No. 1701 eventually brought about a ceasefire, over 1000 Lebanese had been killed, with over one million people having been displaced from their homes, tens of thousands of homes being destroyed and with the country's infrastructure severely damaged.

The UAE urged the international community to move quickly to stop the Israeli offensive and implement the UN Security Council's resolutions.

The UAE's approach, expressed consistently throughout the war, was that the international community, in particular the great powers, should move quickly to stop the Israeli offensive and implement the UN Security Council's resolutions, in particular resolutions No. 1559 and No.1680, to guarantee the independence, security and protection of Lebanon.

Acting on the instructions of President HH Sheikh Khalifa bin Zayed Al Nahyan, the Government provided extensive assistance to the Government and people of Lebanon, to help them cope with the impact of the Israeli attacks (see Foreign Aid). At a political level, the Cabinet moved rapidly to condemn what it described as 'Israeli aggression (and) a barefaced violation of Lebanese sovereignty and the integrity of the Lebanese territories. . . '

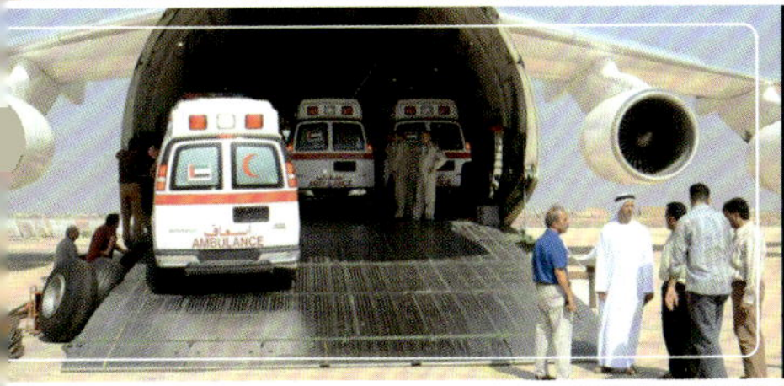

Under the instructions of UAE President, HH Sheikh Khalifa bin Zayed Al Nahyan, the UAE Government provided extensive assistance to the people of Lebanon.

The UAE also condemned strongly the killing of civilians that occurred as a result of Israeli military action. In one such comment, after the killing of several dozen civilians, including old people, women and children, at Qana in late July, Foreign Minister Sheikh Abdullah bin Zayed Al Nahyan described the act as 'a horrible crime' and as 'further proof of the continuing and unchanged Israeli policy of using destructive weaponry for the indiscriminate killing of human beings and of ignoring all international laws and pacts which prohibit the killing of civilians in times of war and armed conflicts.'

Israeli attacks on Lebanon were described as '. . . clear evidence of a contemporary barbarism that threatens global peace and gives rise to a very complicated Arab and international situation that will be difficult to solve in future.'

In comments at the beginning of August, Vice President and Prime Minister HH Sheikh Mohammed bin Rashid Al Maktoum condemned the failure of the international community to act, going on to note that the fact that Israeli attacks were taking place against civilian targets throughout Lebanon showed clearly 'that the (Israeli) target is not Hezbollah alone but the whole of Lebanon.' This, he said, 'is clear evidence of a contemporary barbarism that threatens global peace and gives rise to a very complicated Arab and international situation, which will be difficult to solve in future.'

Foreign Minister Sheikh Abdullah bin Zayed Al Nahyan, as current chairman of the Arab League Ministerial Council, presided over an emergency meeting of the Foreign Ministers in Beirut on 7 August, and shortly afterwards attended the UN Security Council debates that led to the adoption of Resolution 1701.

Following the mid-August ceasefire, the UAE stepped up the dispatch of aid to Lebanon, with, at times, two planeloads of relief aid being dispatched every day. In late August, chairing an extraordinary meeting of the Arab League Ministerial Council in Cairo, Foreign Minister Sheikh Abdullah bin Zayed noted that UN Security Council resolution No. 1701, calling for the ceasefire, should be backed up by further action. 'Resolution 1701 would be hollow if it is not backed up by a series of measures such as speedy return of the displaced, reconstruction of the destroyed areas, exchange of detainees, and resolution of the Shibaa Farms issue', he said.

He went on to promise political, economic and humanitarian Arab support to Lebanon in the aftermath of the aggression. 'The

The Abu Dhabi flagpole stands at 123 metres tall and flies a flag measuring 20 by 40 metres. It was classified [in 2002] in the Guinness World Records as the World's Tallest Unsupported Flagpole.

fact that the Lebanese have demonstrated unity and solidarity during the crisis was encouraging. That unified stand became the basis for the common Arab position. It is on the basis of this common ground that we are working to implement resolution 1701', said Sheikh Abdullah.

The UAE re-launched Emirates Solidarity, its mine clearing project in south Lebanon.

The UAE also announced a re-launching of its programme, carried out following the 2000 Israeli withdrawal from south Lebanon, to remove all mines and unexploded ordnance left as a result of the latest conflict. Ordered by President HH Sheikh Khalifa, the programme is expected to cost up to US$50 million, and was described by the Lebanese Foreign Minister as 'yet another demonstration of the UAE's unequivocal support for Lebanon'.

The UAE continues to believe that the restoration of security, peace and stability in the region, as well as normalisation of relations between all countries, including Israel, cannot be achieved while Israeli occupation of the Palestinian and Arab territories continues and supports an ending of the occupation and creation of an independent Palestinian state with Jerusalem as its capital, within the context of a just and lasting peace agreement.

The UAE is a strong supporter of the United Nations and its various agencies.

Beyond the Arab world, the UAE has pursued a policy of seeking, wherever possible, to build friendly relations with other nations, both in the developing and in the industrialised world. While this policy is implemented at a bilateral level, another important feature of UAE policy has been its support for international bodies, like the United Nations and its various agencies. Through its support for such bodies, it seeks to reinforce the rule of international law, and to support the implementation of internationally agreed conventions, so as to protect the interests of the small, the weak and the powerless.

Throughout the year, the United Arab Emirates continued to extend all possible support to the international fight against terrorism, while emphasising the necessity both of a clear definition of terrorism and of ensuring that terrorism perpetrated by states should not be overlooked.

In response to an outrage in Bombay, India in July that left 183 dead and more than 600 injured, Foreign Minister Sheikh Abdullah bin Zayed Al Nahyan said that 'the UAE condemns in the strongest possible terms this abhorrent criminal act.'

In more general terms, the UAE has continued throughout the year to work on building bilateral relations with countries across the world, one development of note being the continuing of negotiations with the United States on a free trade agreement. These proceeded steadily, despite the overt hostility to UAE investment in the United States shown early in the year following the takeover by Dubai Ports World of the British shipping company P&O, which had extensive operations in the United States.

During the year, there was the usual steady flow of high-ranking visitors from other countries to the Emirates, both from within the Gulf and Arab world, and from further afield.

Among official visits overseas by President HH Sheikh Khalifa during the year were trips to Egypt, Morocco and France, while Vice-President HH Sheikh Mohammed bin Rashid, the Crown Prince of Abu Dhabi and Deputy Supreme Commander of the Armed Forces, HH Sheikh Mohammed bin Zayed, Foreign Minister Sheikh Abdullah bin Zayed and other senior officials also made numerous, important overseas trips, visits to France and Britain being of particular significance.

HH Sheikh Khalifa visiting Morocco in July 2006

As noted at the beginning of this section of the *Yearbook*, the UAE has always sought, since its establishment, to work with and to support the United Nations and its specialised agencies. During late 2005 and 2006, the Ministries of Foreign Affairs and Interior worked closely with the United Nations Children's Fund (UNICEF) on a continuing campaign to ensure the repatriation of young children who had formerly been working as camel jockeys in the Emirates. The practice, fuelled by smuggling rings from their countries of origin, mainly in South Asia, was made illegal in 2005. The UAE's efforts to eradicate the use of children in the sport have been widely acknowledged.

Another important step taken during the year was the approval by the Cabinet in June 2006 of a new law designed to stamp out all trafficking in people, as defined under international conventions. Beneficiaries will include domestic servants, agricultural labourers and those involved in sexual exploitation. As with many such

www.uaeinteract.com/foreign_policy

issues, the successful implementation of such legislation will depend to a considerable extent on collaboration with the countries of origin, and plans were being drawn up during the latter part of the year, in association with international bodies, to identify the most effective ways of enforcing the new legislation.

Characterised by prudence, a support for conciliation and consensus, as well as for international institutions, yet also by a readiness, if necessary, to support the use of force to defend the rights of the weak, UAE foreign policy in the years since the state was established has also been noteworthy for its consistency, thanks to the fact that the architect of the policy, Sheikh Zayed, continued throughout to guide its implementation until late 2004. During 2006, under the leadership of President HH Sheikh Khalifa bin Zayed Al Nahyan, that policy has remained unaltered.

FOREIGN AID

One of the top ten of the world's Red Cross and Red Crescent Societies. it has disbursed over US$460 million in 95 countries in the last year alone.

Since the establishment of the United Arab Emirates, the country has played an active role in the provision of financial aid to developing countries and has been a major contributor of emergency relief to regions affected by conflict and natural disasters.

Much of the assistance has been supplied by Government, but in recent years the UAE Red Crescent has emerged as a major international relief agency. One of the top ten of the world's Red Cross and Red Crescent Societies. it has disbursed over US$460 million in 95 countries in the last year alone.

The philosophy behind the aid policy is two-fold – first, a belief that help for the needy is a duty incumbent on all Muslims and, second, that part of the country's wealth from oil and gas should be used to help other countries that have been less well-endowed.

The philosophy was well-described by former UAE President Sheikh Zayed bin Sultan Al Nahyan:

Foreign aid and assistance is one of the basic pillars of our foreign policy. For we believe that there is no true benefit for us from the wealth that we have unless it also reaches those in need, wherever they may be, and regardless of their nationality or beliefs. That is why we have ensured that our brothers and our friends have shared in our wealth.

The focus of the country's emergency relief programme during 2006 was, not surprisingly, on Lebanon, following the outbreak of the devastatingly destructive conflict in July and August, which caused up to a quarter of the country's population to flee from their homes. The UAE responded with a massive outpouring of support, led by President HH Sheikh Khalifa bin Zayed Al Nahyan, who ordered the provision of US$20 million in aid within hours of the Israeli attack commencing, following this up with more, and larger, sums as the conflict continued.

The country's emergency relief programme during 2006 was focused, not surprisingly, on Lebanon.

On the orders of President HH Sheikh Khalifa, Vice-President and Prime Minister HH Sheikh Mohammed bin Rashid, and the Deputy Supreme Commander of the UAE Armed Forces and Abu Dhabi Crown Prince, HH Sheikh Mohammed bin Zayed, dozens of flights were made by aircraft from the UAE Armed Forces, ferrying relief supplies, including ambulances, medicines, food and clothing,

www.uaeinteract.com/foreign_policy

to Lebanon and to camps for displaced persons in Syria. On the ground, the Red Crescent played an active role in distributing the supplies and in providing assistance for the refugees. A number of persons injured in the Israeli attacks were also flown for treatment in the UAE's hospitals. US$36 million had been spent by the Red Crescent by late August.

Besides the Red Crescent, other charitable organisations, such as the Mohammed bin Rashid Foundation for Charitable and Humanitarian Works, were also instrumental in collecting and distributing relief supplies, while the Emirates Diving Association helped in cleaning up oil pollution along Lebanon's coastline caused by Israeli bombing of fuel tanks

While Government bodies and non-governmental organisations took the lead, private sector companies and individuals also played a role. Television fund-raising campaigns prompted donations of over Dh50 million from the public. Over Dh90 million was donated by the private sector as a whole by late August and the total aid programme, excluding the cost of donated government services, like the use of over three dozen planes to ferry aid supplies, exceeded US$ 135 million, with much more due to flow over the next few months and years as the rebuilding of Lebanon's infrastructure gets under way. This task is essential to enable the displaced to rebuild their homes, their livelihoods and their lives – and the UAE is committed to playing a major part in that process.

The UAE is financing and directing mine clearance operations in south Lebanon.

One of the most important initiatives was the decision to resume a UAE-funded programme, to be carried out in association with the UN and the Lebanese Government and in accordance with UN Security Council resolution No. 1701, to clear mines and unexploded munitions from the south of Lebanon, to make it possible for the inhabitants of the area to resume their normal lives. The first phase of the programme was undertaken following the Israeli withdrawal from south Lebanon in 2000, with tens of thousands of mines being removed.

Other initiatives include a programme for rebuilding schools and hospitals in a number of south Lebanese towns and the restoration of the important fishing port at Ouzai, just south of Beirut, along with the donation of new boats for the fishermen.

While the crisis in Lebanon was a major focus of the UAE's relief programme during 2006, the country continued to give support elsewhere, notably to the people of Palestine. The lead was taken by President HH Sheikh Khalifa, who personally funded the construction of a major housing programme with 3000 apartments, to be called Sheikh Khalifa City, in the Gaza Strip. A Sheikh Zayed City, funded by the former UAE President, has also been built in Gaza.

Other assistance has been provided by the Red Crescent, chaired by Deputy Prime Minister, Sheikh Hamdan bin Zayed Al Nahyan. Working with its Palestinian counterpart, as well as with UN agencies, it has provided over US$120 million in assistance in the last 12 months alone. Some has been in the form of emergency relief, while other help has gone to the social welfare infrastructure both in the Gaza Strip and on the West Bank. One new project during the year was the Dh50 million (US$13.62 million) 'Emirates District', in Khan Yunis in the Gaza Strip, comprising 600 residential units, with associated health, educational, and other facilities.

The Zayed Foundation for Charitable and Humanitarian Works has also funded projects in Palestine, these being carried out in coordination with the Palestinian National Authority and UNRWA, the United Nations Relief and Works Agency for Palestine Refugees in the Near East, while the Mohammed bin Rashid Foundation for Charitable and Humanitarian Works announced in May a donation of Dh10 million (US2.72 million) for the purchase of drugs for Palestinian hospitals.

Elsewhere, the UAE has continued to play a swift and effective role in the provision of emergency relief after natural disasters. Following the devastating tsunami (tidal wave) in the Indian Ocean at the end of 2004, both the Government and the private sector not only rushed rapid relief assistance, but also supported projects to help communities to rebuild their lives. During the course of 2006, for example, a project being carried out by the Red Crescent in collaboration with the United Nations Development Programme (UNDP) saw a new settlement of over 1000 new homes built in the Aceh province of western Indonesia, one of

Over 1000 new homes were built in the Aceh province of western Indonesia.

@ *www.uaeinteract.com/foreign_policy*

the areas most seriously affected by the tsunami. Funded by the UAE President, the settlement will be called Sheikh Khalifa City.

The same rapid response followed by support for reconstruction was displayed after the major earthquake that hit Pakistan and parts of Indian Kashmir in October 2005, and during 2006 the help for the reconstruction process continued. One such project, jointly implemented by the Red Crescent and the United Nations Childrens' Fund (UNICEF) involves the provision of vaccinations and vitamins to around 250,000 children in the areas affected by the earthquake. Overall, the UAE Government committed over US$100 million dollars in aid to Pakistan in the aftermath of the quake.

Sadly, natural disasters are frequent events, and a further need for emergency help arose after the May 2006 earthquake in Java, in Indonesia. A search-and-rescue team from the Abu Dhabi Police was the first Arab team, and only the second team in the world, to reach the areas affected, while Sheikh Khalifa made a personal donation of US$4 million towards the cost of the relief effort.

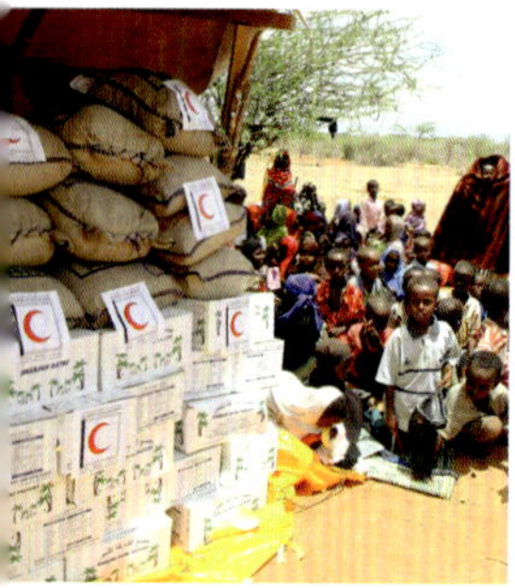

Kenya, Tanzania, Somalia, Djibouti, the Central African Republic and Niger were among recipients of UAE aid.

The programme of emergency relief has also included the provision by the Red Crescent, the Mohammed bin Rashid Establishment and the Zayed Foundation of help to African countries affected by drought or by floods, with Kenya, Tanzania, Somalia, Djibouti, the Central African Republic and Niger being among the recipients.

It is not only people in areas affected by recent natural disasters or by the latest war who need assistance. Millions of people have been displaced by conflict in recent decades, and continue to need help, even when the conflicts that caused their displacement have died down, or have faded from the headlines. Because of this, the Red Crescent and the Zayed Foundation continued during the year to help displaced people in a number of countries, including Azerbaijan and Afghanistan.

Private donations by a number of leading UAE personalities have also been a feature of the UAE's contribution to other countries. During his visit to Egypt in July, for example, Sheikh Khalifa announced a plan to donate funds for a major new residential development, to be known as Khalifa City. Overall, the UAE is now engaged in over 100 development projects in Egypt. During another visit by the President to Morocco, plans were announced for the construction by the UAE of a state-of-the-art hospital. A UAE-backed venture for a residential and tourist complex was also announced.

Overall, the UAE is now engaged in over 100 development projects in Egypt.

Other donations included one by Supreme Council member and Ruler of Ajman HH Sheikh Humaid bin Rashid Al Nuaimi, for a hospital in Syria, which will provide health care for 48 villages in the provinces of Homs and Hama.

Many such aid projects are overseen by the Abu Dhabi Fund for Development (ADFD), which also provides conventional development assistance. Overall, since it was founded in 1971, the Fund has now provided over US$5.4 billion in aid, to over 240 projects in 55 countries, making a real contribution to development of infrastructure in some of the world's poorest nations. New agreements in 2006 included one of US$150 million to Yemen.

UAE commercial institutions also contribute towards the overseas aid programme. Such assistance is often provided as an emergency response to natural disasters. In some cases, though, a longer-term approach has also been adopted. The Emirates Airline Foundation, funded by the airline and by donations from its passengers, is

financing the construction of a floating hospital to serve up to two million people in areas affected by the annual flooding of Bangladesh's Brahmaputra River. The hospital will be operated by a Bangladeshi non-governmental organisation.

The UAE Government also participates in a number of multilateral aid-giving institutions, including the World Bank, the International Monetary Fund (IMF), the International Development Agency (IDA), and other bodies like the OPEC Fund for International Development, the Arab Gulf Fund for the UN (AGFUND), the Arab Bank for Economic Development in Africa (BADEA), the Abu Dhabi-based Arab Monetary Fund (AMF) and the Islamic Development Bank (IDB). A donation of US$2 million was made to the Islamic Solidarity Fund, part of the Organisation of the Islamic Conference, OIC, during the year, to support its humanitarian activities.

INTERNET LINKS

Defence:	www.uaeinteract.com/defence
Development aid:	www.uaeinteract.com/assistance
Diplomatic missions:	www.uaeinteract.com/diplomatic
E-Government:	www.uaeinteract.com/egovernment
Federal budgets:	www.uaeinteract.com/fed_budgets
HH Sheikh Khalifa bin Zayed Al Nahyan:	www.uaeinteract.com/sheikh_khalifa
Higher National Security Council:	www.uaeinteract.com/security
International aid by the UAE:	www.uaeinteract.com/aid
International relations:	www.uaeinteract.com/int_rel
National Consultative Council:	www.uaeinteract.com/ncc
President of the UAE:	www.uaeinteract.com/president
UAE at the United Nations:	www.uaeinteract.com/UN
UAE Cabinet affairs:	www.uaeinteract.com/cabinet
UAE Federal National Council:	www.uaeinteract.com/fnc
UAE Foreign Policy:	www.uaeinteract.com/foreign_policy
UAE Government affairs:	www.uaeinteract.com/governmentaffairs

ECONOMIC DEVELOPMENT

Key factors in the UAE's successful economic performance have been a strong oil market, development of public joint stock companies, enlargement of free zones, a buoyant local stock market and launches of several new mega-projects.

The non-oil sector accounted for 64 per cent of nominal GDP in 2005. Slightly over half of the Dh93.7 billion invested in projects in 2005 was by the private sector.

ECONOMIC DEVELOPMENT

THE ECONOMY

A 20-YEAR PERIOD OF FISCAL DEFICITS in the UAE's consolidated government financial accounts came to an end in 2005 when it posted a Dh38.2 billion surplus. Public revenues rose by 69.3 per cent to reach Dh160.5 billion, while public spending increased by 27 per cent to reach Dh122.3 billion. The resulting surplus contrasted with a deficit of Dh1.5 billion in 2004. This surge in public finances was primarily due to the increase in oil and gas revenues, which rose by 52 per cent in 2005, reaching Dh111.4 billion compared to Dh73.3 billion in 2004.

Astute economic policies provided solid foundations for impressive growth in all sectors.

The country's impressive economic performance during the year led to a GDP growth rate of 26.3 per cent at current prices, while real GDP growth is estimated at 8.2 per cent. Key factors were the strong oil market, active development of public joint stock companies, increased involvement of free zones and buoyant local stock markets, together with launches of a number of significant new projects. Astute economic policies provided solid foundations for impressive growth in all sectors with GDP at current prices reaching Dh485.5 billion in 2005 compared to Dh386.5 billion in 2004 (based on Ministry of Economy figures and Central Bank Annual Report).

According to the Ministry of Economy and the Central Bank, the non-oil sector accounted for 64 per cent of nominal GDP (73 per cent of real GDP), rising by 19 per cent to Dh312 billion, compared to Dh263 billion in 2004. Development of the relatively new private property market in the UAE supported a rise in contribution to GDP of the real estate and business services sector, which formed 11.5 per cent of the non-oil GDP. Likewise, the building and construction sector continued to boom, adding 11.2 per cent to GDP. Meanwhile government investment in education, health and social services boosted the government services sector to 11.1 per cent of non-oil GDP; and infrastructural projects involving transportation, storage and communications contributed 10.4 per cent.

A new private property market in the UAE has boosted the country's economic performance.

GDP AT CONSTANT PRICES 2003–2005 (in millions of dirhams at constant prices)

	2003	2004	2005*
Gross domestic product	301,311	330,511	357,588
Crude oil and natural gas production[1]	91,025	93,625	95,123
Total non-oil sector	210,286	236,886	262,465
Agriculture	8,942	9,806	10,394
Industry	69,494	78,593	85,647
Quarrying	738	790	845
Manufacturing industries	39,170	45,570	47,894
Electricity & water	5,777	6,412	7,214
Construction	23,809	25,821	29,694
Services	131,850	148,487	166,422
Trade	37,993	44,500	51,620
Wholesale & retail trade & repair services	32,293	38,105	44,202
Restaurants & hotels	5,700	6,395	7,418
Transportation, storage & communications	21,121	23,260	26,516
Financial corporate sector	18,954	22,050	25,358
Real estate	23,272	27,046	30,832
Government services	28,222	29,509	30,099
Other services	7,886	8,407	8,911
Less: Imputed bank service charges	5,598	6,285	6,914

* preliminary figures for 2005

Sources: Ministry of Economy and Central Bank Annual Report, 2005.

Notes: 1/ Includes natural gas and petroleum processing industries.

The importance of the private sector in the UAE's growth can hardly be over-emphasised. Out of a total investment in projects of Dh93.7 billion in 2005, slightly over half of this investment (50.9 per cent) was by the private sector, while the public sector accounted for 34.7 per cent and government investment accounted for 14.4 per cent of the total. The largest investments were made in productive sectors (48.7 per cent of the total, or Dh45.6 billion), while the services sector, led by transport, storage and communications,

GDP AT CURRENT PRICES 2003–2005 (in millions of dirhams at current prices)

	2003	2004	2005*
Gross domestic product	321,752	386,535	485,513
Crude oil and natural gas production[1]	92,136	123,261	173,195
Total non-oil sector	229,616	263,274	312,318
Agriculture	9,152	10,100	11,028
Industry	75,061	86,678	105,028
Quarrying	765	828	919
Manufacturing industries	42,215	50,159	61,194
Electricity & water	6,009	6,720	7,935
Construction	26,072	28,971	34,980
Services	145,403	166,496	193,552
Trade	41,985	50,801	61,944
Wholesale & retail trade	35,460	43,458	52,998
Restaurants & hotels	6,525	7,343	8,946
Transportation, storage & communications	24,692	27,263	32,642
Financial corporate sector	19,902	23,374	28,426
Real estate	25,355	30,018	35,920
Government services	30,737	32,463	34,735
Other services	8,557	9,239	9,989
Less: Imputed bank service charges	5,825	6,662	7,395

* preliminary figures for 2005
Sources: Ministry of Economy and Central Bank Annual report, 2005.
Notes: 1/ Includes natural gas and petroleum processing industries.

accounted for Dh40.7 billion. These investments have paid dividends as far as economic growth is concerned and have placed the UAE in an advantageous position in terms of adopting advanced technologies. Indeed, the World Economic Forum (WEF) ranked the UAE in first place in the Arab World and twenty-eighth position worldwide as regards preparedness for technology applications.

Balance of trade figures (FOB) achieved a surplus in 2005 of Dh163 billion against Dh101 billion in 2004. Total exports were

REAL GDP GROWTH

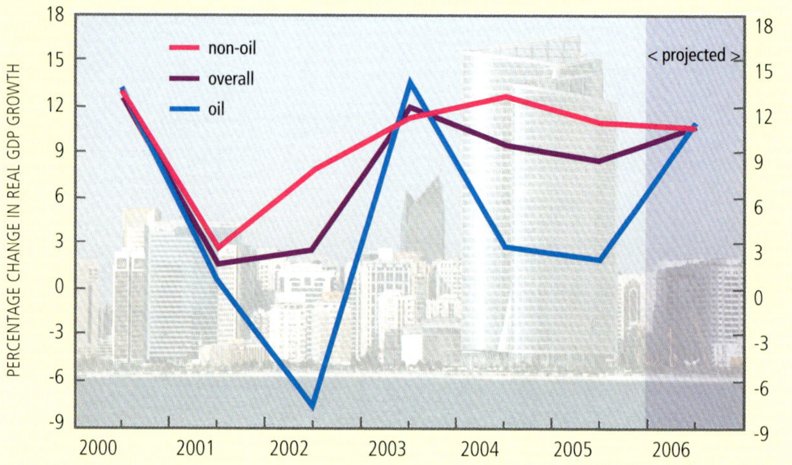

Sources: UAE Authorities and IMF staff estimates

INFLATIONARY PRESSURES

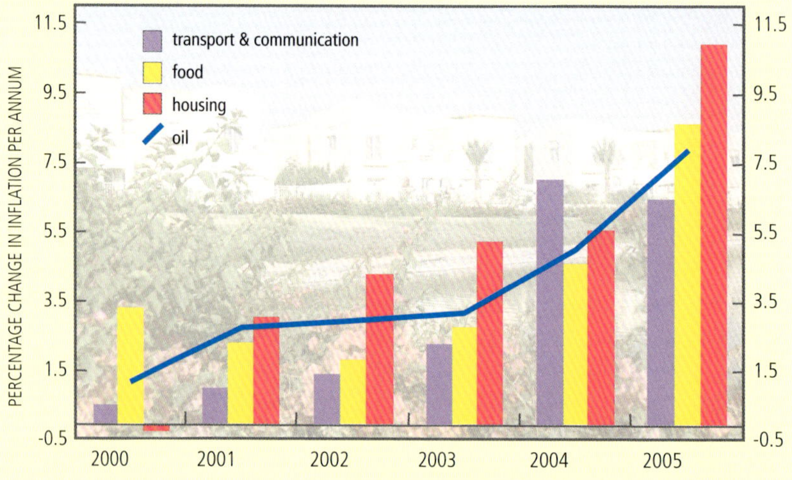

Sources: UAE Authorities and IMF staff estimates

GDP BY SECTOR (in millions of dirhams)

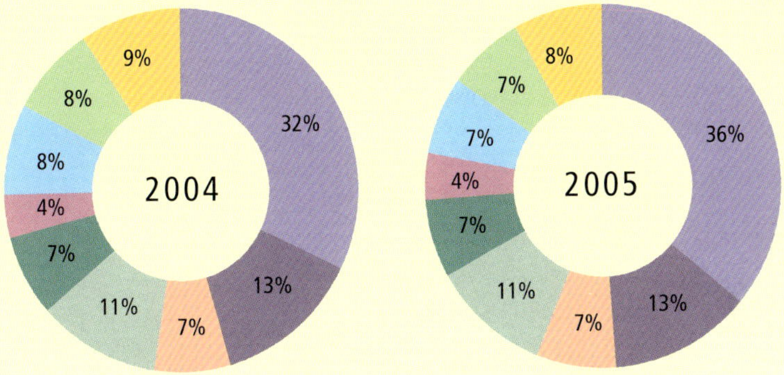

Sectors		2004*	2005**
(1)	**Non-financial enterprises sector**	**335,234**	**427,364**
	Agriculture, livestock & fishery	10,100	11,028
	Mining & quarrying	124,089	174,114
	A. Crude oil & natural gas	123,261	173,195
	B. Other	828	919
	Manufacturing	50,159	61,194
	Electricity, gas & water	6,720	7,935
	Construction	28,971	34,980
	Wholesale / retail trade & maintenance	43,458	52,998
	Restaurants & hotels	7,343	8,946
	Transportation, storage & communication	27,263	32,642
	Real estate & business services	30,018	35,920
	Social & private services	7,113	7,607
(2)	**Financial enterprises sector**	**23,374**	**28,426**
(3)			**34,735**
	Household services	2,126	2.382
(less) Imputed bank services charges		6,662	7,395
TOTAL		**386,535**	**485,513**
Total non-oil sectors		**263,274**	**312,318**

Including agriculture, livestock & fishing; electricity & water; restaurants & hotels, social & personal services and household services

Source: Ministry of Economy * Adjusted data ** Preliminary data little changed from 2004 figures, at Dh334 billion in 2005, while imports rose to Dh261 billion in 2005 from Dh233 billion in 2004. As a result of the increase in oil prices and the increase in production of condensates, the value of oil exports rose by 46.8 per cent in 2005, reaching Dh159.8 billion. The weighted average of oil prices rose from US$36.9 a barrel in 2004 to US$52.9 in 2005.

OUTWARD INVESTMENT

Overseas investments have always formed a key strategy in UAE economic policy.

The UAE is an important participant in global capital markets through several investment institutions, including, among others, the Abu Dhabi Investment Council, the Dubai Ports and Free Zone World, Dubai Holding, and the Abu Dhabi's International Petroleum Investment Co. (IPIC). Its current account has been in surplus since the foundation of the state.

The Abu Dhabi Investment Council was established in mid-2006, to replace the Abu Dhabi Investment Authority. All ADIC's investments are to be tax-exempted in the UAE. The Council will use money set aside by the Government for investment inside and outside Abu Dhabi, and will seek to maintain a balanced portfolio. ADIC will be closely involved in launching major real estate and tourism projects, both within the UAE and internationally.

Dubai Ports & Free Zone World was also established in mid-2006 as an umbrella company to manage DP World, P&O and Jafza.

The UAE's overseas investments have always formed a key strategy in its economic policy. There was considerable activity in this field during the last 12 months with certain investments making world news. Some of the major UAE overseas investments completed in the last year are summarised in the accompanying panels.

INWARD INVESTMENT

The UAE's nominal GDP is expected to grow by 24 per cent to Dh592 billion (US$161.3 billion) in 2006.

Foreign direct investment (FDI) inflow into the UAE achieved a record US$10 billion in 2005, amounting to nearly 34 per cent of the total foreign capital flow of nearly US$29.6 billion channelled into the Arab world. The figure also places the UAE as the top country in the Arab World in terms of attracting inward investment.

The UAE strongly believes that the private sector (both local and foreign) is the true engine of sustained growth. FDI is regarded as crucial in order to transfer knowledge and expertise in areas that are not yet the country's core competencies, open new market opportunities by the creation of new networks and create employment in knowledge intensive and high value-added sectors.

Building on the success of the Jebel Ali Free Trade Zone, the UAE currently has 23 free zones with more under development. Some of the zones cater to service sectors (e.g. Dubai Internet City, Dubai Media City, Dubai Healthcare City, Academic City, Dubai International Financial Centre), while others are industrial zones (e.g. Hamriyah Free Zone, Fujairah Free Zone, Ajman Free Zone and the Gold and Diamond Park). Free-zone companies may be under 100 per cent foreign ownership, enjoy corporate tax holidays, no personal taxes, freedom to repatriate capital and profits, and be free of import duties or currency restrictions.

Outside the free zones, companies may still enjoy tax holidays for most sectors, no personal taxes, freedom to repatriate capital and profits, and no currency restrictions. Foreign ownership is generally set at a ceiling of 49 per cent, though that is under review.

Investments in the productive sector have placed the UAE in an advantageous position in terms of adopting the latest technologies.

FOUNDATIONS FOR GROWTH

Successful development necessitates good planning, adequate investment and professional implementation. The UAE's success is based on all three of these cornerstones. And whilst achievements to date are highly impressive, there is much more to come. Abu Dhabi alone plans to invest over Dh555 billion (US$151.22 billion) in the coming five years. Dh320 billion (US$87.19 billion) will go to the construction sector, Dh120 billion (US$32.69 billion) for development and expansion of the tourism sector, Dh35 billion (US$9.53 billion) for new power and water projects and Dh80 billion (US$21.79 billion) will be spent on expanding the oil and gas sector.

Ever since the foundation of the state in 1971, the UAE's economic strategy has been consistent in terms of maximising the benefits of its oil and gas resources and looking ahead to the day when these non-renewable resources will no longer be available. It has invested heavily in its hydrocarbon industries and utilised their revenues to create a socio-economic infrastructure that is less

CONSOLIDATED GOVERNMENT FINANCES (in millions of UAE dirhams)

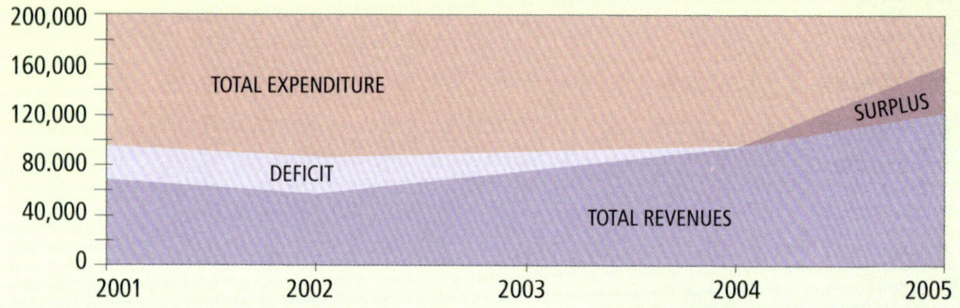

Items In millions of Dh	2004*	2005**
REVENUE	94,751	160,541
Tax Revenue	9,566	10,191
Customs	3,040	3,846
Other	6,526	6,345
Non-Tax Revenue	85,185	150,50
Oil and Gas	73,322	111,377
Joint Stock Corporations	3,322	4,089
Other	8,541	34,884
EXPENDITURE	96,274	122,291
Current Expenditure	80,984	76,940
Salaries and Wages	15,628	16,357
Goods and Services	25,032	24,184
Subsidies and Transfers	11,666	12,665
Other Unclassified	28,658	23,734
Development Expenditure	15,207	13,509
Loans and Equity Participation	83	31,842
Local	3,448	31,436
Foreign	-3,365	406
Surplus (+) or Deficit (-)	- 1,523	+38,250
Financing	1,523	38,250
Changes in net Government Deposits with Banks	-1,777	16,037
Other[1]	3,300	22,213

Source: Central Bank Annual Report 2005 with data drawn from Ministry of Finance and Industry and Local Government Finance Departments
*Adjusted data ** Preliminary data [1] Returns of government's investments.

and less dependent upon oil or natural gas as its main source of income. The success of its policies are apparent wherever one looks in the UAE and indeed in many places around the world. With an average economic growth rate (at constant prices) of 6 per cent over the past ten years (over 9 per cent if you take the period 2003 to 2006) the figures speak for themselves. Diversification has reduced the dependence on petroleum and natural gas from around three-quarters of total GDP in 1980 to approximately one-third of the UAE's GDP today. Although it remains of huge importance to the UAE, the hydrocarbons sector's position as the prime economic contributor to GDP has been overtaken by the non-oil services sector, which accounts for 64 per cent of nominal GDP. On a per capita basis, the UAE's relatively small population and large resources have helped to place it close to the top rung of the world's per capita GDP ranking, with a figure of approximately US$24,000.

The UAE's fiscal surplus in 2005, combined with a decrease in external debt (which fell from over 25 per cent of GDP in 2000/01 to 12.5 per cent by the end of 2005), has boosted the country's financial position, but the Government remains vigilant on the issue of inflation which, according to the Governor of the Central Bank, grew from an annual average of 3 per cent in the period 2001/03 to between 6.5 and 7 per cent in 2005.

Although it remains of huge importance to the UAE, the hydrocarbons sector's position as the prime economic contributor to GDP has been overtaken by the non-oil services sector.

@ *www.uaeinteract.com/economicdevelopment*

ESTIMATE OF UAE BALANCE OF PAYMENTS 2004–2005 (in billions of dirhams)

	2004	2005*
Current Account Balance	**38,889**	**97,257**
Trade Balance (FOB)	**101,231**	**162,801**
Total Exports of Hydrocarbon	142,500	202,156
Crude Oil Exports	108,798	159,761
Petroleum Products Exports	16,243	21,179
Gas Exports	17,459	21,216
Total of Non Hydrocarbon Exports	67,267	82,342
Free Zone Exports	52,587	63,928
Other Exports [1]	14,680	18,414
Re-Exports [2]	124,419	139,506
Total Exports and Re-Exports (FOB)	**334,186**	**424,004**
Total Imports (FOB)	**-232,955**	**-261,202**
Total Imports (CIF)	**-264,722**	**-296,821**
Other Imports [3]	-203,257	-233,521
Free Zone Imports	-61,465	-63,300
Services (NET)	-44,346	-49,837
Travel	-10,575	-11,145
Transport	-2,119	-3,185
Government Services	115	112
Freight and Insurance	-31,767	-35,619
Investment Income (NET)	570	5,900
Banking System [4]	2,362	5,400
Private Non-Banks	296	500
Enterprises of Public Sector	13,912	23,300
Foreign Hydrocarbon Companies in UAE	-16,000	-23,300
Transfers (NET)	-18,566	-21,608
Public Transfers	-17,066	-19,733
Workers Transfers	-1,500	-1,875

[1] Including estimates of other exports from all emirates.
[2] Including re-exports of non-monetary gold.
[3] Including estimate of imports from all emirates and imports of non-monetary gold.
[4] Central Bank and all banks.
[5] Data not available at time of compilation.
* Adjustable figures and preliminary estimates
Source: Central Bank Statistical Report January–March 2006.

ESTIMATE OF UAE BALANCE OF PAYMENTS, continued

	2004	2005*
Capital and Financial Account	**–23,867**	**–68,681**
Capital Account [5]	—	—
Financial Account	–23,867	–68,681
Enterprise of Private Sector	44,411	46,019
Direct Investment	28,629	26,257
Outward	-8,109	-13,773
Inward	36,738	40,030
Portfolio Investment	7,345	22,360
Banks	-647	-12,498
Securities	404	-10,597
Other Investment	-1,051	-1,901
Private Non-Banks	9,084	9,900
Enterprises of Public Sector	-68,278	-114,700
Net Errors and Omissions	-2,193	-19,075
Overall Balance: Surplus (+) or Deficit (-)	**+12,829**	**+9,501**
Change in Reserves (- indicates an increase)	**-12,829**	**-9,501**
Net Foreign Assets with Central Bank	-12,969	-10,166
Reserve Position with I.M.F.	140	665

[5] Data available at time of report.

CONSUMER PRICE INDEX ON MAJOR COMPONENTS 2001–2005

(Annual averages, 2000=100)

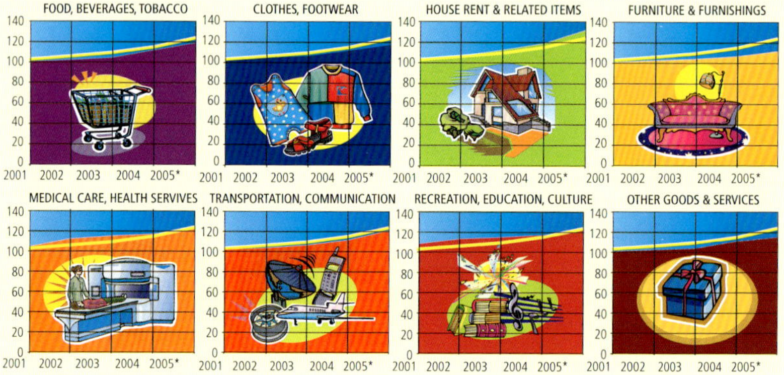

	2001	2002	2003	2004	2005*
Consumer price index	**102.8**	**105.8**	**109.1**	**114.6**	**123.7**
Foodstuffs, beverages and tobacco	101.0	102.4	104.7	112.0	119.2
Ready made clothes & footwear	104.0	104.9	106.6	112.0	117.4
House rent & related housing items	102.7	107.1	112.7	119.0	132.0
Furniture & furnishings	101.0	102.8	104.4	106.9	112.0
Medical care & health services	104.8	112.5	115.3	117.0	123.0
Transportation & communication	102.0	103.8	106.6	111.5	121.1
Recreational, educational, & cultural services	108.3	113.2	114.7	117.1	122.0
Other goods & services	101.0	102.3	103.9	111.1	115.3

Source: Ministry of Economy and Planning and IMF staff estimates
* Figures for 2005 are preliminary.
International Monetary Fund, July 2006: IMF Country Report No. 06/257

This economic growth has been fostered, in part at least, by the removal of barriers to trade and the creation of a relatively liberal business environment. The focus has been on how to help business develop while maintaining good standards of corporate governance. State ownership has played a key role in development of certain sectors, but in recent years there have been moves to reduce this role through a series of privatisation and partnership arrangements. In addition, introduction of free zones and other

SECTORAL DISTRIBUTION OF CIVILIAN EMPLOYMENT 2003–2005 (in '000s)

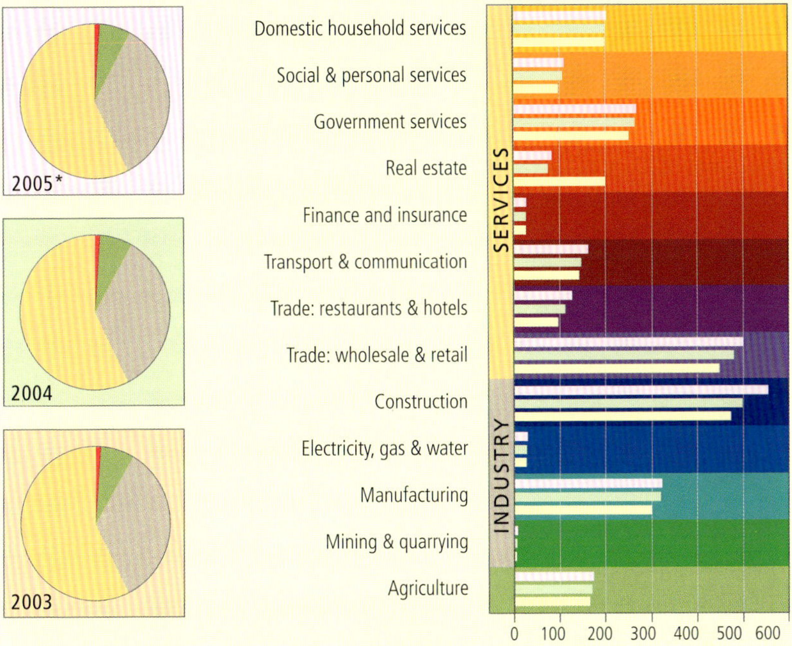

	2003	2004	2005
Civilian employment	2,334	2,459	2,597
Oil sector	28	30	30
Other sectors	2,306	2,429	2,567
Agriculture	166	169	173
Industry	806	852	911
Mining and quarrying	5	6	6
Manufacturing	299	319	322
Electricity, gas, water	28	29	30
Construction	474	498	553
Services	1,334	1,408	1,483
Trade	549	589	628
Wholesale and retail	450	479	501
Restaurants and hotels	99	110	127
Transport and communications	142	148	164
Finance and insurance	27	27	28
Real estate	67	74	81
Government services	250	264	268
Social and personal services	99	106	111
Domestic household services	200	200	203

Source: Ministry of Economy and Planning in IMF Country Report No. 06/257, International Monetary Fund, July 2006

DUBAI PORTS WORLD

IN JANUARY 2006 DUBAI PORTS WORLD (DPW) announced that its offer to purchase Peninsular and Oriental Steam Navigation Co. (P&O) had been recommended for acceptance by the board of P&O. Acquiring P&O's 29 container terminals and logistics operations in 19 countries would make Dubai the world's number three port operator. A shareholder vote in the UK confirmed acceptance of the deal and DPW duly celebrated its success in one of the largest takeovers in history.

• But that was not the end of the story. Shortly after the takeover was announced President George Bush rebuffed criticism that had been raised about potential security risks related to the fact that Dubai Ports World would become managers of significant operations at six major US ports. Four senators and three House members asked the administration to reconsider its approval of the deal. The fact that the sale had been 'rigorously reviewed' by a US committee that considers security threats when foreign companies seek to buy or invest in American industry, the National Security Council, did not seem to satisfy politicians who made political capital from the deal.

• The UAE countered the opposition and its Foreign Minister, Sheikh Abdullah bin Zayed Al Nahyan, pointed out that the UAE had 'worked very closely with the United States on a number of issues relating to the combat of terrorism, prior to and post-9/11. ' The *Gulf Today* newspaper summed up the views of many in the country when it stated that 'The controversy over Dubai Ports World taking control of American ports is unfortunate. It is a commercial deal done in a transparent way within the framework of US laws. Now it is being unjustly politicised'.

• Meanwhile President Bush threatened to veto legislative attempts to thwart the deal. In a bid to dampen down the rhetoric and opposition, DP World offered to postpone its plans to take over the management of six US ports. DP World said it would not take control until lawmakers had been given time to study the deal. The company said it would 'segregate P&O's US operations while it engages in further consultations with the Bush Administration'. The White House welcomed the delay but reiterated that the deal should still proceed because national security was not at risk.

• DP World was scheduled to formally become the new owner of P&O's assets in 19 countries on 2 March 2006, but it faced a last minute attempt to sabotage the deal in the London High Court, which ruled on 4 March 2006 that the deal should indeed proceed despite strong objections from one of the British firm's partners in the United States.

• Meanwhile the US Deputy Treasury Secretary Robert Kimmitt announced that the Bush administration, stung by the vehemence of US political reaction to the deal, would 'launch a fresh review of DP World's proposed management of major US port terminals as soon as it receives a new filing from the company'. He promised that CFIUS would 'take into account the concerns Congress has raised about the acquisition'.

• On the day after the UK court had approved the deal the US Treasury Department stated that it had received an application from DP World to start a second review of the company's purchase of P&O. 'This is a full review without preconceptions,' the department stated, 'We are going to give this transaction a very robust examination'. Rather than prolong this issue further, DP World deflated the situation by offering to sell off its interests in US port management that it had acquired as part of the P&O acquisition.

• The whole experience left many UAE Government officials and investors disappointed that their responsible handling of the issue and their substantial international investment programme had still not convinced ill-informed politicians and members of the American public that DPW is a 'safe pair of hands' and indeed that it has a well-earned record of highly efficient management in port development and administration worldwide.

• DP World announced plans in 2006 to develop new port facilities at a number of strategically placed ports around the world, including Doraleh in Djibouti, Vallarpadam in India, Korea, Ho Chi Min City in Vietnam, Tianjin in China, Port of Callao in Peru and at a number of other facilities under its management in the Middle East, Asia, Europe, Australasia and Latin America. In July 2006 a new umbrella company, known as Ports & Free Zone World, was established in Dubai to manage DP World, P&O and Jafza.

DIRECTIONS OF TRADE: IMPORTS 2003–2005 (as percentages)

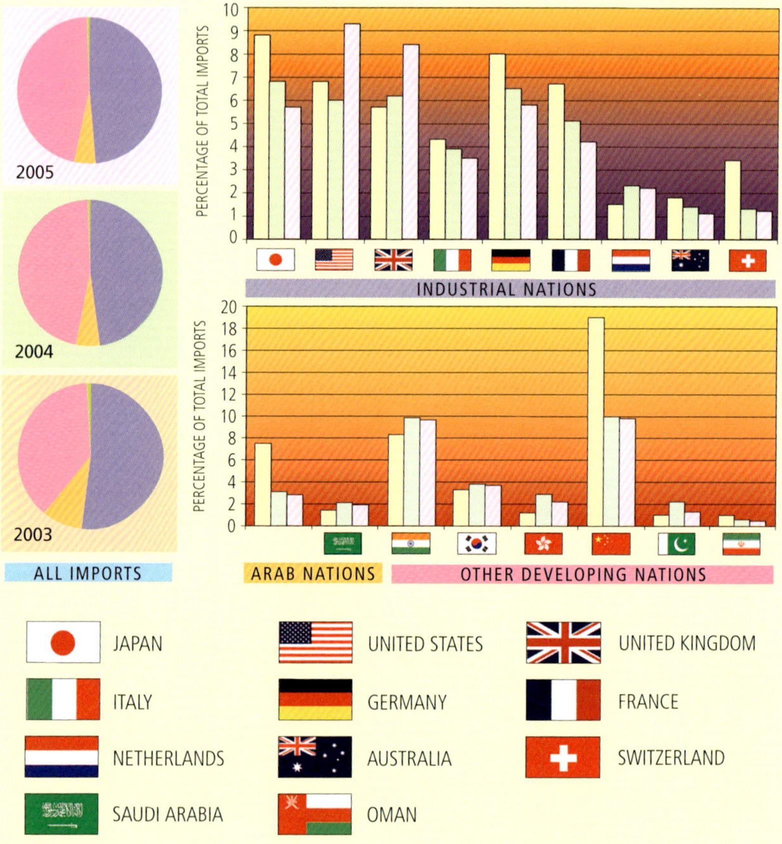

Shown as percentages	2003	2004	2005
Industrial countries	52.0	47.8	48.6
Arab countries	8.9	5.2	4.7
Other developing countries	38.4	46.5	46.1
Other unspecified	0.7	0.5	0.6

Sources: Ministry of Economy and IMF staff estimates.
International Monetary Fund, July 2006: IMF Country Report No. 06/257

DIRECTIONS OF TRADE: IMPORTS 2003–2005 (as percentages)

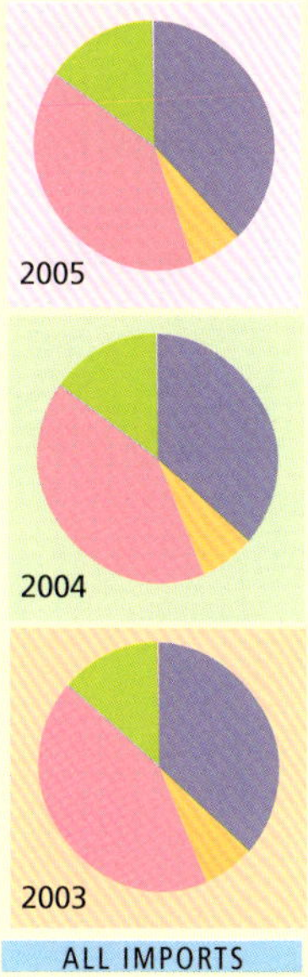

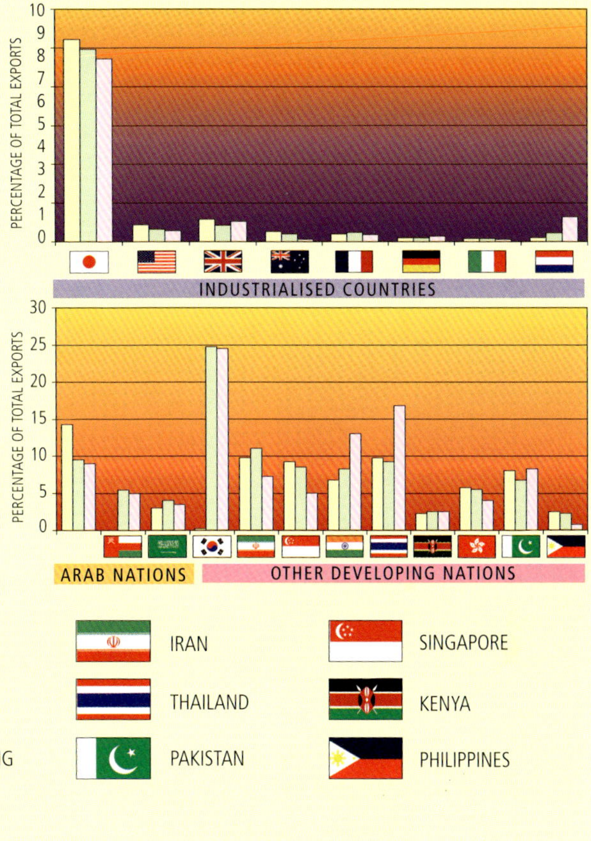

Shown as percentages	2003	2004	2005
Industrial countries	37.8	36.4	36.7
Arab countries	6.9	7.6	7.0
Other developing countries	40.1	41.0	42.6
Other unspecified	15.2	15.0	13.7

MAJOR INTERNATIONAL INVESTMENT IN 2006

- Mubadala, owned by the Abu Dhabi government, acquired a 35 per cent of the equity of the Italian business aircraft maker, Piaggio Aero. Mubadala's other overseas investments include a 5 per cent stake in Ferrari, a 25 per cent stake in Dutch fleet management giant LeasePlan Corporation and a stake in nine oil exploration blocks in Libya. In addition, its development of the Dolphin Project has involved considerable investment in a gas processing plant in Qatar.
- Etisalat extended its international portfolio by making substantial investments in Pakistan, Afghanistan and Egypt, involving 2G and 3G mobile networks and has begun to see profits from its company in Pakistan, u phone. The company is planning to double its international investment from Dh50 billion (US$13.62 billion) to Dh100 billion (US$27.24 billion) over the next few years.

- Wateen Telcom-Pakistan (owned by Abu Dhabi Group) invested in the implementation of a wireless broadband service and data network in Pakistan at a cost of US$200 million.
- ADIA (now ADIC) invested around US$600 million in US company Apollo Management, a new publicly listed private equity fund.
- Dubai International Capital (DIC), the investment arm of Dubai Holding, completed its US$1.3 billion (Dh4.78 billion) acquisition of British engineering group Doncasters from Royal Bank of Scotland. US President George W. Bush approved DIC's takeover of Doncasters, which operates nine plants and employs 1000 people in the US. Its plant in Georgia supplies turbine fan parts and airfoils for American army tanks and helicopters.
- The group had previously invested US$1 billion in DaimlerChrysler, bought Britain's Tussaud's Group for US$1.48 billion, put US$272 million into JD Capital investment company in Jordan and US$150 million into Ishraq, a company formed to develop a hotel chain in the Middle East.
- Dubai Holding LLC mandated Emirates Bank and Standard Chartered Bank to finance the purchase of a 35 per cent equity stake in Tunisie Telecom, the Tunisian Government telecommunication provider.

MAJOR INTERNATIONAL INVESTMENT IN 2006

- Dubai Financial (DF), a subsidiary of the Dubai Investment Group (DIG), the global investment arm of Dubai Holding, acquired an initial 31.5 per cent stake in Greece's Marfin Financial Group, (Marfin), one of the fastest-growing banking groups in Europe. It later raised its stake from 31.5 to 33.6 per cent. This investment provided Dubai Investments with a strong foothold in the Greek banking sector.
- DIG – Real Estate and Hospitality bought a large suburban shopping centre in Berlin for Dh380 million (US$103.4 million) in a bid to create a German multi-tenant retail portfolio.
- Tecom Investments and DIG, both members of Dubai Holding, acquired a 60 per cent controlling stake in the Maltese telecom company Maltacom for Dh1.04 billion.
- An agreement was signed between Emaar and Saudi Arabia to build the King Abdullah City in Jeddah at a cost of nearly SR100 billion.

- Emaar announced three real estate developments in the cities of Islamabad and Karachi, at a projected investment of Dh8.8 billion (US$2.4 billion). The latter were described as 'only a small part of Emaar's commitment to development projects in Pakistan'. Dubai Islamic Bank said it would open as many as 70 branches in Pakistan with an investment of US$100 million (Dh367 million).
- Emaar Properties bought John Laing Homes, the second-largest privately held US homebuilder, for Dh3.856 billion (US$1.05 billion) cash. The purchase creates one of the world's leading real estate developers in residential homebuilding. Emaar's spokesperson said that 'Partnering with John Laing Homes is consistent with our strategy of expanding our business on a global basis beyond Dubai. This agreement will provide Emaar with an important gateway into the US real estate market.' John Laing Homes will be operated as a division of Emaar and its corporate headquarters will remain in Newport Beach, California.
- Damac Properties signed a Memorandum of Understanding (MOU) with the Tanggu District Government located within Tianjin City, People's Republic of China, to develop a mixed-use real estate development in the Trumpet Bay region at a cost of Dh10 billion (US$2.72 billion).

MAJOR INTERNATIONAL INVESTMENT IN 2006

- Damac announced investments in Beirut City Centre in Lebanon and the new Abdali master planned development in Amman, Jordan.
- Istithmar PJSC, a major investment house based in the UAE, completed the acquisition of 230 and 280 Park Avenue in New York City and the classic, Beaux-Arts style Knickerbocker Hotel located in Times Square, NY. It also agreed to acquire Loehmann's Holdings from Atlanta-based private equity company Arcapita for Dh1.1 billion (US$299 million).
- Nakheel, DP World's sister concern, developed Djibouti's first five-star hotel. The first phase of the 400-room waterfront property cost US$150 million.
- Horizon Terminals Limited (HTL) of Dubai, in partnership with Kuwaiti and Moroccan companies, was awarded a 25-year concession to build, own, operate, and transfer (BOOT) an international petroleum storage terminal at the new Port of Tangiers, in the Kingdom of Morocco. The Port of Tangiers is a new US$1.6 billion development.
- On 9 July 2006 Dubai launched 'Dubai World' as a holding company comprising around 20 entities, some of them managing multi-billion-dollar assets. Dubai World will be responsible for holding several government-owned entities that have been busy locating and acquiring assets overseas in recent years. With presence in 30 countries, DP World and P&O are leading Dubai's global business presence. Other big investments have been made by Nakheel, Limitless and Istithmar in real estate and hospitality. With the restructuring, Dubai World becomes one of the largest holding companies in the Middle East, employing 50,000 people in over 100 locations around the world.

legal measures have reduced or removed some of the restrictions on foreign ownership of companies and obligations for branches of foreign companies to recruit UAE agents. The provision of jobs for UAE nationals does, however, remain a high priority for Government, which applies quotas for the percentage of Emirati staff working in banking, insurance, professional, and distribution services.

The provision of jobs for UAE nationals remains a high priority for Government.

Throughout its history the people of this part of the Gulf have been active traders and so it continues today. Apart from oil and gas products (sent mainly to East Asia), the UAE exports aluminium and a range of non-oil goods to other Arab, Indian and European markets. The prime trading activity is however re-exporting, utilising the UAE as a hub for temporary storage and trans-shipment of a very wide variety of goods and materials. Iran, India, and other Gulf Cooperation Council (GCC) countries are prime participants in this re-export business.

GLOBAL INDICES

The UAE's progress in terms of business development is regularly assessed by a number of different global studies. The country's ranking on these scoreboards provides an indication of how others view the UAE's status as a safe and attractive place to do business. Different organisations use different criteria but they usually produce similar, if not identical, results. For example, the Swiss Institute for Business Cycle Research placed the UAE first in the Arab World (twenty-first overall) in its Kof Globalization Index that covered 123 advanced and developing countries and their performance in a selected list of fields during the period from 1970 to 2003; whilst the Economic Freedom Index of the Heritage Foundation and the Wall Street Journal placed the UAE second in the Arab World in its assessment of other business related criteria. Countries that were listed above the UAE in the index are all well-established economies, including in descending order the United States, Sweden, Canada, and Britain.

The UAE is ranked second in the Mena region and thirty-second internationally in the 2006 WEF Growth Competitiveness Index.

STRUCTURAL FRAMEWORK

Economic policy is administered by the UAE Ministry of Economy, which oversees trade policies approved by the Federal Supreme

Individual emirates exercise a high degree of direct control over their own economies, and emirati governments frequently play significant roles in local business development.

Council (comprising the rulers of each of the seven member emirates of the UAE). Whilst the federal Ministry sets economic guidelines and provides the essential administrative framework, individual emirates exercise a high degree of direct control over their own economies, and emirati governments frequently play significant roles in local business development.

The UAE is a contracting party to GATT and one of the original members of WTO. Its Constitution, Commercial Companies Law and Trade Agencies Law form the main structure of federal legal instruments under which business and commerce operate. Within this framework, additional laws, decree-laws, ordinary decrees, and regulations are issued from time to time to deal with specific issues affecting how business is conducted in the UAE.

E-RANKINGS

According to the Economist Intelligence Unit (EIU) working in cooperation with the IBM Institute for Business Value, the UAE's ranking in terms of 'e-readiness', within a list of 68 of the world's leading e-economies, rose from sixtieth, in 2004, to forty-second, in 2005, and thirtieth in 2006. It is in top position among Arab countries, with Saudi Arabia forty-sixth, Jordan fifty-fourth and Egypt fifty-fifth. The rankings evaluated countries based on more than 100 different criteria, organised into six categories: connectivity and technology infrastructure; business environment; consumer and business adoption; and legal and policy. But this is only the beginning in terms of the UAE's commitment to utilise the internet as an enabling tool in both government and business. There is now a focus on developing e-government services between government agencies (intra-government, or G2G), government to business (G2B), and government to citizens (G2C).

E-BUSINESS

The UAE's leading position in use of the internet to facilitate business is well illustrated by the impressive success of the online trading websites such as the G2B and business to business (B2B) pioneer Tejari. This UAE-based company, which specialises in putting government and private organisations in touch with suppliers of goods and services, has processed transactions worth more than US$3 billion since its establishment in June 2000. It is the Middle East's leading B2B online marketplace, providing a secure and affordable online business platform used by more than 5000 trading partners from across the region, and has a capacity to serve 70,000 more businesses through its mylinkDubai.com tie-up with the Dubai Department of Economic Development.

Tejari enables direct procurement savings of 15–20 per cent plus indirect savings of more than 40 per cent. It has grown each year, a clear indication that it is delivering what users need. 2005 results showed a 50 per cent increase in the total number of auctions on the marketplace, combined with a 25 per cent increase in revenues and a tripling in profits. The company has been utilising its success as a horizontal online marketplace to create portals or hubs for specific industries and groups such as the Jebel Ali Free Zone (Jafza), Dubai Tea Trading Centre (DTTC), and the Dubai Department of Economic Development (DED). Each of these special partnerships generate new business for Tejari and its clients. For example, the partnership between JAFZA and Tejari will help more than 5000 companies located in JAFZA to send and receive trade leads, create online company profiles and product showrooms, and find suitable trading partners through the website's secure environment. Similarly, the establishment of 'mylinkDubai.com', accessible to all businesses registered with DED, enables Dubai-based companies to contact more potential partners and undertake more business in the region.

The UAE's leading position in use of the internet to facilitate business is well illustrated by the impressive success of online trading websites such as Tejari.

In addition, Tejari introduced 'Tejari Expert' in 2006. This new strategic consulting service assists companies to manage their buying and selling practices in a structured and organised manner. Organisations such as Gulf Extrusions and Dubai Municipality have been early users of the service. Tejari has also been extending its presence beyond the UAE, opening new offices in Oman and Saudi Arabia, following a rise in demand for online procurement of services from these countries.

At the fifth annual Glocalisation conference held in Ankara, Turkey in August 2006, Tejari signed an agreement with Glocal Forum to create an online portal to provide procurement services to a network

The Glocal Forum is dedicated to improving inter-city relations by means of a merger of global opportunities and local interests.

of more than 100 city administrations across the five continents. The Glocal Forum, an international non-profit organisation bringing together major international institutions like the World Bank and several specialised UN agencies, private sector partners and other global actors to work at local level, is dedicated to improving inter-city relations by means of 'glocalisation', a merger of global opportunities and local interests. One of its major initiatives is the Glocal eCities Network programme to enable cities to modernise their governance processes with the use of information and communication technology (ICT). Under this new initiative, Tejari as the region's largest business-to-business marketplace, will build and manage a dedicated eCities portal and offer online procurement services to Glocal eCities Network members.

DIVERSIFICATION

Diversification of the economy has been a key plank of UAE policy, ever since the founding of the state in 1971. Funded from oil and gas sales, new investments were made initially in hydrocarbon and energy-related industries such as aluminium and petrochemicals.

While those sectors continue to be important, the overall manufacturing base has expanded considerably. The latest technologies and state-of-the-art facilities are now a feature of the UAE's manufacturing base, which includes cement and blocks, ceramics, textiles and clothing, pharmaceuticals, gold and jewellery, and other subsectors. Excluding the oil sector, the manufacturing industries sector contribution to GDP touched 19.5 per cent in 2005. The sector is a major driving force behind the diversification of sources of national income and is expected to continue its growth, facilitated by the availability of efficient infrastructure and communications within the industrial zones, the UAE's relative proximity to suppliers of raw materials (e.g. India and China) and buyers of final products (e.g. EU and Arab countries), together with the availability of private capital.

But it is the services sector that now plays the major role in terms of GDP contribution. A strong focus on transport in terms of ports and airports, shipping companies and airlines, together with efficient road networks, has underpinned a strategic plan aimed at creating a major transport hub between Europe and South-East Asia. Meanwhile the UAE's tourism industry is among the fastest growing in the world. An estimated 6.1 million tourists visited Dubai alone in 2005 and the recently established Abu Dhabi Tourism Authority has set itself a target of increasing Abu Dhabi's annual visitor numbers to over three million by 2015. It plans to achieve this with an expenditure of at least Dh40 billion (US$10.90 billion) during the next ten years. Other emirates are promoting tourism as well.

The manufacturing sector in the UAE is a major driving force behind the diversification of sources of national income.

The financial sector also played a valuable role in boosting the UAE economy in 2005 when banks witnessed an unprecedented boom fuelled in part by massive profits associated with financing applications for oversubscribed IPOs (see below). Islamic banking has also blossomed in the UAE, while the insurance sector has shown robust growth. Projects like Dubai International Financial Centre and the country's two main stock exchanges (in Abu Dhabi and Dubai) have provided a framework for growth in the financial subsector.

The financial sector played a valuable role in boosting the UAE economy in 2005.

BANKING, FINANCE & INSURANCE

Profits more than doubled for many financial institutions in 2005. The impressive gains by UAE banks were driven, at least in part, by profits related to booming local stock markets. The Dubai Financial Market index more than doubled in 2005, while the sister bourse in Abu Dhabi was up more than 80 per cent for the year. Turnover also increased sharply, while investor appetite for initial public offerings (IPOs) reached frenzied heights.

Rising markets led to increased sales of mutual funds, with lucrative performance fees for generating exceptional returns (most fees were based on absolute returns, rather than outperforming a benchmark). Many banks own brokerage subsidiaries, with fees rising sharply in line with turnover. Most important, though, were the extraordinary revenues from interest and arrangement fees on lending to investors buying IPO shares.

National Bank of Abu Dhabi (NBAD) stressed this fact when unveiling the bank's 127 per cent increase in net profit for 2005

The impressive gains by UAE banks were driven, at least in part, by profits relating to booming local stock markets.

to Dh2.billion (US$708 million). 'Buoyant local equity markets have helped our results this year,' the bank's CEO stated. Investment banking revenues more than tripled, contributing 43 per cent of group earnings. It was a similar story for many of the UAE's 21 locally owned banks.

In July 2006 Abu Dhabi Commercial Bank (ADCB) announced a record net profit for the first half of the year of Dh1198 million against Dh844 million for the same period in 2005, an increase of 42 per cent. The bank's chairman attributed the strong results to growth in core businesses complemented by the bank's participation as a receiving bank in the first quarter IPO issues. According to figures from Ernst & Young, UAE firms raised US$1.9 billion through IPOs in 2005, up from just US$500 million the previous year. Established listed firms raised even more through rights issues and banks made extra profits from financing the massive oversubscriptions for these primary issues. The 800 times oversubscribed IPO for Abu Dhabi's Aabar Petroleum illustrates the point. The firm wanted to raise just Dh485 million in capital, but attracted Dh385 billion in subscriptions – more than the UAE's gross domestic product. Most of that money was borrowed.

The participation of Abu Dhabi Commercial Bank in the public offerings of many new companies accounted for 30 per cent of the bank's total revenues in the first quarter of 2006.

Loans and deposits related to two massive initial pubic offerings (IPOs) accounted for 45 per cent of eight UAE banks' total assets in the first quarter of 2006. Banks lending to individuals to finance IPO subscriptions generated significant revenues from interest and fees – the cost of subscribing being measured in a multiple of the allocation rather than a percentage of the allocation, bringing huge gains to the banks. Reporting on the performance of Abu Dhabi Commercial Bank at the end of the first quarter of 2006, its chairman stated that a net profit surge of 182 per cent was linked to the bank's participation in the public offerings of many new companies, an activity that accounted for 30 per cent of the bank's total revenues for the period.

Two major IPOs took place in the UAE during the period, including 'du', the country's second telecoms operator, which was 167 times oversubscribed, attracting Dh400 billion. The subscription set a world record, according to Bloomberg News. Banks treat IPO-related

income differently on their balance sheets, some declaring it as interest income and some as fee income.

But the fall in stock markets towards the end of the first quarter changed the climate for launching new IPOs as a crisis of confidence gripped investors across the world's biggest oil exporting region. Dubai's main index fell almost 60 per cent in the first half of 2006 and it was not until late July that activity in this field began to pick up again with Dubai-based shipping company Gulf Navigation Company starting the ball rolling with a US$248 million initial public offering. The company, which transports crude oil and chemicals, offered investors a 55 per cent stake, or 910 million new shares at Dh1 (US$0.272) each.

Meanwhile shares in mortgage lender Tamweel debuted at three times the IPO price in July 2006, but tumbled soon after as leveraged investors bailed out to book what gains they could. Tamweel's IPO in March had been more than 500 times oversubscribed.

Officials from the Central Bank and the Ministry of Economy were actively considering changes to the rules associated with IPOs.

Massive oversubscriptions in IPOs generated significant revenues for the banks.

Massive oversubscriptions were of concern to the UAE Government, which drafted reforms to the country's securities law aimed at curtailing the situation. The aim is to move towards a more conventional method of IPO pricing, with investment banks acting as book runners.

TRADE

In 2005, the UAE was the third largest US trading partner in the Middle East.

Free trade is considered to be a *sine qua non* for improving competitiveness and productivity. The UAE considers that high tariff barriers and technical barriers to trade would only result in a stagnant and inefficient private sector. It is in this spirit that the UAE has signed several free trade agreements (FTA) and embarked on negotiations, either individually or through the GCC. Bilateral preferential agreements signed with Syria, Jordan, Lebanon, Morocco and Iraq accord both the UAE and its co-signatories preferential access for certain specified goods. The FTA between the GCC and the EU, in final stages of negotiation during 2006, covers market access for industrial and agricultural products, trade in services, intellectual property, rules of origin, government procurement, investment and legal and institutional arrangements. It is expected to boost trade between the two regions from its current level of 40 billion euro to at least twice that figure. Meanwhile a comprehensive FTA has been under negotiation for some time with the United States of America. Trade between the US and the UAE amounted to US$10 billion (Dh36.7 billion) in 2005, making it the third largest US trading partner in the Middle East. Talks to establish FTAs have also begun with both Australia and New Zealand.

The UAE is a staunch advocate of removal of trade barriers and fostering of greater international trading ties.

A staunch advocate of removal of trade barriers and fostering of greater international trading ties, the UAE, along with all other GCC member states, is a signatory of GAFTA (The Greater Arab Free Trade Area).

Goods imported into the UAE from countries with most favoured nations (MFN) status are subject to the GCC Common External Tariff (CET), which averaged around 5 per cent in 2005/06. Over

400 basic food items and pharmaceuticals are duty-free. Tobacco products attract up to a 100 per cent tax rate, depending on the item. Average tariff protection in 2005 was 5.3 per cent for manufacturing activities, 5 per cent for mining and quarrying, and 3.3 per cent for agriculture.

With the exception of oil, gas and petrochemicals, the primary export centres in the UAE are free zones that provide logistical, administrative and financial advantages for exporting or re-exporting companies. These free zones are exempt from the licensing, agency, emiratisation, and national majority-ownership obligations that apply in the domestic economy. There are many success stories among the companies operating from the UAE's free zones, with major enterprises using the UAE as a base to compete efficiently in the international market place.

UAE free zones provide logistical, administrative and financial advantages for exporting and re-exporting companies

Approximately 70 per cent of the UAE's trade passes through Dubai, whose trade increased by 30 per cent in 2005 compared to the previous year. India took over from China as the largest importer, due largely to high figures for gold imports. Dubai handles 10 per cent of the world's physical gold each year. Total trade passing through Dubai ports increased from Dh215.73 billion in 2004 to Dh280.46 billion in 2005. Dubai maintained its status as a major re-exporter, with a total of Dh78.82 billion worth of goods moving through the city's ports in 2005, representing a 38.22 per cent increase over 2004. Total imports increased by 27.75 per cent from Dh149.04 billion in 2004 to Dh190.40 in 2005 and exports grew by 16.39 per cent from Dh9.64 billion to Dh11.22 billion. One of the biggest segments is the re-export of machinery, electrical and electronics equipment, with Dh45.23 billion being imported and Dh20.89 billion being re-exported.

Dubai maintained its status as a major re-exporter in 2005.

REVISION OF COMMERCIAL AGENCIES LAW

The close relationship between local traders and international manufacturers in the UAE is regulated by the Commercial Agencies Law, which was revised in June 2006 to bring greater clarity into the situation and to ensure that matters of dispute can be fairly dealt with by the UAE courts. Revisions introduced to the law support an open economy that encourages local and international investment from people of all nationalities. The new law allows principals and agents the freedom to mutually agree the duration and other terms of their contracts. Once the signatories to a commercial agency agreement have set a specific duration for their contract, the executive authority (Ministry of Economy) will allow the agency to be terminated or deregistered at the end of its term. If the contract does not give a fixed term, the agency agreement will be deemed to exist for an indefinite period. In the event of any dispute arising in connection with the contract, the matter is now brought before the courts for a decision. The law took effect immediately upon publication and therefore Articles 8, 9, 23 of the old law were replaced with Articles 8, 9 and 23 of the new law and Articles 27 and 28 of the old law were repealed.

MANUFACTURING & INDUSTRIAL DEVELOPMENT

Food processing and packaging is a growing ingredient in the UAE's manufacturing sector.

The policy of diversification, which has had such a positive impact on the UAE economy, has taken place at all levels, from street-side metal manufacturers to larger scale factories. Indeed, some of the huge factories that play such an important role in the UAE economy had their beginnings as much smaller ventures with just a few employees. This diversification that is so visible throughout the UAE has not happened by chance. It has been part of Government policy since the founding of the state in 1971, and the governments of individual emirates have played a key role in this process. Initially the UAE took advantage of its established oil and gas operations to develop related industries, such as petrochemicals, fertilisers, cement and aluminium. Subsequently, the range of manufactured goods widened to include electronic items and light machinery for export. Currently, major growth areas include capital-intensive high-technology industries supplying, among other items, security and safety equipment; information technology equipment; medical equipment and services; construction products; air conditioning and refrigerating equipment; environmental and pollution control equipment; and sporting equipment.

The UAE took advantage of its established oil and gas operations to develop related industries, such as petrochemicals, fertilisers, cement, and aluminium.

Import substitution and strong local markets are driving forces for further growth in the UAE manufacturing sector. If one excludes the free zones (of which there are over 23 and Jebel Ali alone imports over US$20 billion worth of manufactured goods a year), the UAE imports around US$35 billion of manufactured goods and exports US$2.4 billion worth each year, mostly in the form of aluminium, other articles of base metal, and plastic and rubber articles.

In June 2005 a law was issued for the establishment of the Khalifa Fund to support and develop small and medium-size enterprises (SMEs). The new organisation established by the fund, named Bidaya, provides financial support and technical assistance for SMEs, and had an initial capital of Dh300 million (US$81.69 million).

INDUSTRIAL CITIES

Industrial development requires a coordinated infrastructure and the UAE has therefore focused on a number of 'industrial cities' where all the necessary support facilities are provided and where clustering of production units creates time- and cost-saving synergies.

Abu Dhabi has made substantial progress in promoting industrial growth. Much of this effort, coordinated by the Higher Corporation for Specialised Economic Zones, has been directed at establishment of many industrial cities in the emirate, including ICAD1 and ICAD2. HCSEZ acts as a catalyst and enabler, providing investors with an integrated state-of-the-art infrastructure and services in these business-friendly economic zones. It aims to attract and promote industries that are knowledge-, energy- and capital-intensive.

Specialised business-friendly economic zones provide investors with an integrated state-of-the-art infrastructure and services.

Minimum bureaucracy and maximum efficiency are two of the prime factors that have attracted companies to site their projects in the ICAD centres. Swift issuance of government permits and licences, allocation of suitable land for factories, a fully developed infrastructure and a wide range of dedicated business support services are further aspects listed as key to the success of the ICAD programme. These high-value strategic industry clusters are playing an important role in transforming Abu Dhabi into an industrial, services and logistics hub connected to both regional and global markets. Key sectors positioning themselves in ICAD include basic metals, building products and construction materials, oil and gas services, agriculture and food processing, paper and wood products, automotive industries, logistics services, high-tech industries, financial services, pharmaceutical and medical companies, and chemical and petrochemical industries.

THE GENERAL HOLDING CORPORATION

The General Holding Corporation (GHC), a wholly-owned entity of the Abu Dhabi government, together with the Higher Corporation for Special Economic Zones, is responsible for devising and implementing the industrial diversification strategy of Abu Dhabi and the establishment of specialised clusters of industry within special economic zones. GHC owns, in addition to Emirates Iron and Steel Factory, Emirates Cement Factory in Al Ain, Anabib Pipe Factories and Emirates Food Industries (Aghzia).

THE UAE OFFSETS GROUP (UOG)

The UAE Offsets Group has created four joint stock companies with thousands of citizens as shareholders, and brought in technical expertise and know-how for establishment of new business ventures.

The UAE Offsets Group was established in 1992 to implement the UAE Offsets Programme and to act as a conduit between international contractors and the local private sector for the creation of commercially viable, profitable and sustainable joint ventures. It is now playing a pivotal role as a think-tank for setting up joint ventures. UOG has implemented over 25 successful ventures with a combined paid-up capital of Dh5 billion (US$1.3 billion). It has also created four joint stock companies with thousands of citizens as shareholders, and brought in technical expertise and know-how for establishment of new business ventures ranging from shipbuilding, aircraft leasing and fish-farming to district cooling, agriculture, waste management and energy.

UOG plays the role of a conduit between the joint venture partners. Offsets ventures should yield profits of up to 60 per cent of a contract's value over a period of several years – the typical duration of an offset obligation is seven years – to earn offset credits that are evaluated at several milestones during the life of each offset project. The performance of the joint ventures is closely monitored by UOG and, if defence contractors fail to fulfil obligations, they are required to pay liquidated damages of 8.5 per cent on the unfulfilled portion of the obligation.

For defence contractors with small obligations, UOG has formed the Alfiah Fund. This is an investment vehicle whereby defence contractors can earn credits based on the Fund's performance rather than setting up independent offsets projects. The Alfiah Fund, managed by the First Gulf Bank (FGB), is capitalised at US$10 million and seeks to maximise returns from a diversified portfolio of investments in civilian ventures under the UOG programme. Initial investment by the Fund in a single project ranges from US$500,000 to US$3.5 million.

MUBADALA DEVELOPMENT COMPANY

Mubadala Development, an investment company wholly owned by the Abu Dhabi government, was established under Emiri decree No. 12 of 2002. It has a mandate to form new companies or to acquire stakes in existing companies in the UAE or abroad and to focus on generating sustainable economic benefits for Abu Dhabi Emirate through partnerships with local, regional and international investors. The company invests in a wide range of sectors, including energy, utilities, real estate, public-private partnerships, and basic industries and services, in order to diversify and further develop the economy of Abu Dhabi.

Dolphin Energy, owned 51 per cent by Mubadala, is responsible for the Dolphin Gas Project, the first cross-border natural gas network in the GCC. Natural gas from Qatar's North Field passes through Dolphin's giant gas processing plant at Ra's Laffan. The plant strips out valuable commercial by-products and the resulting dry gas is transported by pipeline to Abu Dhabi via Dolphin's 370-kilometre export pipeline. This innovative and brave venture was on schedule to commence transport of up to 2 billion cubic foot per day of natural gas from Qatar to the UAE in late 2006 or early 2007 and supply gas to Oman from 2008.

Dolphin began upgrading the Eastern Gas Distribution System (EGDS) in 2006, enabling the company to efficiently deliver its gas from Qatar to its customers in Abu Dhabi, Dubai and the Northern Emirates during 2007 and subsequently Oman in 2008. The company also announced that it is studying the possibility

The Dolphin Gas Project is the first cross-border natural gas network in the GCC.

Dry gas is transported by pipeline to Abu Dhabi.

of a second stage expansion to produce another 1.2 billion cubic feet per day of gas in Qatar.

Other Mubadala investments in the energy field during 2005/06 included expansion of the oil and gas global portfolio of its wholly owned subsidiary, Liwa Energy Limited. An agreement for development of the Mukhaizna heavy oil field in Oman is an example of Mubadala's interest in regional energy projects. The current production of the field is approximately 10,000 barrels per day. Liwa Energy and their partners in the project expect to implement a large-scale steam flood to increase production from the field to 150,000 barrels per day within the next few years.

Another venture for Mubadala in Oman is its agreement to work with Oman Oil Company to develop the Salalah Methanol Project. The project entails the development, construction and operation of a 3000 tonne per day state-of-the-art methanol plant, using natural gas, supplied by Ministry of Oil and Gas through Oman Gas Company, as feedstock.

Liwa, in partnership with Occidental Petroleum and Woodside Petroleum, has also obtained oil concessions in Libya.

In addition to investments in the energy field, Mubadala has a wide variety of business interests including utilities, real estate, public-private partnerships and basic industries and services.

Mubadala's varied business interests include, among others, shareholdings in 'district cooling' company, National Central Cooling Company (Tabreed); property company, Aldar Properties PJSC; shipping company, Eships (formerly CCU); shipbuilder, Abu Dhabi Ship Building Company (ADSB); aviation and pilot training company, Horizon International Flight Academy; UAE University Development and Management Project in Al Ain; Imperial College London Diabetes Centre in Abu Dhabi; IT company, Injazat Data Systems; and automobile companies, LeasePlan Corporation and Ferrari; and Al Hikma Development Company that is developing a modern campus for the UAE University on a BOOT (Build Own Operate and Transfer) basis. Al Hikma will act as the lead operator and has assigned Khadamat Facility Management Company, a joint venture between Mubadala Development and SERCO PLC of the UK, to provide support services, maintenance and day-to-day operations for the campus.

As we discuss below, in February 2006 Mubadala also took major strides towards establishment of an Abu Dhabi aluminium smelter.

METAL INDUSTRIES

Aluminium

Aluminium smelting is moving from strength to strength in the UAE with prospects of developing the world's largest aluminium smelter in Abu Dhabi and Dubai's Dubal hardly pausing for breath in its own impressive expansion plans. By mid-2006 Dubal had already sold its entire production for the year, amounting to 861,000 tonnes of aluminium. But not all of the action is taking place in the UAE itself. Abu Dhabi Water and Electricity Authority (ADWEA) recently acquired a 40 per cent stake in a new 325-kiloton aluminium smelter to be built on the Batinah coast of Oman, at Sohar. It is in partnership on the project with Oman Oil Company and the multinational aluminium company, Alcan. The project is expected to commence production in 2008. In March 2005, Dubal entered into a provisional agreement with one of India's engineering and construction conglomerates (Larsen and Toubro) to build a Dh3.67 billion combined bauxite mining and alumina refinery in India's Orissa state.

Aluminium smelting is moving from strength to strength in the UAE.

But the heart of the UAE's aluminium investments remain firmly centred within its own borders. Perhaps the most impressive of these developments, still on the drawing board, is the massive smelter, which is planned for Abu Dhabi. This is based on a Joint Development Agreement (JDA) between Mubadala, owned by the Abu Dhabi government, and Dubal that entails construction and operation of a more than US$6 billion world-class green-field aluminium smelter complex with 1.2 million tonnes capacity a year and related facilities at Taweelah in Abu Dhabi. This will make it the largest single-site aluminium smelter in the world. The two entities will jointly develop, construct, own and operate the complex at the new Khalifa Port and Industrial Zone in Taweelah. The smelter is to be developed in two phases and the first phase is expected to be operational in 2010, with front engineering and design studies scheduled for completion in 2007.

A joint venture between Mubadala and Dubal entails construction of the largest single-site aluminium smelter complex in the world, Emirates Aluminum Limited (EMAL).

Later in the year, the General Holding Company signed an agreement with the world aluminium giant, Comalco, part of the

Rio Tinto group, to study the feasibility of another smelter, possibly to be located in Abu Dhabi's western industrial zone of Ruwais.

The aluminium business extends far beyond the smelting process and the UAE intends to participate in all profitable aspects of the sector. A joint steering committee with senior officials from Mubadala and Dubal has been formed to look into possible business opportunities and to study the creation of a UAE-based centre for excellence, research and development in the aluminium industry. The steering committee is also mandated to study and develop the economic basis for other upstream and downstream integrated investment opportunities in the aluminium industry such as production of calcined coke, development of aluminium rolling mills and possible applications in the automotive industry.

This historic deal between Dubal and Mubadala will result in creation of more than 4000 jobs, of which a large percentage will be taken up by UAE nationals.

This historic deal between Dubal and Mubadala will result in creation of more than 4000 jobs, of which a large percentage will be taken up by UAE nationals. The project will also add value to the local energy pool, creating an industrial venture that will have over 2 million tonnes capacity as well as raw material production and downstream applications. Demand for aluminium is growing at an annual rate of 4 per cent or 1.3 million tonnes a year.

The market for Dubal's aluminium is very strong. The company sold 600,000 metric tonnes in 2005 and following its June 2006 announcement that it had no more aluminium for sale during the rest of the year, it announced its own plans for further development – a major Dh700 million (US$190 million) Phase II expansion plan that will increase production capacity by 60,000 tonnes a year to 920,000 tonnes. The expansion plan is part of Dubal's roadmap to increase the total production capacity to 1.5 million tonnes per annum and comes on top of a Dh380 million capacity enhancement programme initiated by Dubal in 2004, taking its total investment to more than Dh1 billion (US$272 million) so far.

In keeping with its environmentally aware policies, 20 per cent of the total investment in the expansion will be spent on environmental protection plants. The project will be managed in-house by UAE national engineers with assistance from SNC-Lavelin, international experts in aluminium expansion projects.

Electric Cables

Dubai Cable Company (Ducab) manufactures low- and medium-voltage electric cables and is a 50:50 joint-venture between the Dubai and Abu Dhabi governments. Ducab's sales revenues increased by 30 per cent in 2004 to US$187 million (Dh687 million). The company has recently expanded its business by entering into new export markets in Iran, India, Jordan, and Tanzania under major projects and distribution agreements.

Ducab recently made a capital investment of Dh125 million (US$34 million) to set up a copper rod casting plant in its Abu Dhabi factory premises. The move was part of the company's strategy for backward integration of processes, mainly to cater for its raw material requirements needed for the manufacture of high quality power cables. The new plant will be able to produce up to 160,000 tonnes of 8 millimetre copper rod a year and will be equipped with the most advanced technology and equipment to ensure superior quality and high yield.

Dubai Cable Company has recently expanded its business into new export markets in Iran, India, Jordan and Tanzania.

Ducab is also well known as the supplier of Ducab Connect cable accessories. The company has always placed an emphasis on quality control and is certified to ISO 9001:2000 quality management systems and ISO 14001 environment protection systems. In late 2005 Ducab acquired ISO 9001:2000 certification for its Abu Dhabi plant.

Steel

National demand for steel is currently estimated at approximately 2.5 million tonnes per year and is forecast to reach 4 million tonnes per year in the medium term. A steel factory, with an initial capacity of 500,000 tonnes of 10 to 32 millimetre diameter steel per annum, in the Mussafah Industrial Area, in Abu Dhabi, uses imported raw material. Substantial expansion plans for this complex, which forms part of Emirates Iron and Steel Factory, were announced in January 2006. Once completed, annual output capacity will reach a total of approximately 2 million tonnes of rebar and wire rod. The expansion will be built on 1.5 million square metres of land adjacent to the existing operations and will include two new rolling mills and an integrated steel plant

Steel factory expansion plans will increase annual output capacity to approximately 2 million tonnes of rebar and wire rod.

comprising a direct reduction plant utilising HYL technology and associated steel melt shop. In addition, a jetty dedicated to the handling of raw materials will be constructed.

Steps have also been implemented to further increase Abu Dhabi's steel production capacity with the construction of a Phase II steel plant manufacturing flat products. Taken together, these expansions will generate an output of 4 million tonnes of steel products per year.

Magnesium Alloy

A magnesium alloy plant is under construction at Sharjah's Free Zone. The magnesium smelter project is being promoted by the Sahari Group of Abu Dhabi and Normans of Albania, with a 50 per cent stake each in the project. The plant's initial production capacity will be 20,000 tonnes per year of magnesium products, to be increased to 60,000 tonnes upon completion. Raw material (magnesium) will come from mines in Albania. The production is expected to be exported.

PETROCHEMICALS AND FERTILISERS

Abu Dhabi is planning to grow its petrochemicals industry, both as a result of existing facilities expansion and through the establishment of new projects.

The UAE's oil and gas industry has spawned a major associated petrochemicals industry that produces a variety of materials including plastics, melamine, fertilisers and urea. Abu Dhabi has several major petrochemical and fertiliser industrial complexes: the Ruwais Fertiliser Industries Company (Fertil), the Abu Dhabi Polymers Company (Borouge), and Abu Dhabi Fertiliser Industries Company (Adfert).

Abu Dhabi is planning to grow this sector, both as a result of existing facilities expansion and through establishment of new projects that will produce derivatives such as melamine, polyethylene (PE), polypropylene, polyvinyl chloride (PVC), vinyl chloride monomer (VCM), linear alpha olefins and aromatics. Prior to new developments, in mid-2006, Fertil was producing 1850 tonnes per day of urea and 1340 tonnes per day of ammonia. Of this it was exporting 100,000 tonnes per annum of liquid ammonia and more than 625,000 tonnes per annum (tpa) of urea. The recent expansion programme at Fertil should add 1.2 million tpa of urea to its production. The new plant is due for completion by the fourth quarter of 2008 and the additional urea production of about 1.2 million tpa will come on-stream in mid-2010. In addition to enabling useful utilisation of flue gas CO_2, the new technology will also make a welcome contribution to environmental preservation through reduction of CO_2 emissions.

Other fertiliser companies include Adfert, Kemira and Spic. Adfert can produce up to 200,000 tpa of water-soluble and granular compound fertilisers and also produces liquid and suspension fertilisers. Dubai's first fertiliser plant, a joint venture between Kemira Agro Øy of Finland (49 per cent) and the local firm Union Agricultural Group (51 per cent), has the capacity to produce 6000 tpa of water-soluble compound fertilisers. A second fertiliser plant developed by the same group, called the Kemira Emirates Fertiliser Company (KEFCO), produces around 60,000 tpa of phosphate and nitrogenous fertilisers, and was brought on-stream in 2001 in the Jebel Ali Free Zone. A much larger plant (developed by Spic Fertilisers and Chemicals) with a capacity to produce 600,000 tpa of ammonia and 440,000 tpa of granular urea came on-stream in mid-2005. The plant is being supplied with 40,000 million btu/day of natural gas feedstock by Dubai Supply Authority (Dusup) and exports all its output to India.

PLASTICS

Since the completion of its production site in Ruwais in 2001, Borouge has become a leading supplier of value-adding specialist plastics materials for applications such as water, gas and industrial pipe systems, power and telecommunications cables, advanced packaging, medical devices and automotive components. This has brought the company an annual turnover of US$860 million in 2005. At the present time the petrochemical complex, which cost an estimated US$1.2 billion to develop, includes a 600,000 tpa ethane cracker that supplies ethylene feedstock to two 225,000 tpa polyethylene units. It produces up to 580,000 tonnes of Borstar bimodal high-, medium-, and linear low-density polyethylene per year. Combining good processability with excellent mechanical properties, Borouge Borstar products are claimed to be stronger,

Borouge is a leading supplier of value-adding specialist plastics materials for applications such as water, gas and industrial pipe systems, power and telecoms cables, advanced packaging, medical devices and automotive components.

lighter, environmentally friendly and more malleable than conventional polyethylene, resulting in material savings of up to 30 per cent.

Notwithstanding its excellent results to date, Borouge has significant expansion plans. The multi-billion Borouge-2 expansion project in Abu Dhabi is due for completion by mid-2010. This will be one of the world's largest plastics projects and will triple production capacity at the existing Ruwais facility. The project will encourage the growth of downstream industries and increase the company's capacity to serve growing markets in the Middle East and Asia. The ground-breaking expansion project comprises an ethane cracker that will produce 1.4 million tonnes of ethylene per annum and the world's biggest 752 kta olefins conversion unit. Its two Borstar enhanced polypropylene PP plants will have a combined annual capacity of 800,000 tonnes, while the Borstar enhanced PE plant will have an annual capacity of 540,000 tonnes.

CEMENT

Cement consumption in the UAE was 2920 kilograms per capita, or nine times the world average.

The UAE cement sector, one of the oldest manufacturing industries in the country, continues to be extremely buoyant. Per capita cement consumption (PCC) in the UAE during 2005 was 2920 kilograms against the GCC's 2025 kilograms and a world average of only 320 kilograms. Contributing factors have included rising oil prices, an increase in inbound investment, both by nationals and by fellow Gulf Cooperation Council (GCC) nations, low interest rates and access to credit, a relatively free economy and liberal real estate laws. These have contributed to an unprecedented rise in construction activities and associated cement consumption.

Demand for cement increased from 5.8 million tonnes per annum in 2001 to around 14 million tonnes per annum during 2005. Cement manufacturers increased their capacities extensively to meet the sharp rise in demand. But despite these measures there was still a shortfall in the supply-demand chain and this was met by imports from India and the Far East. The shortage led to a rise in the cement prices from Dh265 to Dh270 per tonne compared with Dh135 to Dh145 during 2000/01 when there was excess supply. At times during 2004 and 2005 the cement market was frenzied and demand was so high that the retail prices of the standard 50 kilogram bag reached Dh25–27 as compared to the mid-2006 level of around Dh16.

In April 2006 cement and clinker production were estimated at 14.7 million tonnes and 8.4 million tonnes, respectively. Limestone is available locally, but bauxite, iron ore, and gypsum are imported. Factories operating throughout the country produce clinker and Portland cement; one factory in Ra's al-Khaimah manufactures white cement. Approximately 70 per cent of the market is concentrated amongst the top six companies. There are around eight integrated cement companies (with clinker and grinding facilities) in the UAE and another four to five grinding units. Gulf Cement Company (GCEM) was the market leader with a 17 per cent share of the total cement capacity of the UAE during 2005, followed by Sharjah Cement and Industrial Development Company (SCIDC) with 15 per cent share. Fujairah Cement and National Cement followed next with 12 per cent and 10 per cent share respectively. However, by late 2006 the Union Cement Company (UCC) had become the largest player in the market, followed by SCIDC and GCEM.

There are around eight integrated cement companies (with clinker and grinding facilities) in the UAE and another four to five grinding units. Gulf Cement Company (GCEM) was the market leader with a 17 per cent share of the total cement capacity of the UAE during 2005, followed by Sharjah Cement and Industrial Development Company (SCIDC) with 15 per cent share.

Other developments in this field are being revealed on a regular basis. In mid-2006 the Emirates Cement Factory, owned by Abu Dhabi's General Holding Company, announced a new plant to be set up in Fujairah. The new unit, Arkan Building Materials Company, was to be capitalised at Dh1.75 billion (US$476 million), of which Dh857.5 million (US$234 million) would be raised through an initial public offering (IPO). The new plant will have a capacity of 3.1 million tonnes per annum. Fifty-one per cent of Arkan is to be owned by GHC and 49 per cent by the public shareholders.

Also in 2006 Ro'ya Industrial Company announced that it would establish the Ro'ya Cement Factory at a cost of Dh1.5 billion (US$408 million) and a planned production capacity of 3.6 million tonnes a year. This plant is to be located at the Hamriyah Free Zone in Sharjah. Ro'ya leased 1 million square metres at HFZ for 25 years to build its new factory, whose construction is expected to take two years.

Pioneer Cement Industry company also announced a new project for Ra's al-Khaimah with a 1 million tonnes production capacity.

PHARMACEUTICALS

Pharmaceutical products Federal Law No. 4 of 1983 is the main law regulating the pharmaceutical industry. The Ministry of Health is responsible for licensing pharmaceutical companies, both in the customs territory and in the free zones. Pharmaceutical imports account for about 1 per cent of the entire import bill of the country. Despite a developing manufacturing base within the UAE, the local market remains 80 per cent dependent upon imported medicines, whilst most of those produced in the UAE are primarily for export. The establishment of special free zones such as Dubai Healthcare City (DHC) has provided a boost for local production.

At the present time there are about ten pharmaceutical and related products manufacturing companies in the UAE. The leader is Gulf Pharmaceutical Industries, known as Julphar, which is based in Ra's al-Khaimah. Julphar is a composite corporation having seven manufacturing plants. Five are situated in UAE and one each in South America and Europe. In addition to the manufacturing plants, Julphar also has several wholly owned subsidiaries that work as independent entities and provide a large network for distribution, warehousing, transportation and pharmacy management in UAE as well as in Oman. Julphar also owns several other support units, such as a printing and packaging unit; and plastic dosing cup and aluminium pilfer-proof cap manufacturing plants.

Julphar employs a workforce of about 1500 worldwide and manufactures more than 275 products.

Julphar employs a workforce of about 1500 worldwide and manufactures more than 275 products. The company's primary manufacturing plants are located at the Ra's al-Khaimah site where four plants produce oral and topical products, penicillin, antibiotics, injectable products, topical antiseptics, surgical rubbing solutions, syrups, suspensions and over-the-counter pharmaceuticals, as well as consumer products such as household disinfectants. The company has a production capacity of over 1 billion units.

Until recently Julphar was the only significant UAE-based manufacturer, but it has been joined in the last few years by newcomers including Neopharma in Abu Dhabi, Global Pharma and Gulf Injects in Dubai and Medpharma in Sharjah.

Neopharma is a large-scale producer of tablets, capsules and liquid orals. Costing around US$25 million to build, the company is Abu Dhabi's first state-of-the-art pharmaceutical facility. Its plant, spread over an area of 100,000 square metres, encompasses two independent production blocks – one dedicated for the manufacture of general products and the other exclusively used for manufacturing betalactam products.

Globalpharma, making a wide range of products including tablets, capsules, dry syrups, liquid oral syrups and suspensions, is a subsidiary of Dubai Investment PJSC. Whilst Dubai Investments holds 65 per cent equity in Globalpharma, the remaining 35 per cent is held by Kopran Ltd, one of the leading healthcare concerns in India. The Globalpharma site is situated in Dubai Investment Park, about 50 kilometres from the heart of Dubai City. The factory has two separate manufacturing units, for penicillin and non-penicillin products, with the utilities in a separate block.

Gulf Inject manufactures, in technical collaboration with Fresenius AG, of Germany, intra-venous (I.V.) fluids. It produces the I.V. Fluids using the 'form-fill-seal' technology, which is widely accepted as the safest and most aseptic technology to manufacture I.V. Fluids. Manufacturing facilities conform to the US Federal Standards 209 E.

The UAE also has three manufacturing facilities for the production of disposable medical syringes in Dubai, Sharjah and Abu Dhabi.

CERAMICS

RAK Ceramics' latest facility in the UAE is the world's largest single ceramic products plant. The company invested Dh735 million (US$200 million) to boost its combined annual capacity to 100 million square metres of ceramic tiles. It now accounts for 5 per cent of the total world production of ceramic tiles and it has also formed a new company, in which it holds a 50 per cent stake, to produce 15 million pieces of ceramic tableware per year.

RAK Ceramics owns the world's largest single ceramics product plant, accounting for 5 per cent of the total world production of ceramic tiles.

The company's UAE factories are located 20 kilometres south of Ra's al-Khaimah City, along the highway to Dubai. While it runs the business from its UAE base, it has also established an extensive international network of factories. In 2005 it announced a new joint venture with the world's largest producer of adhesive substances and ceramic fixing grouts, Laticrete International. The new company, Laticrete RAK Co. LLC, whose factory is located in Ra's al-Khaimah, is able to produce 100,000 tonnes of adhesive material and ceramic fixing grouts.

Company milestones in 2005/06 included opening of its ninth plant (capacity 30,000 square metres per day); receiving ISO 9001–2000 approval from BVQI; starting its fourth overseas tiles projects in Iran with a production capacity of 10,000 square metres per day; doubling capacity to 34,000 square metres per day at its China tiles plant; doubling capacity to 20,000 square metres per day at its Sudan plant; sales at its UAE operations reaching Dh1 billion (US$272 million) for the year; starting its fifth overseas tiles project in India with a capacity of 20,000 square metres per day; commencing work on its second overseas sanitaryware plant with a production capacity of 1000 pieces per day in India; and also commencing production at its tenth tile plant in Ra's al-Khaimah, which has a capacity of 45,000 square metres per day.

There are approximately 350 outlets in Dubai's Gold Souq and between them they display about 20 tonnes of jewellery at any given time.

GOLD & JEWELLERY

Dubai imported 522 tonnes of gold in 2005, up from 502 tonnes in 2004. A survey released in 2006 indicated that shoppers in the UAE spend on average 30 times more on gold than the rest of the world. Seventy per cent of gold buyers were from South Asia, followed by 22 per cent from East Asia, and with Arab and European consumers accounting for 4 per cent each of the total. The UAE provides ample opportunity for gold lovers to purchase fine quality jewellery. There are approximately 350 outlets in Dubai's Gold Souq and between them they display about 20 tonnes of jewellery at any given time. UAE shoppers buy an average of 30 grams of gold annually compared to the global average of less than 1 gram.

According to the World Gold Council regional office in Dubai, annual gold consumption in the UAE, in terms of sales, registered a 21 per cent increase in 2005 compared to the previous year (from Dh5.1 billion in 2004 to Dh6.2 billion in 2005). The figures place UAE as one of the top ten gold consuming countries in the world. In terms of tonnage, the UAE gold consumption (jewellery and investment) increased from some 96 tonnes in 2004 to 106 tonnes in 2005.

In March 2006 the Dubai Metals and Commodities Centre (DMCC) changed its name to the Dubai Multi Commodities Centre (DMCC) in order to reflect the broader brief of acting as an exchange for a variety of commodities in addition to gold and silver. Since its launch in 2002, the commodities centre has diversified into diamonds and has plans to launch futures trading in energy and several agricultural commodities. By late 2006 DMCC had almost a thousand registered free-zone businesses in various commodity sectors, including gold and precious metals, diamonds and coloured stones, tea and energy.

In June 2006 the UAE Government decided that the Dubai Diamond Exchange (DDE) should act as the sole gateway for imports and exports of polished diamonds in the UAE. The Exchange had previously been recognised as the single point of entry for rough diamonds and implements the Kimberly Process Certification Scheme in the UAE. The latter is a UN initiative meant to resolve conflict diamonds and involves the issue of a certificate by the diamond office at the source to certify that diamonds have been mined under legitimate conditions. The UAE is one of the largest trading centres in the world for rough diamonds, with the total trade in rough diamonds in Dubai jumping 46.25 per cent in 2005, to US$3.734 billion, up from US$2.553 billion in 2004. Dubai exported diamonds valued at US$2.248 billion in 2005, while imports for the same period touched US$1.484 billion.

The Dubai Gems Club (DGC), launched under the auspices of DMCC in mid-2006, is an exclusive trading platform dedicated to gemstones. Membership was initially restricted to about 25 companies with priority given to registered members of the DMCC free zone. Respecting the privacy of traders, in keeping with the international norms of the coloured stones and diamonds trade, Dubai Gems Club does not disclose statistics or details of trade transactions conducted through the Club, unless specially requested by the traders themselves. Housed in the premises of the Dubai Gem Certification Unit, Dubai Gems Club also offers members

In June 2006 the UAE Government decided that the Dubai Diamond Exchange (DDE) should act as the sole gateway for imports and exports of polished diamonds in the UAE.

The UAE is one of the largest trading centres in the world for rough diamonds.

easy access to the world's first ISO certified gem certification service for diamonds, gemstones, pearls and jewellery items from globally recognised certification bodies.

FILM PRODUCTION

The UAE's attractiveness for film-makers is based upon a number of socio-economic and physical characteristics. Film companies can operate in free zones on a tax free basis and be 100 per cent owned by international investors. The companies enjoy all the benefits of the UAE's liberal economy and they are also close to a large reservoir of potential finance. Add to that a wide variety of stunning scenery, an excellent climate for more than half the year, first class international flight connections, state-of-the-art communications, and one of the highest standards of living in the world and it is easy to understand the attraction.

Dubai Studio City

Dubai has created its own free zone aimed specifically at the film industry. Designed to accelerate the growth of the broadcast, film, television and music production industries, Dubai Studio City, still under development, is an ultra-modern facility integrating every component under one roof. Spread across 186,000 square metres, it includes production, post-production, equipment rental, business centre and satellite facilities, among others. It will also have residential areas, hotels, an entertainment centre, film schools and training institutes. This unique combination of world-class infrastructure, qualified professionals and productive networking environment will make it the ideal location for creative people to unleash their imagination.

Film companies can operate in free zones on a tax free basis and be 100 per cent owned by foreign investors.

Ra's al-Khaimah's Media City

Ra's al-Khaimah's Media City, at an early stage of development, is also attracting investors from the international film world. Mirage Holdings, a spin off of the USA company, Nickelson Entertainment Group (NEG), recently announced plans to set up one of the largest film and post-production centres in the world in Ra's al-Khaimah. The ambitious proposal states that the new facilities will be located on a 2 million square metres plot of land close to Emirates Road.

In addition to that plan, RAK Media City also signed agreements with Century Media Networks Incorporated, a South Asian group, which leased the first 20,000 square metre plot and is involved in television production and satellite up-linking.

OIL & GAS

The UAE has confirmed hydrocarbon reserves standing at 97.8 billion barrels of oil and 6 trillion cubic metres of natural gas. Based on current knowledge, the UAE's oil reserves account for 9.6 per cent of the world's total oil reserves. This ranks the UAE in fifth place in terms of the size of its oil reserves, and fourth in respect to its natural gas reserves.

The UAE currently produces around 2.8 million barrels of oil per day (b/d) and plans to raise its daily production capacity to 3.5 million b/d in the next few years. Abu Dhabi owns more than 90 per cent of the UAE's oil and natural gas resources. Dubai produces around 140,000 b/d of oil (6 per cent of the country's production) and substantial quantities of gas from offshore fields (with a major condensate field onshore); Sharjah is the third UAE hydrocarbon producer. On the East Coast, Fujairah is the second largest bunkering port in the world (handling about 1 million tonnes of fuel from neighbouring countries per month). Natural gas has been gaining in importance as a local energy source and is increasingly used by households and local industries, including for power generation and water desalination. Exports of gas have also increased. Oil and gas production is handled by the Abu Dhabi National Oil Company (ADNOC), or by subsidiaries in which ADNOC is the majority shareholder in partnership with international companies. The sharp rise in oil and gas prices on world markets, which began in 2004, continued through 2005 and much of 2006, resulting in higher than anticipated revenues from oil and gas sales. The industry is making significant investments to upgrade drilling, processing and transport facilities so that strong demand can be adequately met.

OIL

Exxon & Upper Zakum

In early 2006 ExxonMobil was formally awarded a 28 per cent equity interest for 20 years in Abu Dhabi's Upper Zakum oilfield. ADNOC retained 60 per cent share in the field and Japan Oil Development Co. (Jodco) continues to hold the remaining 12 per cent. Upper Zakum is one of the world's largest fields, contributing significantly to Abu Dhabi's production, and with potential for substantial production growth. ExxonMobil, with ADNOC and Jodco, will provide support to the joint operating company Zadco, which aims to increase production to around 750,000 barrels per day. Current production by the Zakum field is about 520,000 barrels per day. The US company is establishing an ExxonMobil Technology Centre in Abu Dhabi to apply the industry's most advanced technology to Upper Zakum in areas of reservoir management, well management and production operations. It will also provide support for training and personnel development.

UAE Energy Minister Mohammed bin Dhaen Al Hameli is the President of OPEC for 2007.

New Oil Fields in Abu Dhabi

Three new oil fields in Abu Dhabi were placed under development in 2006. As part of its expansion plans ADNOC's subsidiary Abu Dhabi Company for Onshore Oil Operations (ADCO) commenced work on Ruwais, Qusaihwira and Bida Al Qemzan, with an estimated Dh12.85 billion expected to be invested in drilling operations and construction of new production and support facilities. The greenfield developments are aimed at producing a total of at least 155,000 b/d.

Oil & Gas City is to be a tax-free zone set up by Abu Dhabi to create a cluster of companies involved in hydrocarbon industries.

Abu Dhabi Oil & Gas City

The Emirate of Abu Dhabi plans to set up a Dh4 billion (US$1.09 billion), tax-free zone for the energy industry, Oil & Gas City, which will start operations by the end of 2007. The City seeks to attract offshore firms that offer services such as consulting, financing, project management, and engineering, procurement and construction. The new development plans to provide work visas within 24 hours and allow repatriation of capital.

Dubai Oil Resources

It was announced in August 2006 that the Dubai government will take control of its offshore oil resources from 2 April 2007 following the ending of its agreement with the Dubai Petroleum Company (DPC) to operate the oilfields. DPC is owned by ConocoPhillips and part of the DPC/Dubai Marine Areas Limited

(DUMA) consortium involving interests from France's Total; Spain's Repsol YPF; and Germany's RWE Dea AG, a subsidiary of RWE AG and Wintershall AG, a subsidiary of BASF. It will end its role as operator, marking the end of Dubai's first offshore oil concession.

Dubai oil will continue to be freely traded in the international oil market under contracts established by the government and Dubai Petroleum Establishment (DPE), a new entity wholly owned by the Dubai government. From April 2007 DPE will be responsible for operating the oilfields and for all future business related to the production of oil and gas in Dubai. Petrofac, a UK-based company with extensive operations in the UAE, has been awarded a contract to operate the offshore fields for DPE.

Habshan to Fujairah Oil Pipeline

A strategic project that would pump UAE oil across the country to the bunkering port of Fujairah, thus avoiding the Straits of Hormuz, has been under investigation by IPIC from Abu Dhabi. A feasibility study being undertaken by Tebodin was commissioned by IPIC in July 2006 and involves a 350-kilometre 48-inch pipeline to carry crude from Habshan to Fujairah.

Oil Refineries & Their Products

Downstream development of refineries, petrochemical plants, and other related industries has created an integrated oil and gas sector. The UAE has five refineries with a combined capacity of more than 1.14 million b/d. The progressive build-up of refining capacity since the 1980s has made the UAE a sizeable net exporter of refined products; although their share in the total oil exports remains modest at about 10 per cent, it is on an upward trend. Furthermore, Abu Dhabi has been considering plans to further increase refinery capacity at Ruwais and also to build a new refinery at Fujairah. Four of the existing five UAE refineries are owned by the respective emirates; two are operated by Abu Dhabi Oil Refining Company (Takreer) and owned by ADNOC.

The UAE is planning to increase its refining capacity to 1.1 million barrels per day from a present level of 600,000 barrels per day.

Takreer's refining capacity is now over 500,000 b/d, making it a major regional operator. Other refineries are in Dubai, Sharjah and Fujairah. The Emirates National Oil Company condensate refinery

(ENOC), owned by Dubai Emirate, with a capacity of 120,000 b/d, began operations in Dubai in May 1999. Metro Oil, owned by the Fujairah government, owns a 90,000 b/d refinery. A 71,250 b/d privately owned second-hand unit was set up in Sharjah by the private Sharjah Oil Refining Company in 2001. The Metro Oil and Sharjah refineries were not operating in 2005/06.

Abu Dhabi Oil Refining Company known as Takreer is owned by ADNOC and presently operates two oil refineries with a capacity of over 500,000 barrels per day. It is in the process of expanding its Ruwais refinery. Meanwhile the International Petroleum Investment Company (IPIC) of Abu Dhabi is planning to build a new refinery in Fujairah.

As noted above, Takreer is keen to expand its Ruwais refinery. In April 2006 companies were invited to submit technical bids for a conceptual study contract covering a major expansion of this facility. Estimated to cost around US$3 billion, the proposed expansion of the Ruwais refinery would take the nominal capacity from its present level of 300,000 b/d to 415,000-b/d and increase its range of end-user products to include unleaded petrol, naphtha, aviation turbine fuel, liquefied petroleum gas (LPG), kerosene, gas-oil, bunker fuel and other hydrocarbon derivatives.

Products refined by Takreer are sold to international buyers at regional market prices by ADNOC, while domestic sales are undertaken by ADNOC Distribution, a separate legal entity in the ADNOC Group. Oil products are also marketed by ENOC and Emirates Petroleum Products Company (EPPCO). Petrol or gasoline prices are fixed by the UAE Government and are the same throughout the country. Gasoline of 95 and 98 octane is sold at fixed prices (Dh6.25 and Dh 6.75 a gallon in 2006), whilst all other domestically refined products such as diesel, jet oil, naphtha, bunkering oil, etc are sold at market rates. The mid-2006 price for diesel was Dh7.8 a gallon. Around 6 million tonnes of refined products per annum are sold domestically, while twice that quantity is exported.

Fujairah New Refinery

The International Petroleum Investment Company (IPIC) of Abu Dhabi signed a memorandum of understanding (MOU) in July 2006 with ConocoPhillips for a feasibility study on a 500,000 b/d refinery to be located in Fujairah. Subject to final approval of the project, it is envisaged that ConocoPhillips will retain 49 per cent of the project and IPIC will own 51 per cent. The project replaces an earlier plan for Takreer to build a refinery in Fujairah.

Fujairah Oil Treatment Plant

Fujairah Oil Technology, a 50:50 joint venture between Nevada-based SulphCo Inc. and the Fujairah government, was due to commission a Dh91 million (US$25 million) oil-upgradation plant in late 2006. It is the first such facility in the Middle East capable of treating 210,000 barrels per day. SulphCo's patented process employs ultrasound technology to 'desulphurise' and hydrogenate crude oil and other oil-related products. The company's technology upgrades sour heavy crude oils into sweeter, lighter crudes, producing more gallons of usable oil per barrel. Reports stated that the cost of treating a barrel of crude varied from US$0.18 to US$0.20 including electricity, manpower and raw materials, while the upgrade value of the oil is boosted by US$10 per barrel. Subject to success of the existing plant, there were plans to install an additional 200,000 to 300,000 barrels of processing capacity in Fujairah by the first quarter of 2007, with an additional 200,000 to 300,000 barrels of processing capacity by the end of 2007.

Environmental Measures

ADNOC and its subsidiaries have led the way in terms of environmental protection and 'greener' solutions to industrial projects. Part of this policy has been a constant striving for cleaner fuels. It was with this in mind that Takreer recently installed a new catalytic reformer plant with a capacity of 12,000 b/d and an isomerisation plant with a capacity of 19,000 b/d, improving the quality of refined gasoline and increasing capacity. The new units reduce aromatics and benzene content enabling production of higher grade fuels. Sulphur levels have been lowered further by introduction of a new gas oil hydrotreater of 15,000 b/d capacity and also revamping the existing 22,000 b/d gas oil hydrotreater by changing the catalyst. The 'greener' diesel complies with the latest international specifications that are due to come into force in 2010.

ADNOC and its subsidiaries have led the way in terms of environmental protection and 'greener' solutions to industrial projects. Part of this policy has been a constant striving for cleaner fuels.

Reduce, Recover, Reuse

Takreer recently acquired the cooperation of Japanese companies to enhance flare gas recovery. Agreements were signed by Takreer with the Japan Cooperation Centre, Petroleum (JCCP) and the Toyo

Engineering Corporation (TEC). The flare gas recovery project is expected to take 25 months at a total cost of US$15.622 million. Implementation of the projects will reduce the emission of noxious pollutants, particularly combustion emissions such as nitrogen oxides (NOx), carbon monoxide (CO) and (CO_2). It also makes financial sense and is in line with the general trend of 'Reduce, Recover and Reuse', which is a catch-phrase adopted by refineries worldwide.

Bi-fuel Vehicles

Dual fuel engines, comprising compressed natural gas (CNG) and conventional gasoline (petrol), are being tested by ADNOC in two experimental cars. It is possible to switch between the fuel types whilst driving. With a range of 450 kilometres using only CNG, plus 400 kilometres on gasoline, the total range without the need to refuel is over 800 kilometres. ADNOC Distribution believes that this type of car can result in a significant reduction in harmful emissions and environmental pollution. Savings due to the lower price of CNG compared to gasoline should encourage consumers to favour bi-fuel and CNG-powered cars. Meanwhile a CNG refueling service is being installed at ADNOC stations throughout Abu Dhabi. Sharjah is also promoting natural gas vehicles and ADNOC Distribution set up four stations there for gas conversions of cars and fuelling of converted vehicles. A gallon of natural gas costs Dh4 and converting a car costs less than Dh5000.

GAS

With its proven gas wealth exceeding 6 trillion cubic metres at the beginning of 2006, the UAE is the fifth largest gas power in the world and is one of the top LNG producers.

The UAE is pumping billions of dollars into projects to boost its hydrocarbon production, set up more gas-related industries and increase oil extraction from its fields by gas injection. With its proven gas wealth exceeding 6 trillion cubic metres at the beginning of 2006, the UAE is the fifth largest gas power in the world and is one of the top LNG producers. Its sprawling LNG complex on Das Island produces in excess of 8 million tonnes per year. Government figures indicate that the UAE produced a record 65 billion cubic metres of natural gas in 2005 compared to 50 billion cubic metres in 2000. A portion of this gas is used to enhance oil recovery by injection into underground reservoirs. From around 7.5 billion cubic metres in 2000, injected gas increased to more than 14 billion cubic metres in 2005.

The Dolphin Gas Project

The Dolphin Project, approaching a key stage of development in 2006, has been established to bring gas from the Qatar gas field to the UAE and Oman. A development and production sharing agreement was signed in 2001 between the UAE Offsets Group and the State of Qatar, under which, initially, up to 2 billion standard cubic feet of natural gas are to be supplied from Qatar to the UAE daily, beginning in 2007. Dolphin's main customers are Abu Dhabi Water and Electricity Authority (ADWEA), the Union Water and Electricity Company, the Oman Oil Company, and the Dubai Supply Authority. The Dubai Supply Authority is responsible for sourcing and securing Dubai's natural gas requirements; it is currently acquiring these from ADNOC, and has signed a 25-year gas sales agreement with Dolphin Energy, with deliveries to commence once the project comes on-stream. Dolphin's main shareholder is the Abu Dhabi government, with 51 per cent ownership, and two foreign partners, Total and Occidental Petroleum, each with 24.5 per cent of the equity.

Dolphin Energy's Dolphin Gas Project is the largest single energy initiative ever undertaken in the Middle East. Dolphin will be a unique source of clean, new energy for the Southern Gulf.

Hamriyah Gas Pipeline Project

Dana Gas and Emarat completed and commenced operations of the first phase of the Hamriyah gas pipeline project in June 2006. The project involves jointly developing the region's first common-user pipeline for gas transportation to power stations and industrial customers, and is being built, owned and operated jointly by the two companies in a 50:50 partnership. The first phase of the project involved the construction of a 10-inch pipeline connected by a hot-tap to an existing Emarat pipeline and pressure-reducing station, delivering gas to the new Hamriyah power station belonging to Sharjah Electricity and Water Authority (SEWA).

The remaining phase of the project entails the construction of a 48-inch gas pipeline to connect the gas hub of Sharjah at Sajaa to the fast-growing industrial area at Hamriyah, a distance of 32 kilometres. With a capacity of 1 billion cubic feet of gas per day, the pipeline, due for completion in late 2006, will be one of the largest in the UAE, and will be used to deliver both domestic and imported gas supplies for the three users: SEWA, FEWA and CNGCL, the gas marketing affiliate of Dana Gas.

Ra's al-Khaimah Concessions

In August 2006 Indago Petroleum entered into a new joint petroleum concession agreement with the Ra's al-Khaimah government over the offshore Saleh field and relinquished the Ra's al-Khaimah onshore licence. The Saleh concession area encompasses a field located 42 kilometres offshore and is a multi-well, multi-platform development that has been producing since 1984. After peaking at approximately 70 million standard cubic feet (mmscf/d) gas rate and 13,000 b/d condensate rate in 1986 the production has declined as a result of pressure depletion and encroaching water. Saleh production now currently averages approximately 100 b/d of condensate and small amounts of gas. The gas/condensate product is treated at the onshore processing plant in Ra's al-Khaimah operated by Rakgas, which also processes production from the Indago-operated Bukha field.

The joint venture (Indago as operator with 40 per cent and Rakgas with 60 per cent) intends to conduct a full study of the field, including the processing and interpretation of a 3D seismic volume that was acquired previously. Indago hopes to improve significantly imaging of the sub-surface geology using the latest seismic processing techniques and equipment. Indago believes the field could have remaining, unrealised potential that may result in the drilling of additional production wells to enhance production rates and increase the recoverable reserves.

Umm al-Qaiwain Gas Field

Umm al-Qaiwain's Ruler signed an agreement in 2006 with the Atlantis Holding Norway AS for the development of the Umm al-Qaiwain offshore gas field discovered by the company in 2001. The project includes construction of an automatic loading quay and the laying of a 75-kilometre underwater pipeline between the offshore wells and the delivery facility. It is planned that most of this gas will be sold to Ra's al-Khaimah, which will participate in construction of pipelines for gas delivery. Total investment in the project is estimated at US$130 million.

ALTERNATIVE ENERGY

A pioneering initiative, Al Masdar, was announced in 2006 with the aim of engaging top global energy companies together with the Abu Dhabi government in order to create the region's first alternative energy and resource conservation project. Land has been granted, a special economic zone proposed and a fund of US$100 million has been offered so that a state of the art institute can be set up to look at both alternative energy and resource conservation technologies. The initiative has the potential to contribute to the transformation of Abu Dhabi from a consumer to an exporter of technology. The funding is in support of a 'clean technology fund' to co-invest with private sector partners in domestic and foreign companies focused on emerging technologies.

Abu Dhabi Future Energy Company (ADFEC) launched a US$250 million Masdar Cleantech Fund in partmership with Credit Suisse in September 2006.

Supported by partners that include many major energy and technology bodies such as BP, Shell, Occidental Petroleum, Total, Mitsubishi, Mitsui, GE, and Rolls-Royce, the Masdar initiative will focus on the development and commercialisation of advanced innovative technologies in renewable energy, energy efficiency, carbon management and monetisation, water usage and desalination. The new entity will operate closely with ADNOC, ADWEA, the Environmental Agency–Abu Dhabi (EAD), the Abu Dhabi Education Council and other involved government departments. The project is expected to start by 2009 and begin to show results by 2015.

In addition to setting up a company that will develop solutions to cut pollution, the initiative has three other components – an innovation centre to support the adoption of sustainable energy technologies; a special economic zone for investors and developers of renewable energy technologies and products; and an educational institute offering graduate degrees in renewable and sustainable energy in partnership with Imperial College London and RWTH Aachen University in Germany.

@ *www.uaeinteract.com/economicdevelopment*

TOURISM

Plans laid in the late 1980s and early 1990s to create an entirely new tourism industry have exceeded expectations. Tourism is now worth more to Dubai than its income from oil. Abu Dhabi has also invested in developing a tourism industry and has announced a number of ambitious projects in this field. All the other emirates consider tourism as an important factor in their future growth and prosperity. With the wisdom of hindsight, this makes sense. The UAE has warm shallow seas, rich in marine life, long sandy beaches perfect for sun-bathing and relaxation, a climate that delights for much of the year and the resources to mitigate against the discomfort of excessive heat through innovative construction and cooling projects. The addition of first-class shopping malls, leisure and sporting facilities also ensures that boredom is never an issue. The UAE is the 'right flying distance' from some of the world's most populous markets, from the Middle East and Western Asia to Europe, and it has excellent airports and seaports. Its natural and cultural heritage is rich and varied and its people are educated, friendly and hospitable. It is a long-standing melting pot of cultures where foreigners feel at ease. Emiratis have always welcomed visitors: it is not the nature, but the scale of things that has changed.

ABU DHABI

Tourism in Abu Dhabi increased by 17 per cent in the first half of 2006 and is poised to continue growing at an even faster rate. Total investments in the emirate's tourism sector will reach Dh40 billion by 2015.

Over Dh3.7 billion was earned from tourism to Abu Dhabi in 2005, amounting to 1.2 per cent of Abu Dhabi's total GDP or 3 per cent of non-oil GDP. While this figure is still much less than that for Dubai, which received 6.1 million visitors in 2005 compared to 1.2 million for Abu Dhabi, the scale of tourism-related planning in the country's capital city and surrounding land suggests that Abu Dhabi's tourism sector is, like that of Dubai, set for almost exponential growth. Tourism planning and marketing is the task of Abu Dhabi Tourism Authority (ADTA), whose target (in mid-2006) was to achieve three million hotel guests (per year) by 2015, half as business travellers and half as leisure tourists. In order to meet that target, hotel room capacity needs to increase from 8000 to 25,000, so ADTA expects to see 17,000 more rooms added to the Abu Dhabi inventory over the next eight to nine years.

The image of Abu Dhabi as an attractive tourist destination has been massively boosted by a sustained media and advertising campaign linked to present facilities and planned developments. For example, coverage of Abu Dhabi's participation at the World Travel Market in London and EIBTM in Barcelona in December 2005 resulted in 581 articles on 800 pages in the local and international press. But the emerging phenomenon of Abu Dhabi and Dubai achieving some of the highest rankings on the international tourism map is underpinned by much more than words and advertising. It is delivering a reality that lives up to visitor expectations and sometimes even exceeds the 'hype'. And there is much more to come.

Completion of Abu Dhabi's new airport is expected to contribute to the unprecedented boom in tourism. The project is upgrading the capacity of the airport to 50 million passengers in the long term, with the first phase scheduled for completion by 2010. In addition, the Abu Dhabi-based Etihad Airways, like Emirates in Dubai, has greatly increased the accessibility of Abu Dhabi to international travellers and is a lynchpin in the emirate's tourism development planning.

Completion of Abu Dhabi's new airport is expected to contribute to the unprecedented boom in tourism. The project is upgrading the capacity of the airport to 50 million passengers in the long term, with the first phase scheduled for completion by 2010.

A key component of strategic tourism development is ADTA's Saadiyat Island project. This will transform the 27-square-kilometre natural island only half a kilometre north-east of the capital city into a major tourism destination with 29 hotels, one being a 'seven-star' property. The island will also house the world's largest Guggenheim Museum of Modern Art and a wide range of other key attractions. Such grand thinking, supported by both the means and the will to carry them through to fruition, mean that growth targets for Abu Dhabi's tourism development are likely to be adjusted upwards at fairly regular intervals.

Other recent developments in this sector in Abu Dhabi include significant resort projects on Al Lulu Island, Al Reem Island and at Al Raha Beach; a new International Exhibitions complex, which will complement efforts being made to encourage incentive and other tourism in the emirate; plans for a tourist complex, with a 350-room five-star hotel in the Mabain Al Jirsein area; the Sir Bani Yas Island project, aimed at making the island an environmental and tourist destination; and eco-tourism developments such as the Al Watbha Wetland Reserve.

The property development company Aldar also has advanced plans for a large number of new hotels to be built in Abu Dhabi within the next three to seven years. These hotels will significantly increase the annual room offering in the city and many of those planned are of a very high standard. For example, In early 2006 Aldar signed an agreement with the multiple award-winning Banyan Tree Group to operate and manage the exclusive Al Gurm Resort and Spa in the UAE capital, scheduled to open in the last quarter of 2007.

Abu Dhabi National Hotels (ADNH) has also announced that it is undertaking two major hotel projects at a cost of Dh1.508 billion (US$411 million). This includes a 265-room, five-star hotel and two serviced apartments towers, an office tower, a retail mall, 50 chalets, a beach club and adventure water-world, to be completed in mid-2008, part of The Gate project. ADNH is also redeveloping its Gulf Hotel into a new waterfront resort at a cost of Dh502.79 million (US$137 million). Hotel projects from Fairmont and Rotana are already under construction, both of which will combine resort environments with extensive meeting and event facilities, while Four Seasons has announced a 300-room property, opening in 2008.

In addition, Emirates Palace Hotel, the new landmark for the city of Abu Dhabi, is playing an increasingly significant role in providing a world-class venue for major meetings and a sophisticated holiday retreat for both business and leisure visitors.

Dubai has over 300 hotels and over 110 hotel apartments. New developments such as the emirate's three 'palms' are adding many new hotels.

DUBAI

Hotels in Dubai are steadily increasing with 302 hotels and 111 hotel apartments recorded by Dubai Municipality's Statistics Centre in June 2006. The world-famous man-made offshore developments along Dubai's coast, such as The Palms and The World, will support numerous hotels and resorts. A concentration of land-based hotels along the Sheikh Zayed Road/Al Barsha Road includes at least 12 new projects that add 2948 rooms to the emirate's 'room-bank'. Among these is the five-star, 250-room Armani Hotel in the Burj Dubai development, due to open in 2008, and the five-star, 400-room Kempinski Hotel in the Mall of the Emirates. Meanwhile new developments on Dubai's Jumeirah coast involve at least seven hotel and resort developments and the coastline north of Dubai Creek is also receiving attention with six confirmed hotels and resorts.

In addition, Dubai specialises in giant shopping malls and is building numerous theme parks and other attractions. Plans were unveiled in 2006 for a Dh99 billion ($US27 billion) resort and entertainment complex, the Bawadi project, spread over 13 million square metres in Dubailand. This will feature a cluster of 31 hotels, offering more than 29,000 hotel rooms, including the world's largest hotel, the 6500-room Asia Asia hotel. This is expected to accommodate more than three million tourists by 2016. The first phase of the project, which includes the Asia Asia Hotel, will be operational by 2010.

The emergence of Dubai as a top holiday destination is also attracting the attention of the cruise lines. Dubai's weather and tourism infrastructure are supporting development of a new cruise destination for the industry that lacks a viable turnaround port when winter strikes the Mediterranean, Alaska, North Europe and the Baltic.

Dubai's Department of Tourism and Commerce Marketing (DTCM) is constantly active in promoting the emirate as a tourism destination of worldwide significance. It mounts regular media and advertising campaigns and is a major presence at regional and international travel markets and fairs. The 'home' and regional market is of growing significance with over two million Arab hotel guests staying in Dubai in 2005. There was also a significant increase in the number of German hotel guests to Dubai in 2005 with their numbers totalling 264,298, an increase of 12 per cent from 2004.

The Bawadi project alone will add 31 hotels and 29,000 hotel rooms to Dubai's room bank.
The world's largest hotel with 6500 rooms will form part of this development in Dubailand.

SHARJAH

The Sharjah Commerce & Tourism Development Authority (SCTDA) is responsible for promoting its particular attractions to visitors, including the emirate's numerous top-class heritage, arts and cultural sites, museums and interpretive centres. It does this through an active publishing programme, road shows, advertising and participation at travel fairs. As with Dubai, the regional market is important, with visitors from the Gulf countries accounting for 30 per cent of tourism to the emirate in 2005. Promotions such as Sharjah Summer Promotions 2006 tend to boost these figures.

More visitors mean an increased demand for hotels and the Sharjah tourism sector expected investments in the range of Dh1.5 billion to Dh2 billion in 2006, including three to four new hotels. SCTDA reported that the number of hotel occupants rose by 10 per cent to reach 688,299 guests during 2005, compared to 622,133 in 2004.

Each emirate has included tourism in its development plans. Sharjah is continuing to develop its cultural strengths and is investing in new hotels; Umm al-Qaiwain is building a major marina; Ajman is creating a big hotel and residential complex; Ra's al-Khaimah's tourism master plan includes hotels, islands and a mountain resort; whilst Fujairah is capitalising on its East Coast location with beach hotels and water sports.

AJMAN & UMM AL-QAIWAIN

Both Umm al-Qaiwain and Ajman are capitalising on their natural assets to assist in tourism development in these tiny emirates. Umm al-Qaiwain is focusing on a major marina development that should be a major attraction for both residents and tourists, whilst Ajman is launching an extensive new tourist development on the Emirates Road.

RA'S AL-KHAIMAH

The Ra's al-Khaimah government has adopted a tourism master plan that embraces a number of large-scale developments, including luxury hotels, residential complexes, an offshore island and the redevelopment of the creek area. The plan also includes the development of a mountain complex – Jebel Jais Mountain Resort – complete with a five-star hotel, luxurious residential units, a snow slope and a climbing and abseiling centre. Some Dh5 billion is being spent on building luxurious four- and five-star hotels along the seafront and more money is expected to be invested in developing the mountain areas. The tourism master plan also includes the promotion of Ra's al-Khaimah's heritage sites.

RAK Properties' development at Mina Al Arab, a complex containing 14 hotels, is expected to become one of the elite resort destinations in the region with its mixed-use leisure and holiday facilities. In addition, the already established five-star Al Hamra Fort Hotel and Beach Resort will be part of a redeveloped complex containing a new hotel – Al Hamra Palace. The latter is due to open at the end of 2007 and will offer 400 rooms, 37 suites, a golf course and five restaurants.

The foundation stone for a Dh850 million (US$231.6 million) Wow RAK theme park project on 120 acres in the Khor Qurm region was laid in August 2006. Planned as a complete family entertainment venue, the development will include two adjacent theme parks with a capacity to cater to 15,000 visitors per day, and a non-ticketed shopping and entertainment plaza. The project, which is expected to provide a huge boost to the emirate's tourism figures, is scheduled for completion in 2008.

Ra's al-Khaimah may also soon become a destination for space tourists! Space Adventures Ltd, which has already sent tourists into space, has announced plans to develop a commercial spaceport in Ra's al-Khaimah, from where it will operate suborbital flights. The project will cost US$265 million (Dh975 million). The Russian-built suborbital vehicle called 'Explorer' will have the capacity to transport up to five people to an altitude of nearly 100 kilometres in space.

Ra's al-Khaimah is being considered as a possible base from which to launch space tourism in the form of sub-orbital flights.

FUJAIRAH

Fujairah currently attracts around 250,000 visitors a year, both from within the UAE and from overseas, but it has significant plans to further develop its tourism industry and is also planning to expand its airport to attract more charter airlines.

Located on the UAE's East Coast, Fujairah can offer both fine beaches on the Gulf of Oman and the solitude and adventure of the nearby mountains and valleys, a combination not available elsewhere. The focus of new hotel developments is in the north of the emirate, between Bidiya and Dibba, where the Meridien Al Aqah is to be joined by several other hotels, with investors including the Abu Dhabi-based Rotana Group and German tour operator TUI. Projects include the five-star Kempinski Fujairah Resort, the Robinson Club and the Fujairah Dana (Pearl) development on a peninsula and group of small islands being reclaimed off the coast near Al Aqah. One major development that was announced in 2006 is Fujairah Paradise, a multifaceted project located on the shores of the Gulf of Oman, involving construction of 1000 luxury villas, a five-star hotel, and a shopping mall.

REAL ESTATE

The UAE has been described as the world's most buoyant property market. In 2005 it dominated the Gulf construction sector with Dh130.6 billion (US$35.42 billion) worth of projects under construction, accounting for 63.7 per cent of the total value of projects under construction in the GCC states. Saudi Arabia occupies the second slot with Dh28.9 billion, with Qatar (Dh16.88 billion) in third place, followed by Kuwait (Dh12.8 billion), Bahrain (Dh7.34 billion) and Oman (Dh5.1 billion). Much of the success of the real estate sector is attributable to new property laws that regularise the purchase of land and property for nationals and grant varying degrees of property rights to non-nationals. Whilst the property market has already reached massive proportions in Dubai, other emirates are now developing this sector.

The UAE has been described as the world's most buoyant property market. In 2005 it dominated the Gulf construction sector with Dh130.6 billion (US$35.42 billion) worth of projects under construction, accounting for 63.7 per cent of the total value of projects under construction in the GCC states.

ABU DHABI

Abu Dhabi's real estate sector is expected to receive investment of over Dh100 billion in the next ten years. With current residential occupancy levels reaching 90 per cent and hotel occupancy at 80 per cent, the residential and tourism sectors are likely to witness the major share of this investment. There is a clear convergence between the government's vision and that of the private sector and introduction of advanced financial instruments and retail products aimed at facilitating property investment are boosting the growth of the real estate sector.

Residential and tourism property projects unveiled in Abu Dhabi during 2005 and the first half of 2006 exceeded expectations. Nearly Dh200 billion worth of projects, including the Al Raha Beach Development (Dh53.94 billion), Najmat Abu Dhabi (Dh30 billion) development on Al Reem Island, the Lulu Island project, the Abu Dhabi Airport expansion (Dh24.9 billion), Mohammed bin Zayed City (Dh14 billion), 'Between The Bridges' project (Dh800 million) and The Gate project, among others, were unveiled with many more in the pipeline.

The public-private paradigm that epitomises development in Abu Dhabi was underpinned by the establishment in 2006 of a public joint stock company, the Tourism Development & Investment Company (TDIC). Wholly owned by ADTA, TDIC will spearhead development of the emirate's tourism and real estate assets, in particular its flagship Saadiyat Island project. Major development parcels are being offered on this key offshore island development to UAE and Gulf investors on a freehold basis and, in accordance with the new property law promulgated in 2005 that allowed for the extension of leasehold property rights to non-nationals in designated investment areas, non-GCC investors are being offered 99-year leases or 50-year renewable leases. The Abu Dhabi Tourism Authority expects to attract investment of about Dh100 billion over three phases of development from 2006 to 2018.

In accordance with the new property law promulgated in 2005 that allowed for the extension of leasehold property rights to non-nationals in designated investment areas, non-GCC investors are being offered 99-year leases or 50-year renewable leases on Saadiyat Island.
The Abu Dhabi Tourism Authority expects to attract investment of about Dh100 billion over three phases of development from 2006 to 2018.

Aldar

Aldar Properties PJSC is a key player in the real estate sector in Abu Dhabi with extensive and rapidly expanding residential, commercial and amenity portfolios. Some of Aldar's significant developments include the Abu Dhabi Central Market district, a fully integrated mixed-use scheme that is redefining the heart of Abu Dhabi City, the Imperial College of London Diabetes Centre in Abu Dhabi City, the headquarters of Mubadala Development Company and the Environment Agency – Abu Dhabi, and the Al Jimi Mall expansion in Al Ain.

Ferrari and Aldar launched Ferrari World in November 2005. Located near Al Raha, this will be an exciting new themed entertainment and leisure project based on the prestigious Ferrari motoring brand. The development is scheduled to open to the public in 2008.

Raha Gardens, developed by Aldar, is being built on 665,000 square metres of a heavily landscaped area and incorporates villas, townhouses, and a full range of facilities for residents. All of the 1388 villas to be constructed have been pre-sold to UAE nationals. The project is adjacent to the dynamic Al Raha Beach development which occupies an area of 6.8 million square metres of prime beachfront on the Abu Dhabi–Dubai highway.

Aldar is also planning to build a series of hotels in the emirate.

Surouh

Surouh Real Estate is developing Al Lulu Island adjacent to the Breakwater. This will be a new waterfront bustling with mixed-use commercial, residential, cultural and recreational facilities. Shams Abu Dhabi is also being developed by Surouh on 1.32 million square metres of Al Reem Island. Predominately urban in character, Shams Abu Dhabi will encompass residential and commercial buildings, hotels, and leisure and recreation facilities. The signature 83-storey (379 metres) Sky Tower will be one of a group of eight towers that form the Gate project on the land entrance to Al Reem. The first phase will be finished in 2009 and the entire project is scheduled for completion at the end of 2011.

Dana Abu Dhab'si real estate project is a Dh34 billion development being executed by Al Qudra and comprising 34 towers, a four star hotel and other leisure facilities.

Surouh will also build the first golf course development in Abu Dhabi. The Dh998.24 million (US$272 million) Golf Gardens will be constructed around the existing Abu Dhabi Golf Club, the home of an annual European PGA event. Golf Gardens will have 389 residential villas and townhouses and the Gardens Club will be situated in the heart of the development.

First Gulf Bank

First Gulf Bank launched two major Dh645million developments in Abu Dhabi in 2006, Ocean Terrace and Seashore Villas. Ocean Terrace is a 99-year leasehold tower project located at the waterfront of the first phase of the Reem Island in Abu Dhabi. Seashore Villas, meanwhile, is a unique modern style villa community located at the Officer's City in Abu Dhabi. FGB is offering conventional and Islamic financing of up to 90 per cent of the value of the residences, which is available for nationals and expatriates, whether residing in the UAE or not.

Capital Centre, a Dh8 billion (US$2.17 billion) business and residential micro-city, is being built around Abu Dhabi's Exhibition Centre.

Damac Properties

Damac Properties marked its entrance into the lucrative Abu Dhabi real estate market with the launch of two projects. Dolphin Towers is a three-tower structure, including 400 one-, two-, and three-bedroom luxury condominiums and ten sea-facing townhouses, to be located at the Al Raha Beach development. Oceanscape is a mixed-use undertaking, including 184 one-, two-, and three-bedroom apartments with state-of-the-art finishing and eight townhouses on Al Reem Island.

DUBAI

Investment in real estate in Dubai in mid-2006 stood at Dh165 billion (US$44.95 billion), up from Dh11 billion (US$3 billion) in 2000. Between 2000 and 2005 the number of residential buildings in Dubai increased by more than 42 per cent, to 79,000 buildings from 56,000. This compares with a modest growth in residential buildings of 6.7 per cent in the previous five years. The number of residential units, meanwhile, surged 63 per cent over the five years to about 238,000 at the end of 2005.

Over Dh165 billion has been invested in Dubai's real estate sector. New legislation provides a basis for freehold ownership of land and property for UAE and GCC citizens and allows the same rights to expatriates in designated areas.

In March 2006 the Dubai government issued Dubai Law No. 7, which legalises freehold ownership of land and property for UAE and GCC citizens while allowing the same rights to non-GCC expatriates in designated areas. The law was issued nearly four years after the government first announced that it would extend freehold ownership to expatriates, grouped under three Dubai-government owned entities Emaar Properties, Nakheel and Dubai Properties. More than 13,000 expatriate families have already moved to their new homes without securing title deeds in their names, while another 7000 were expected to move in by the end of 2006. The new law paves the way for expatriate homeowners to register their properties in their names with Dubai Lands and Properties Department. The law was followed by a number of new by-laws that identify the freehold areas in Dubai and determine the registration fees and procedures. Reform of the property law, which has been in the pipeline for some time, has encouraged development on an unprecedented scale in Dubai.

Most people have by now heard of massive offshore tourism and residential developments such as The Palm projects and The World, being developed by Nakheel Properties, as well as the themed entertainment complex at Dubailand, part of Dubai Holdings portfolio, but these are only some of the mammoth projects being pursued by real estate companies in the emirate. Others include the massive Dubai Waterfront, Dubai World Central and Dubai Business Bay (see section on Urban Development in Infrastructure).

Emaar Properties has been at the forefront of real estate development in the UAE.

Emaar

Emaar Properties PJSC has been at the forefront of real estate development in the UAE where local projects include the US$20-billion Burj Dubai development with its majestic centrepiece tower approximately 800 metres in height. Across Dubai, Emaar has launched more than 50 real estate projects and delivered about 13,000 residential units in projects such as the Arabian Ranches and the Greens. Its Dubai Marina project, when completed, will add more than 100 towers to the emirate's skyline and it has ventured into neighbouring Umm al-Qaiwain, where it teamed up with regional investors to develop a US$3 billion marina development.

Two more huge Dubai developments are in the pipeline. However, at its 2006 AGM held in February, the company announced that the shift of focus from now on would be towards the larger global market and to a diversification of projects. Naming the strategy 'Vision 2010' the developer intends to become a global player not only in real estate but across a variety of other sectors, including hospitality, education, retail and health care. By 2010 Emaar expects 80 per cent of its real estate investments will be outside the UAE.

Emaar will expand its retail business through the construction of 100 malls across the region and Indian subcontinent at a cost of about US$4 billion. A further US$3 billion will go into creating a chain of ten Giorgio Armani-branded hotels across the world. But real estate will remain its core business. Asia, the US and Europe have all been targeted as areas of interest. Saudi Arabia makes up its largest commitment to date, with Emaar's share of investment in

Across Dubai, Emaar has launched more than 50 real estate projects and delivered about 13,000 residential units in projects such as the Arabian Ranches and the Greens.

Massive tourism and residential development have radically altered Dubai's coastline.

Nakheel's developments include the Arabian Canal, Discovery Gardens, Ibn Battuta Mall, International City, Jumeirah Islands, Jumeirah Golf Estates, Jumeirah Park, Jumeirah Village, The Lost City, the three Palm projects at Jumeirah, Jebel Ali and Deira, and the 'World'.

the US$27 billion King Abdullah Economic City standing at about US$10 billion. Other major projects in the Middle East are planned in Egypt, Morocco, Syria, Pakistan, and Jordan.

The company's profits jumped 180 per cent to cross Dh4.73 billion for the year ended 31 December 2005, compared to the previous year's Dh1.691 billion. Property revenues increased by Dh3.11 billion or 59 per cent to Dh8.36 billion for the year ended 31 December, compared to Dh5.24 billion in 2004. Earnings per share increased to Dh0.85 per share for 2005 from Dh0.33 per share for 2004. 2005 was a significant year for the company whose regional expansion represents a total investment of more than Dh150 billion (US$40.87 billion).

Limitless

Launched in 2006, the appropriately named Limitless is a new property development company under the control of Dubai World, the holding company that includes Nakheel, Istithmar, Ports Customs and Free Zone Corporation and DP World. As well as investing in real estate abroad, Limitless will assume responsibility for the International City, a 300-hectare residential project and Jumeirah Village South, a 750-hectare residential cluster, from Nakheel, its sister concern. Limitless is also planning to launch a Dh44 billion (US$12 billion) mixed-use project, currently under construction in Dubai. Codenamed Project A, a section of the 7-million-square-metres project will be commissioned by the second quarter of 2007.

Real Estate Funds

In April 2006 Dubai Holding created a new corporate entity, Sama Dubai, to consolidate its real estate investment activities. The entity's mission is to leverage synergies across international real estate activities, to create a portfolio of world-class interlinked real estate businesses. In June 2006 Sama Dubai announced the establishment of a new real estate fund of approximately Dh22 billion (US$5.99 billion) to be developed over a decade. The joint venture will create real estate sub-funds to attract investors, with each fund being dedicated to a Sama Dubai project.

The Palms have been created by Nakheel. This model shows part of the 'trunk' of the Jumeirah Palm which will open in 2007.

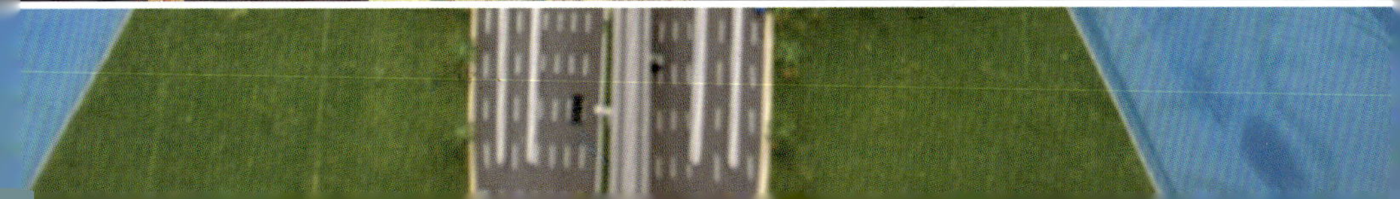

Office tower building in Sharjah

In April 2006 local investment bank Emirates Financial Services announced the launch of a Dh75 million (US$20.4 million) property fund, Carnelian I, which will invest in short-term opportunities in the UAE's booming real estate sector.

AJMAN

Ajman is also making strides in real estate development following liberalisation of its property laws to include the grant of leasehold to expatriates. In mid-2006 the Ajman government launched a Dh15 billion mixed-use development featuring 72 residential and commercial towers. Located on the Emirates Road, which is linked to the other emirates of Ra's al-Khaimah, Umm al-Qaiwain, Sharjah, Dubai and Abu Dhabi, the project is expected to feature lakes and parks, a shopping district, mosques, five-star hotels, educational and medical facilities.

UMM AL-QAIWAIN

The government of Umm al-Qaiwain is committed to development of real estate projects and, as already mentioned, has linked up with Emaar to create a new development surrounding a purpose-built marina. Umm al-Qaiwain Marina will be a vast master-planned waterfront community located on the shore of Khor al-Beidah. The blueprint envisages residential villas and apartments – the majority either waterfront or beachfront created on the site. Some of the villas with waterfront views will be built on a large island with gated access and a series of smaller private islands will offer luxury waterfront villas. In addition, resort and hotel rooms as well as parks and recreational areas, retail facilities, schools and community centres are planned.

Sharjah has a buoyant real estate sector. Its largest single project under development is Nujoom Islands, an Dh18 billion investment located near Hamriyah. The scheme will increase Sharjah's coastline by 18.64 miles (30 kilometres).

RA'S AL-KHAIMAH

In November 2005 the RAK government issued a decree permitting expatriates to enjoy freehold ownership of property developed in selected developments in Ra's al-Khaimah. The legislation was preceded by a grant of 4.6 million square metres of strategically located land to RAK Properties PJSC to be used in proposed residential and industrial projects.

In January 2006 RAK Properties contracted with the China-based China Harbour Engineering Company (CHEC) for the construction of the marine works for the Mina Al Arab project in Ra's al-Khaimah for an estimated Dh67 million (US$18.25 million). This complex will contain numerous hotels, 25,000 accommodation units, shops and a theme park. RAK Properties has also launched, 'Julfar Towers', a residential and commercial development in the centre of Ra's al-Khaimah, which is scheduled to be ready by 2007, and it is responsible for Mangrove Islands, a low-rise residential and commercial building development. A community area complete with a golf club, 2000 luxury villas, schools and shopping malls is also being planned for an area on Emirates Road and will be completed in 2009.

View of harbour and Ra's al-Khaimah City

Another major project under way is Al Hamra Village, an 1800-unit residential complex with a shopping mall and two hotels, one of which will be of seven-star standard. The five-star Al Hamra Fort Hotel and Beach Resort, already established in the area, will be part of the complex, along with the brand new Al Hamra Palace Hotel. The latter is due to open at the end of 2007 and will offer 400 rooms, 37 suites, a golf course and five restaurants.

FUJAIRAH

Real estate developments in Fujairah are primarily concentrated along the Gulf of Oman coastline. The Fujairah Dana (Pearl) development is a combination of villas and hotels being built on a peninsula and reclaimed islands off the coast near Al Aqah, whilst 'Fujairah Paradise' is a multifaceted project that is expected to cost around Dh2 billion. Other projects in the planning stage include a large residential community in one of the more secluded valleys, yet close to the coast, and a smaller community at Ghurfa, just south of Fujairah City.

'Emirates Flag' is a cluster of 21 commercial buildings costing Dh7 billion that is planned for Ra's al-Khaimah.

AVIATION

The aviation industry in the UAE is experiencing a period of phenomenal growth. This success story is intimately connected with the country's drive to increase tourist and international transfer figures by investing in airport development and the establishment of new national airlines. The General Civil Aviation Authority (GCAA), a federal autonomous body set up in 1996 to oversee all aviation-related activities in the UAE, is tasked with the regulation of these airlines and the creation of the necessary infrastructure to establish civil aviation services compatible with twenty-first century requirements. The GCAA has been extremely active in negotiating 'open skies' air services agreements with countries across the globe, in line with the UAE's interest to expand its economic, trade, cultural and tourist relations with other countries.

Air traffic in the UAE is increasing year by year as airports are expanded, new ones built, and more airlines choose to include the UAE in their flight schedules. This trend continued in 2005 and 2006 with an 8.5 per cent rise in air traffic during the first half of 2006. Overall 80 per cent of traffic movement comprised landings and departures, 3 per cent domestic flights and 17 per cent overflights (no change since 2004). Just over half (52.9 per cent) of the UAE's total air traffic during that period was handled by Dubai. This was followed by Abu Dhabi with 11.2 per cent, Sharjah with 9.7 per cent, Fujairah with 0.9 per cent, Ra's al-Khaimah with 0.5 per cent and Al Ain with 0.2 per cent.

Etihad, one of the world's fastest growing airlines with a current US$8.9 billion order for 29 new aircraft, has far-reaching plans to expand its international route network. Passenger levels are expected to grow by 150 per cent from 1.2 million in 2005 to 3 million by the end of 2006, with equally strong cargo growth.

Emirates airline accounts for almost 20 per cent of air traffic movements in the UAE, while Gulf Air accounts for 9 per cent and Saudi Arabian airlines 5 per cent, Qatar Airways has 8 per cent and Etihad, in early 2006 had 2 per cent – a figure that is increasing rapidly as this ambitious new national airline adds new aircraft to its fleet and new routes to its schedule. The other 300 or so active carriers account for the remaining 43 per cent.

ETIHAD

As already indicated, one of the key facts in the growth of Abu Dhabi airport has been the success of the Abu-Dhabi based Etihad Airways. Although the airline only commenced commercial operations in November 2003, Etihad has experienced an impressive period of growth in this short space of time. One of the key contributing factors to the record performance is the unprecedented speed at which Etihad Airways flight network has expanded. Early in 2006 the airline celebrated the launch of 30 international destinations in 30 months, including Brussels, Johannesburg, and Toronto. Sixteen new destinations, including Lahore, Islamabad, Peshawar, Jakarta, Manila, Manchester, Paris, Dhaka, Casablanca, Doha, Jeddah, Muscat, Kuwait, Khartoum and New York were added in 2006, highlighting the airline's goal to link major population centres in the East and the West. In addition frequencies have been increased on popular routes such as Abu Dhabi–Paris. Etihad is on-target to achieve its ambition of flying to 70 world-wide destinations by 2010.

Etihad Crystal Cargo

Etihad Crystal Cargo, the cargo division of Etihad Airways, is also experiencing significant growth and is expected to double its turnover of Dh361.50 million (US$98.5 million) in 2005 to over Dh734 million (US$200 million) in 2006. Crystal handled 115,000 tonnes of cargo in 2005, about 50 per cent of the cargo uplifted from Abu Dhabi airport. Cargo tonnage is expected to double in 2006 to 230,000 tonnes and to increase significantly in future years. Etihad's new facility at Abu Dhabi airport will be equipped to handle more than 500,000 tonnes annually.

With engine efficiency improvements and design changes that increase payload capabilities up to 20 tonnes per flight, some of the new aircraft, that have recently joined Etihad's fleet, particularly the Airbus A330-200 and Boeing 777-300ER will play a significant role in cargo expansion.

Etihad was voted the 'World's Leading New Airline' at the World Travel Awards in September 2006. It was the third year in a row that the airline earned this accolade.

Fleet Acquisitions

Etihad Airways' record order worth (Dh32.7 billion) US$8.9 billion for the new Airbus and Boeing fleet was made in 2004. As well as purchasing five Boeing 777-300ER aircraft, Etihad has also ordered 24 Airbus aircraft – four A340-500s, four A340-600s, 12 A330-200s and four double-decker A380s. The fifth Boeing 777-300ER, the last of Etihad's existing order of ultra long-range aircraft, was delivered in May 2006 and Etihad also took the delivery of its first Airbus 340-500 in June 2006, as well as the delivery of the fifth Airbus 330-200.

One of the new batch of Boeing 777-300ER commenced its first commercial flight to London's Gatwick airport in March 2006 increasing Etihad's profile in the UK, a profile which is already high due to the airline's 66 strong fleet of London taxis, all branded with a specially commissioned Etihad Airways livery.

Etihad Airways launched its Dh250 million (US$68.1 million) Aviation Academy at the end of 2006. The Academy has training facilities for pilots and cabin crew, including simulators, as well as other operational staff. An important part of the Academy is a management training programme for UAE nationals, including stints abroad.

EMIRATES

Emirates, with a 70 per cent share of all new Middle Eastern orders for long-haul aircraft, plans to triple its capacity over the next eight years. If Emirates meets this target, it will become the world's largest long-haul carrier by 2012.

Emirates airline, based in Dubai, has been one of the major success stories of the aviation industry, not only in the Middle East but across the globe: IATA statistics indicate that in 2005 Emirates ranked among the top-ten airlines in the world in terms of passengers (13.98 million) carried and kilometres (59.3 million) flown.

Emirates will receive delivery of one new aircraft per month on average over the next six years. The airline forecasts that its fleet will comprise at least 156 aircraft by 2010 when it is expected to serve 101 destinations and carry some 26 million passengers. Emirates chose the 2005 Dubai Air Show to place the largest-ever order for Boeing 777 aircraft, valued at US$9.7 billion and comprising 24 Boeing 777-300ERs and ten Boeing 777-200LR.. Emirates will have 54 Boeing 777-300ERs by 2014, making it the single largest aircraft type in fleet.

Emirate's impressive growth is built on the airline's successful strategy and financed from profits and commercial borrowing. The company's 2006 annual report confirmed that, despite sky-high fuel costs, the group turned in a record profit for its eighteenth financial year in a row, posting a 5.8 per cent rise in net profit at Dh2.8 billion (US$762 million) for the year ended 31 March 2006, against Dh2.7 billion in 2005. Fuel costs accounted for 27.2 per cent of total operating costs, compared to 21.4 per cent in the previous year. Though Emirates levied fuel surcharges on tickets, it only recovered 41 per cent of the incremental costs.

The airline carried 14.5 million passengers in 2005/06, 2 million more than the previous year's 12.5 million. The passenger seat factor increased to 75.9 per cent, up 1.3 percentage points from the previous year, led by an increase in traffic by 20.2 per cent. The breakeven load factor remained relatively low at 60.3 per cent. Well known for its long haul flights, Emirates has also become a dominant carrier within the Middle East region. Its development of this market has been on a consistent fast-track ever since 1986 when it flew to its first Middle East gateway other than Dubai, Amman in Jordan. By mid-2006, Emirates was serving 12 cities in the Middle East with 140 flights a week.

Emirates, which hopes to take delivery of Airbus A380 super jumbos in the near future, also invested Dh73 million (US$20 million) to expand its crew training facility at the Emirates Training Centre in Garhoud. In order to serve its expanding operations the airline has been hiring new cabin crew at a rate of 60 per week, due to rise to 100 per week as larger aircraft, especially the A380s, join the fleet. By 2011, Emirates expects to have more than 14,000 cabin crew on its payroll.

An Airbus A380 in Emirates livery flying past Burj al-Arab.

Emirates SkyCargo

Emirates SkyCargo moved over 1 million tonnes of freight in 2005/06 an increase of 21.5 per cent over the previous year; while the division's revenue grew by 29.2 per cent to US$1.2 billion, accounting for a record 21.2 per cent of the airline's transport revenue. In mid-2006 Emirates SkyCargo freighters operated to 26 destinations. The new Cargo Mega Terminal, scheduled to begin operations in December 2006, has a capacity to handle 1.6 million tonnes – a necessary development to improve capacity of the current facility, which handles 817,957 tonnes. The company has also completed development of its new generation SkyChain, an automated central cargo reservation and business management application that enhances logistics efficiency, increases productivity and provides highly accurate information through seamless communication with customers and service providers.

The success of its cargo division is reflected in the numerous awards for excellence received by the carrier in 2006, including

'Best Cargo Airline to the Middle East' (eighteenth year running), 'Best Cargo Airline to the Far East' (second year running), and 'Best Cargo Airline to Australia', at the prestigious Cargo Airline of the Year Awards 2006 run by *Air Cargo News*.

SHARJAH

Air Arabia, the region's first budget airline, commenced operations from Sharjah in October 2003 and now serves destinations in Amman, Afghanistan, Kochi, Jaipur, Istanbul (Air Arabia's first European destination), Syria, Egypt, Jordan, Bahrain, Lebanon, Kazakhstan, Sri Lanka, Saudi Arabia, Sudan, Qatar, Kuwait, Oman, and Yemen. Passenger figures crossed the 2 million milestone in March 2006. Air Arabia received its first new Airbus A320 in March 2006 and the additional three on order will raise the fleet to eight in 2006.

RAK AIRLINES

RAK Airways, the newest of the national airlines, took delivery of its first aircraft, a Boeing 737-300 in mid-2006, in time to commence operations at the end of 2006. More aircraft are in the delivery pipeline for 2007 and it hopes to fly at least ten Airbus in the next three years, to begin with a mix of A319s and A320s, and A330s at a later stage. The airline will initially fly to other GCC countries, Iran, Egypt, Lebanon, India, Bangladesh, Sri Lanka, Pakistan and the Philippines.

GAMCO

Gamco continues to deliver on its strategy of becoming the leading provider of services for airlines in the UAE.

Abu Dhabi-based Gulf Aircraft Maintenance Company (Gamco) earned a net profit of Dh88 million in 2005 on revenues totalling Dh1.28 billion, compared to Dh1.069 billion for the year 2004, an increase of 20 per cent in revenues and a record 105 per cent jump in profits over the previous year. The introduction of new services, such as maintenance of the new Boeing 777-300ER, was a major factor behind this growth. The year 2006 continued to be a busy one for Gamco as they prepared to service new aircraft, including the A340-500 and A340-600, as well as the A380 when it is ready.

PRIVATE JETS

The number of private jet movements in and out of Dubai International Airport increased by 57 per cent to 6216 in 2005 over 3940 in 2004, and movements in the first quarter of 2006 were 24 per cent ahead of the first quarter of 2005, according to data released by the airport's Executive Flight Services. The Middle East market for luxury private jet travel looks set to build on this growth, as the benefits and convenience of private air travel are well understood in the corporate sector, and by tour operators and luxury hotel property owners from the Maldives, Greece and Cyprus – all within four hours' flying time of Dubai.

DAE, a UAE-based conglomerate focused on the global aviation market, is seeking to invest US$15 billion in ten years in manufacturing and services in the aviation sector.

SHIPPING & SHIPBUILDING

ABU DHABI

Abu Dhabi Ship Building

Abu Dhabi Ship Building (ADSB) reported a net profit of Dh46.2 million on revenues of over Dh577 million for 2005. With earnings per share (eps) up to Dh2.40, both net profit and eps have increased by more than 22 per cent over the previous year's performance, which was also a record high at that time.

ADSB is currently working on shipbuilding projects that include the six vessel 'Baynunah' naval Corvette programme, 64-metre and 42-metre naval landing craft, four fast supply vessels, and a 40-metre crew boat. The company also has major projects under way for the mid-life refit of two missile patrol boats and combat system upgrades on six 45-metre missile patrol boats. In addition, ADSB performs nearly 200 ship-repair jobs every year.

Abu Dhabi Ship Building Company constructs a range of commercial and naval vessels.

ADSB is a Public Joint Stock Company (PJSC) listed on the Abu Dhabi Securities Market (ADSM). The firm was set up in 1995 through cooperation with the UAE Offsets Group (UOG) and has built a strong reputation for high quality construction and repair of both military and commercial vessels. Ten per cent of the company is owned by the Abu Dhabi government, 40 per cent by Mubadala Development Company, and 50 per cent by more than 6000 UAE national shareholders.

DUBAI

Dubai Drydocks

Dubai Drydocks launched its US$60 million new building panel line and steel structure assembly facility in July 2006. In 2005, ship repairs accounted for 70 per cent of the 27-year-old facility's turnover, followed by ship conversion and new build businesses in equal parts. This is expected to change with shipbuilding contributing about half of the company's revenues in the next few years. A contract to build four 6200-tonne bunker tankers at Dubai Drydocks was awarded by Gulf Energy Maritime in December 2005. Dubai Drydocks has also been constructing hulls for two semi-submersible drilling rigs for Norwegian group Aker Kvaerner. The ship conversion business has also been keeping Dubai Drydocks busy as demand for floating production, storage and offloading (FPSO) vessels has grown due to high energy prices.

Dubai Maritime City

Dubai Maritime City will be one of the world's most comprehensive maritime complexes and a hub for businesses from maritime management to product marketing, marine research, recreational ship design and construction.

Dubai Maritime City has progressed according to plan in 2005/06. Reclamation work was virtually completed while ground improvements were well under way. The ship-lift assembly was scheduled to commence operations in the first quarter of 2007, with the preparatory construction of the ship-lift platform beginning in October 2006. When completed, Dubai Maritime City will serve as one of the world's most comprehensive maritime complexes, located on a 216 hectare man-made peninsula between Port Rashid and the Dubai Dry Docks and surrounded by the waters of the Arabian Gulf.

More than 270 ship-repair companies operating at Jadaf Dubai were planning to move to Dubai Maritime City once its construction is completed. The city will be the hub for maritime businesses from the marine services sectors, including marine management, product marketing, marine research and education, recreation, ship design and construction.

Sharjah Maritime City

Keen to attract heavy industries, Sharjah is also developing an exclusive zone for shipbuilding and related maritime businesses.

The Maritime City will cover 1 million square metres and have facilities for drydocking, shipbuilding, ship design, warehousing and support services.

AGRICULTURE

The UAE produces dates, green fodder, vegetables, and fruit (mainly citrus and mangoes) together with livestock in the form of goats, sheep, camels, cows, and horses, as well as meat and poultry, eggs, and milk. It is one of the world's top breeding centres for Arabian horses. The country is 100 per cent self-sufficient in dates, 83 per cent in fresh milk, 50 per cent in vegetables, 38 per cent in eggs, 28 per cent in meat, and 18 per cent in poultry.

The Government provides significant technical, financial and physical assistance to farmers who are faced with considerable challenges in terms of high temperatures, poor soil quality, high salinity and restricted freshwater availability. Farming is generally undertaken on small units that deliver their produce direct to market or to centralised processing units.

Main imports include horses, sugar, chicken, and oil. There are also sizeable imports of raw agricultural products for re-exportation after their processing in the free zones. The main exports are sugar confectionery, animal or vegetable fats and oils, miscellaneous edible preparations, products of the milling industry, dates, and vegetables. The main markets for the UAE's exports of agri-food products are other GCC members, Iran, Pakistan, EU countries, and the United States.

Unfortunately farming has depended on fossil water resources that are becoming depleted and there is insufficient rainfall to recharge aquifers. The depletion rate has been estimated at 2126 million cubic metres per year, but this figure does not include the possible recharge of the local aquifer from fossil water lying under neighbouring countries, such as the Eastern Arabia Aquifer. According to the FAO, over-extraction of groundwater has led to a lowering of the water table by more than 1 metre on average per year since 1979, while sea-water intrusion is increasing in the

The UAE is 100 per cent self-sufficient in dates, 83 per cent in fresh milk, 50 per cent in vegetables, 38 per cent in eggs, 28 per cent in meat, and 18 per cent in poultry.

coastal areas. Although desalination plants (17 main plants located in Abu Dhabi, Dubai, and Sharjah with a total desalination capacity of about 710 million cubic metres per year) have compensated for the receding water table, agriculture has been restricted by this water shortage (although it has been estimated that over half total expenditure on electricity and water is spent on irrigation).

In the face of these obstacles the UAE deserves full credit for what has been achieved in the field of agriculture. Since the early days of oil revenues in the mid-1970s, the cultivated area has increased from around 15,000 hectares (ha) to a current figure of about 260,000 hectares, or 3.1 per cent of the UAE's total territory, with an additional 4 per cent covered by forests of palm trees and other drought resistant species.

The cultivated area has increased from around 15,000 hectares (ha) to a current figure of about 260,000 hectares, or 3.1 per cent of the UAE's total territory, with an additional 4 per cent covered by forests of palm trees and other drought resistant species.

Abu Dhabi accounts for 87 per cent of the country's land mass so it is natural that most farming is located there. The Ministry of Environment and Water (MEW) supports agricultural production throughout the Emirates and is in charge of coordinating agricultural, forestry, and fisheries policy, as well as promoting irrigated agriculture and the management of groundwater resources, the construction of dams for flood control and groundwater recharge, and the operation and maintenance of the hydro-meteorological network. The operation of laboratories, pest and disease control, quarantine, inspection services, veterinary services, and forestation are also under its purview.

The task of water management on a federal level is undertaken by the General Water Resources Authority, which also coordinates with the other interested agencies and formulates rules and regulations on matters relating to water, including the registration of the water-well drilling companies and licences for drilling (see section on Electricity and Water in Infrastructure).

MUNICIPAL GARDENS & PLANTATIONS

Abu Dhabi Municipality, responsible for parks and city gardens, roadside planting and more extensive tree-planting projects, recently reported that over 2228 hectares of cultivated lawns and 2180 hectares of date-palm trees were under their management in Abu

The UAE produces dates, green fodder, vegetables, and fruit (mainly citrus and mangoes) together with livestock in the form of goats, sheep, camels, cows, and horses, as well as meat and poultry, eggs, and milk.

Dhabi at the end of 2005. Outside Abu Dhabi City they were caring for around 4000 hectares of date-palm trees, 2187 hectares of 'pasturage', and 34,108 hectares of forestry. The Public Parks section propagated 47,552 plants, distributed 55,135 seedlings and sold 3437 in 2005. Around 120 wells were drilled (amounting to a total drilling depth of 28,572 feet) and 178 fountains were built. Abu Dhabi has 23 public parks with a total area of 170,800 hectares.

Tomatoes are one of the most successful fruit and vegetable crops in the UAE.

AGRICULTURAL LAND

Agricultural land is generally privately owned and managed. However, the government does run some experimental farms, nurseries, forestation schemes, and public gardens. Whilst foreign companies may enter this market as minority partners in local companies, agricultural land must be owned by UAE nationals.

In order to kick-start agriculture the Abu Dhabi government has for many years operated a policy of granting land to UAE citizens, preparing it for farming, and supplying fertilisers, pesticides, seeds, and irrigation. Once the farmer has grown his produce. the government buys part of the production (mainly vegetables and dates) at set farm-gate prices, and resells at set prices through the Abu Dhabi Municipality outlets.

HELPING FARMERS

Assistance to farmers includes investment and production subsidies; reclamation and distribution of agricultural land; provision of necessary equipment and training; large-scale planting of palm trees to create suitable shaded areas for farming; provision of fresh water and seeds; provision of, and guidance on, the timely use of fertilisers; and marketing support. Livestock producers receive a free veterinary service for treatment and vaccination of their animals. Fodder farms that supply most of the animal feed requirements are supported with free land, seeds, fertilisers, and free irrigation. Sales of fodder in Abu Dhabi are organised by the Abu Dhabi Municipality.

Research focuses on four main areas: increasing the production of palm trees, dates, and fruit such as citrus and mangoes; fodder, pastoral, and wild plants; long-term research on agricultural

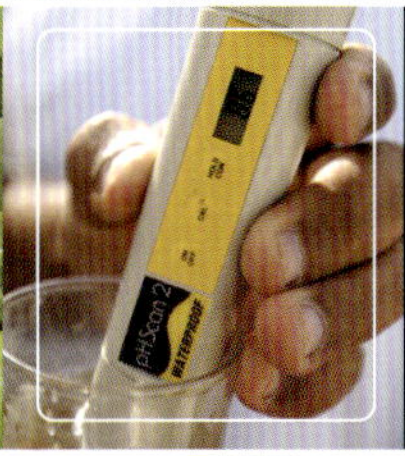

The government's experimental and demonstration farms in the Al Dhaid region grow a wide variety of crops under controlled conditions.

diseases; and research on plants grown in greenhouses. The MEW is also financing research on the types of fodder that can withstand the country's climatic conditions and survive on little water. Studies are under way on combating salinity and the capacity of different types of fodder plants to withstand high salt content in the soil. Research is also encouraged on biological control methods as an alternative to the use of insecticides to combat agricultural diseases. Another avenue of research concerns the production of alternate vegetable products in greenhouses. The UAE also hosts the International Centre for Biosaline Agriculture, an applied research and development centre located in Dubai that aims to develop and promote the use of sustainable agricultural systems that use brackish water to grow crops.

Dates are harvested in late summer.

DATES

The bountiful date-palm tree is at the very roots of the UAE's growth as a flourishing society. Almost anywhere that one looks in the UAE there are live date-palm trees, dates, products made from the tree or signs that the tree has inspired architecture or landscaping. The tree's fruit, the sweet tasting date, is the UAE's main crop. Date-palm cultivation plays a key environmental role in afforesting portions of the desert. Over 40 million date palms have been grown in the UAE; 16 million line the roads. New technologies of irrigation, tissue culture and cloning, disease control, harvesting and fertilisation have boosted date production. One high-tech date producer is Al Wathba Marionnet, a UAE Offset Group enterprise established in 1997 currently exporting dates and using tissue culture to produce about 300,000 date palms a year.

A Jebel Ali free-zone company has introduced a new technology to produce fructose syrup from dates. Concept Food Industries claims to be the first company in the world to use this technology, which also delivers a high protein animal feed as a by-product. The facility has the capacity to extract 35,000 tonnes of high fructose syrup yearly from dates. The new facility is expected to boost government-sponsored efforts to improve date-palm cultivation within the UAE.

OTHER PRODUCE

The Al Ain vegetable packing factory, owned by the Emirate of Abu Dhabi, started operations in 1987 with the aim of processing local agricultural surplus. The factory comprises lines for pickled vegetables (with an annual capacity of 3000 tonnes), frozen vegetables (500 tonnes), and tomato paste (60,000 tonnes).

The Abu Dhabi-based Grand Mills for Flour and Animal Feed Company's production capacity has increased from 200 to 800 tonnes of flour per day since its inception in 1998. One animal feed mill produces over 50 varieties of fodder. Meanwhile a new mill, with a capacity of 30 tonnes per hour, produces feeds for poultry, fish, and other purposes.

The Dubai Investments Company, founded in 1995 by the Dubai government to invest in local companies to improve their productivity, is a joint-venture shareholder in the Edible Oil Company (Dubai) LLC project, in partnership with the Swiss-based CAM Group. Its Jebel Ali Free Zone seed-crushing plant, for the production of edible oil, has a capacity of around 1500 tonnes per year.

POULTRY & DAIRY PRODUCTS

Recognising that scale is a crucial factor in poultry and food production in general, the public-shareholding Abu Dhabi National Foodstuff Company (Foodco) has been expanding its production and marketing bases beyond its present borders. During 2006 it established a new office in Bahrain. The company is headquartered in Abu Dhabi with branches in Dubai and Al Ain and already is a volume supplier of frozen poultry, meat and vegetables to Saudi Arabia, Oman, Qatar, Bahrain, Kuwait, Yemen, Iran and Egypt. In addition to dealing in a wide range of premium brands, export and distribution of essential commodities like rice, sugar, salt and cooking oil are key elements of Foodco's portfolio of services. Foodco announced a 46 per cent increase in net profits in the year ending 31 December 2005, compared with the same period the previous year. The net profits reached Dh133 million (US$36.24 million) as compared to Dh72 million (US$19.61 million) in 2004. The company also reported a rise in the share price from Dh3.12 in 2004 to Dh4.14 in 2005.

The Abu Dhabi National Foodstuff Company (Foodco) supplies frozen poultry, meat and vegetables to a number of countries in the Middle East, as well as exporting and distributing essential commodities such as rice, sugar, salt and cooking oil.

Some UAE poultry farming companies suffered set-backs in 2005, initially caused by increased competition and narrow or non-existent profit margins and later compounded by fears of bird flu causing a reduction in chicken consumption. While Ra's al-Khaimah Poultry and Feeding Company posted a net profit of Dh23.3 million (US$6.35 million) for 2005 (compared to Dh6.4 million or US$1.74 million the previous year), it made this gain from trading on the stock exchange rather than from normal operating profits.

The total value of the dairy trade in 2005 was Dh1.2 billion (US$327 million) against Dh950 million (US$258 million) in 2004. Total imports increased 32.2 per cent from Dh801 million (US$218.25 million) in 2004 to just over Dh1 billion (US$272 million) in 2005, while exports rose 168 per cent to Dh76 million (US$20.7 million) compared to Dh28 million (US$7.63 million) in 2004. The value of re-exports was pegged at Dh123 million (US$33.51 million), a jump of 2.3 per cent. The surge in imports is attributed to the growth in the UAE's population, fuelled mainly by the rise in the expatriate workforce resulting from the country's thriving economy.

Al Ain Farms for Livestock Production reported a 17.5 per cent increase in its 2005 annual sales at Dh260 million (US$70.84 million), up from Dh219 million (US$59.67 million) the previous year. In 2005 Al Ain Farms' raw milk production increased by 15 per cent and the production of pasteurised milk increased by 11 per cent. Juice sales went up by 50 per cent. The company remains the prime vendor of fresh milk in the UAE.

The Al Ain-based farming company also increased its chicken production by 3 per cent to a capacity of 3866 tonnes of chicken meat. Egg production rose from 60 million to 64.8 million in 2005, a 7 per cent increase. The company also launched many innovative products in 2005, such as a morning breakfast drink, cappuccino and Arabian coffee drinks, which have been well accepted in the market.

Al Ain Farms' production research and development department has also developed a camel milk ice cream in three delicious flavours, which they began marketing in late 2006. Another innovative project undertaken by Al Ain Farms is the manufacture and marketing of camel milk chocolate through a joint venture between Al Ain Farms and H.M. GmbH of Austria.

CONTROL OF LIVESTOCK GRAZING IN ABU DHABI

Law No. 13 for 2005 deals with the grazing of livestock in the emirate. The law mandates a committee to identify grazing farms, their owners and livestock prior to their registration. The committee is also required to assess the number of traditional wells and to submit a report on them to the relevant authority. In addition, it is responsible for submitting recommendations on maintenance of wells, preserving pasturage and any other matter relating to grazing. The committee will also specify grazing areas, excluding public lands, lands under development for agricultural and residential purposes, lands allocated for government entities and any lands exempted by the Executive Council.

The regulations prohibit the use of bicycles, vehicles and all other automobiles and equipment in grazing operations. They also restrict cutting or burning of plants, littering, hunting or harming animals and birds, collecting eggs, destroying nests, and bringing animals infected with communicable diseases to the pasturage areas.

ORGANIC FARMING

There is increased interest in organic farming in the UAE and this is being led by the Ministry of Environment and Water. Currently the UAE has set up a number of experimental farms where organic farming is being carried out and recently certified its first private organic farm. The certification of organic farms in the UAE has been made more flexible than it is in other nations to encourage farmers to make the switch. In order to gain national certification as an organic producer within the UAE, farmers must not have sprayed their crops with prohibited chemicals for at least one year. International certification standards are more rigorous than this and individual farmers will make their own arrangements to meet these standards so that produce may be exported as 'organic'.

FISHERIES

Marine and fisheries resources have always occupied an important place in the UAE and still do so today. Apart from supporting a traditional way of life that can be traced back to archaeological sites in the region dating from 7500 years ago, these resources still provide an important source of income, food and recreational opportunity for many residents of the country. Typical of the global trend, and in response to a growing demand for fishery and marine products, the last three decades have seen increased use of UAE fisheries and marine resources. During this period, the traditional commercial fishing sector has substantially invested in modern fishing fleets, while there has also been a significant increase in other uses of fisheries and marine resources. The advent of a modern way of life and a growing tourism industry has augmented the use of fisheries and marine resources for recreation.

All this has inevitably led to concern regarding the sustainability of the use of the fisheries resources. In particular, questions pertaining to depletion of the fish stocks, habitat degradation, and over-fishing have been raised. A recently completed report undertaken by EAD (previously ERWDA) in Abu Dhabi in association with the former UAE Ministry of Agriculture and Fisheries (now replaced by the Ministry of Environment and Water) and Australian/New Zealand consultants highlighted some of these issues, including a catastrophic decline in some stocks of commercial fish species.

Fish are sold fresh, soon after they are landed.

FISHING METHODS

A variety of fish are caught, including sharks and rays, catfish, lizardfish, flatheads, groupers, jacks, grunts, mojarras/silver-biddies, angelfish, parrotfish, wrasses, rabbitfish, barracudas, ponyfish, snappers, threadfin bream, emperors, seabream, goatfish, turbots, flounders and tonguesoles. Over-exploitation and degradation of the environment have been major causes of the overall decline in fish stocks in the area. Environmental degradation includes temporary or permanent elimination of important nursery areas by land reclamation and dredging, and increased pollution by discharge of liquid and solid wastes into the marine environment.

The dhow-based fishery, responsible for the majority of commercial fishing in UAE waters, comprises mostly small commercial operations. Wooden dhows are usually about 12 to 20 metres in length, powered by 150 to 300 horsepower inboard diesel engines. Dhows typically fish with baited basket traps (*gargoor*, plural *garagir*), trawls, hook and line and trolling lines. Drift nets used to be a dominant fishing method, especially for large pelagic species. These nets, known as *al hayali*, are now banned by law, except in tightly regulated circumstances.

Trap fishing using *garagir* is the most common fishing method. Formerly made from interwoven palm fronds, the traps are now manufactured from galvanised steel wire of 1 to 1.5 millimetres thickness, imported from the Far East. *Garagir* are usually made as dome-shaped traps with a base diameter of between 1 to 3 metres supported by reinforced steel bars and a funnel-like entrance. These traps are usually set in the afternoon and the fish are retrieved after three or four days in the early morning. A variety of baits are used inside the traps, including green algae, ground dry fish, dead fish and bread. Over 80 per cent of landed fish are caught in these traps. They mostly comprise groupers (*hamour*), emperors (*shaeri*) and grunts together with snappers, sea bream, parrotfish and rabbitfish. The advent of GPS navigation systems has enabled some Emirati fishermen to set these traps along the seabed without any pick-up buoys on the surface. Once they have located their vessel adjacent to the recorded position of the fishing gear they use a grappling hook dragged across the seabed in order to snag the line and lift the traps. This method prevents the possibility of poaching and leaves the sea surface clear of floating lines that can foul propellers.

A *gargoor* fish trap woven from palm fronds. Most are now made from stainless steel wire.

Gillnets (*al-liekh*) are often set on the seabed. They catch a variety of fish, including grunts, sea bream, emperors, goatfish, rabbitfish, pomfrets and others. Fishing by hook and line (*hadaq*) is specifically used for the capture of groupers, cobias, grunts, jacks/trevallies, emperors, sea bream and Spanish mackerel. Long-lines (*manshalla*) are sometimes used, which may have 10 to 20 extra smaller lines and hooks. These are good for catching requiem sharks and groupers.

Apart from gillnets, two other types of fishing nets are used. Beach seines (*yaroof*) can be up to 40 metres or more in length. One end of the seine is moved rapidly from the shore in a wide arc in an effort to surround fish, both ends of the seine then being pulled to shore. Fishing by this method remains fairly common on the UAE's East Coast, and can be seen, for example, at Fujairah and Dibba, the fishermen frequently accompanied by large flocks of feeding gulls and terns. Speedboats with outboard motors and four-wheel drive vehicles are used today to pull these seine nets to the shore, but traditionally this was done by a large group of men. This method was especially good at catching mojarras/silver-biddies, flathead mullets and rabbitfish. Many other fish are also caught, including small needlefish and jacks/trevallies.

Also sometimes used is the bell-shaped cast net (*salieya*), which has small weights around its base to make it sink. This is only used at times of year when fish such as the Indian oil sardine and flathead mullets are abundant in shallow inshore waters.

Fishing boats and small craft in Fujairah harbour

Fixed shore traps or *hadrah* were traditionally built by driving a row of palm fronds and wooden stakes, but are now made with steel or iron poles and wire mesh or nylon netting. In the UAE, these traps are used during the summer months to catch the blackspot snapper, needlefish, jacks/trevallies, sea bream, mullets, barracuda and rabbitfish and, occasionally, other bottom species.

REGULATIONS

Recreational fishing in the region is growing rapidly and is largely carried out from small motorboats operating relatively close to shore. A licensing system for all recreational fishing, whether from boats or from the shore, was introduced in the Emirate of Abu Dhabi in 2002 as a by-law under Federal Law No. 23 for 1999 on Exploitation, Protection and Development of Marine Bio-Resources. The licences for recreational fishing allow only handline and rod and reel. All fishermen over the age of 18 must obtain a licence, valid either for a year or for a week, although children can continue to fish in the company of a licence holder. Recently, a new licence category, the traditional fishing licence to cater for national fishermen who do not fall under either commercial or recreational fishing categories, was introduced. Competent authorities in each emirate are responsible for licensing. In Abu Dhabi, licences for both commercial and recreational fishing are issued by EAD, with an upper limit of 1000 being set on commercial licences.

Fishing boats are now only permitted to sail if their national or GCC owner or captain is aboard. The Frontier and Coast Guard patrols stop any boat that violates this rule. Fixed or drifting *hayali* fishing nets are banned in Abu Dhabi waters. Each fishing boat formerly carried 20 to 50 drift nets, which often caught and drowned endangered species such as dugong, dolphins and turtles. The nets also damaged commercial fish stocks, catching fish that were not brought to market or fish of no commercial use. Problems still remain, however, such as the removal of fins from sharks for lucrative trade with the Far East. This has decimated the shark population of the Arabian Gulf in recent years.

AQUACULTURE

The focal point of aquaculture in the UAE is the Marine Resources Research Centre (MRRC) of the Ministry of Environment and Water. Based in Umm al-Qaiwain and founded under the terms of a technical cooperation programme between the UAE and Japan, it has succeeded in developing a suitable technology for growing rabbitfish from induced spawned eggs to marketable size fish. Work has also been carried out on shrimp-farming, both at Umm al-Qaiwain and on Abu al-Abyadh Island in Abu Dhabi.

A fish farm off the coast of Fujairah

The International Fish-farming Company (ASMAK) was set up under the UAE Offsets Programme with a total capital of Dh300 million (US$81.74 million). The company specialises in fish- and shrimp-farming and its projects include the Middle East's largest commercial hatchery for finfish in Umm al-Qaiwain and other facilities at Dibba in Fujairah and in Ra's al-Khaimah, the latter two having a combined capacity of 3200 tonnes of fish. One of the objectives of the company, which also operates in Oman and Kuwait, is to replace wild-caught fish, thus reducing the pressure on fish stocks. Fish-farming is likely to be developed further in the future and both ASMAK and the MRRC at Umm al-Qaiwain are active in promoting the industry.

www.uaeinteract.com/economicdevelopment

INTERNET LINKS

Agriculture:	www.uaeinteract.com/agriculture
Automobile industry:	www.uaeinteract.com/auto
Business and entrepreneurs:	www.uaeinteract.com/entrepreneurs
Coinage:	www.uaeinteract.com/coins
Commodities:	www.uaeinteract.com/commodities
Corporate governance:	www.uaeinteract.com/corporategovernance
Date palm:	www.uaeinteract.com/datepalm
Diamonds and gemstones:	www.uaeinteract.com/gems
Dubai Gold & Commodities Exchange:	www.uaeinteract.com/dgcx
Economic development:	www.uaeinteract.com/economicdevelopment
Economy:	www.uaeinteract.com/economy
Fishing:	www.uaeinteract.com/fishing
Food:	www.uaeinteract.com/food
GDP:	www.uaeinteract.com/gdp
Gold:	www.uaeinteract.com/gold
Horticulture:	www.uaeinteract.com/flowers
Hotels:	www.uaeinteract.com/hotels
ICAD, Abu Dhabi Industrial City:	www.uaeinteract.com/icad
IMF Publications on the UAE:	www.uaeinteract.com/centralbank_imf
Industrial development:	www.uaeinteract.com/ind_dev
Industry:	www.uaeinteract.com/industry
Insurance:	www.uaeinteract.com/insurance
International investments:	www.uaeinteract.com/int_inv
Investments in UAE:	www.uaeinteract.com/uaeinvestments
Oil and Gas:	www.uaeinteract.com/oilgas
Oil news and data:	www.uaeinteract.com/opec
Specialised Economic Zones in Abu Dhabi (ZonesCorp):	www.uaeinteract.com/zonescorp
Stock markets:	www.uaeinteract.com/shares
Taxation:	www.uaeinteract.com/tax
Technology sector:	www.uaeinteract.com/technology
Tourism:	www.uaeinteract.com/tourism
Trade agreements:	www.uaeinteract.com/tradeagreements
Trade and the UAE:	www.uaeinteract.com/wto
Trade:	www.uaeinteract.com/trade
UAE Central Bank1:	www.uaeinteract.com/centralbank
UAE Central Bank2:	www.uaeinteract.com/uaecb
UAE Offsets Group:	www.uaeinteract.com/offsets
UAE Population Census:	www.uaeinteract.com/census
WTO Report on the UAE, 2006:	www.uaeinteract.com/wto_report

INFRASTRUCTURE

The new era of economic transition is characterised by public-private partnerships that are playing key roles in infrastructure development.

Abu Dhabi has embarked on a major remodelling of buildings and roads in the city centre. Downtown Abu Dhabi is being redefined by the Central Market mixed-use redevelopment, costing in the region of Dh2.6 billion.

INFRASTRUCTURE

The booming UAE economy, as outlined in the previous chapter, is fuelling infrastructure development on an unprecedented scale. This has been depicted as a 'new era of economic transition', characterised by a public-private partnership that is gradually taking over the role traditionally held by government in infrastructure development. Housing, tourist, industrial and commercial facilities, education and healthcare amenities, transportation, utilities, communications, ports and airports are all undergoing massive redevelopment, radically altering the urban environment in the UAE. Reform of property laws has also added impetus to urban development.

URBAN DEVELOPMENT

ABU DHABI

In Abu Dhabi more than US$100 billion (Dh367 billion) will be invested over the next four to five years on infrastructure projects. In addition to major investment in energy and industry, plans include a new airport, a new world-scale port and industrial zone in Taweelah, another port and industrial zone at Mussafah, the 11,000-unit Showayba City at Mussaffah, Mohammed bin Zayed City, the completion of several projects at Shahama, Khalifa Cities A and B, and the building of massive mixed-use communities on Saadiyat Island, Reem Island, Lulu Island and at Al Raha Beach. Many of these projects will also go some way towards meeting the infrastructural needs of a rapidly increasing and urbanised population.

Abu Dhabi has already embarked on a major remodelling of buildings and roads in the city centre. Downtown Abu Dhabi is being redefined by the Central Market mixed-use redevelopment, costing in the region of Dh2.6 billion. This is scheduled for completion in early 2008, but the first phase of the project, the souq area, could be handed over to the original owners by the end of 2007.

Housing, tourist, industrial and commercial facilities, education and healthcare amenities, transportation, utilities, communications, ports and airports are all undergoing massive redevelopment, radically altering the urban environment in the UAE.

www.uaeinteract.com/urban

Abu Dhabi's signature Corniche

Abu Dhabi's signature Corniche is a delightful seafront esplanade close to the heart of the city. Extensive new highways, bordered by shimmering skyscrapers, landscaped walks and play areas sweep past Mina Zayed and along the coast towards the Breakwater, the site of Marina Mall, a heritage centre and villas. In the wake of its recent Dh300 million extension, at 47000 square metres, Marina Mall is now the largest retail development in Abu Dhabi.

The opening in 2005 of the exotic and luxurious Emirates Palace Hotel on the white sandy beach to the east of the Breakwater bridge spearheaded the new enthusiasm in Abu Dhabi for tourism-related infrastructure development, much of which has already been discussed in the section on tourism and real estate in the chapter on Economic Development. However, it is Abu Dhabi's plans for its numerous offshore islands such as that proposed for Saadiyat that have really caught the imagination.

Island Projects

The Saadiyat Island project is the largest single mixed-use development in the Arabian Gulf. The intention is to transform the 27-square-kilometre natural island, just 500 metres offshore to the north-east of Abu Dhabi City, into a premier international tourist destination with spectacular beachfront. But this will also be an integrated residential community with a full complement of commercial, leisure and tourism facilities, as well as civic and cultural amenities.

Extensive new highways, bordered by shimmering skyscrapers, landscaped walks and play areas sweep past Mina Zayed and along the coast towards the Breakwater, the site of Marina Mall, a heritage centre and villas.

Much of the island to the east is characterised by ecologically sensitive mangrove reserves, which will be protected and also form a feature of the development. Quality conservation and environmental practices will also be employed throughout the development, including best practices for the conservation of energy and water.

Ground-clearing work commenced in May 2006. The Dh128 million (US$35 million) enabling works contract, which will clear the way for the construction of infrastructure, is being carried out by the Abu Dhabi-headquartered Al Jaber Group.

Al Lulu Island adjacent to the Breakwater will be a new waterfront bustling with mixed-use commercial, residential, cultural and recreational facilities. Shams Abu Dhabi is being developed on 1.320 million square metres of Al Reem Island, off the northern coastline of Abu Dhabi Island. Predominately urban in character, the Shams Abu Dhabi project will encompass residential and commercial buildings, hotels, and leisure and recreation facilities. Eight towers on the land entrance to Al Reem will form the prestigious Gate project.

Emirates Palace Hotel

Al Raha

Dredging and reclamation is also well under way on another major mixed-use development that will change the face of the emirate. Al Raha is the new gateway city district of Abu Dhabi on the Abu Dhabi–Dubai road. Eight individual, carefully-designed precincts are planned on an area of 6.8 million square metres, to include 60 towers amid exclusive low-rise residential developments. Khor Al Raha will be the first precinct to be constructed. Creation of the land mass that will shape this prime waterfront development is obviously an integral part of this project.

Exhibition Complex

Construction of a new exhibition complex under the auspices of Abu Dhabi National Exhibitions Company is progressing smoothly, with the first phase of the Dh8 billion project on schedule to host the internationally recognised IDEX 2007 defence exhibition and conference. The complex is close to major hotel developments, a short distance from Abu Dhabi Airport, and approximately 75 minutes from Jebel Ali, Dubai.

The opening in 2005 of the exotic and luxurious Emirates Palace Hotel on the white sandy beach to the east of the Breakwater bridge spearheaded the new enthusiasm in Abu Dhabi for tourism-related infrastructure development.

Roads and Public Transport

Abu Dhabi Public Transport Department (PTD) is constantly updating the transportation element of its 20-year plan to meet the challenges presented by the spiralling increase in traffic on Abu Dhabi's roads: between 2001 and 2006 the total number of vehicles, including trucks and buses, had increased by over a quarter of a million, from 31,472 in 2001 to 237,891 on 15 January 2006. Looking to the future, the PTD are also taking into account the impact of the massive new developments on the

www.uaeinteract.com/roads

Abu Dhabi Traffic Police

Traffic on Abu Dhabi's roads increased significantly in recent years. A massive roads development project is under way to deal with this issue.

surrounding areas, some of which are described above. This involves vastly improved road and bridge networks in Greater Abu Dhabi, including the islands of Saadiyat, Hodairiyat, Mishairib and Lulu and the onshore satellite towns of Bani Yas, Shahama and Al Wathba, as well as major redevelopment of the road network on Abu Dhabi Island, including the Corniche and internal roads such as Hamdan, Khalifa, Al Salam, Falah and Hazza streets. Meanwhile, work continues on the much-needed Dh900 million (US$245 million) Abu Dhabi third crossing project, approach roads and interchanges.

In addition, the transport plan envisages revamping the public transport system, including the provision of additional buses (together with air-conditioned bus stops), and restrictions on taxis in the central area. The most significant proposal, however, is the construction of a metro system that would eventually link up with the Dubai Light Rail to ensure smooth travel for metro users between the two emirates.

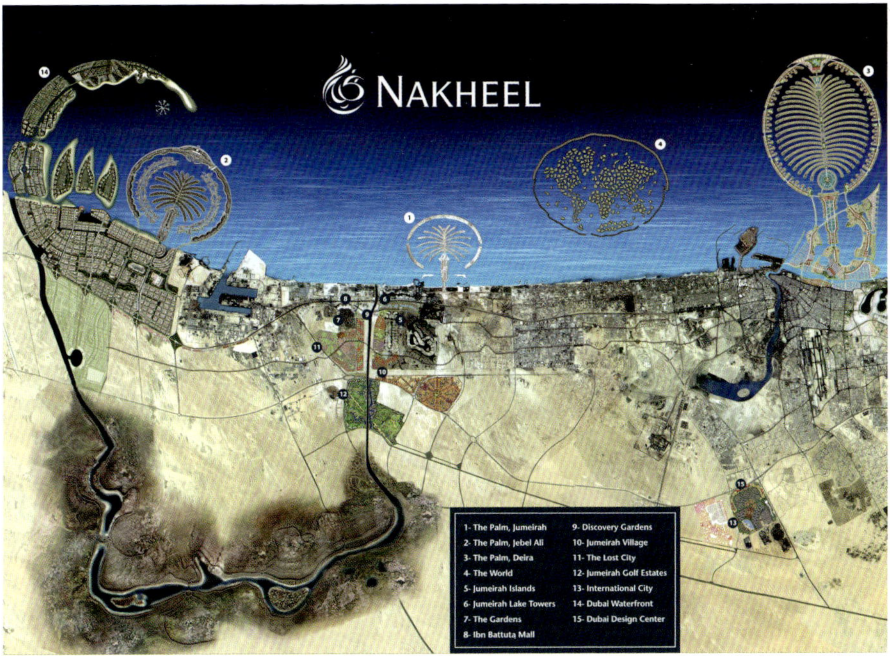

DUBAI

Massive infrastructural development has been taking place in Dubai City for some time. Huge mixed-use complexes and industrial, educational and medical cluster developments are under construction throughout the emirate, many of them, such as Dubai Waterfront and Dubai World Central, of gigantic proportions. Again much of this development has been fuelled by a promise of reform of the property laws that took place in 2006 (see section on Real Estate in Economic Development).

Dubai's coastline is being re-structured to maximise the extent of seafront.

Islands

As discussed in the previous section of this *Yearbook*, the date-palm-shaped, man-made islands known as The Palm Jumeirah, The Palm Jebel Ali and The Palm Deira, and the islands of 'The World' have significantly added to the landmass of Dubai Emirate. Construction work on The Palm Jumeirah is advanced and residents commenced moving into properties there at the end

Three 'Palms' are under development by Nakheel, Palm Jumeirah, Palm Jebel Ali and Palm Deira. In addition 303 man-made islands have been built forming 'The World'.

Part of 'The World'

of 2006, five years after land reclamation began. This signals the end of phase one of construction, which includes approximately 1400 villas on 11 of the island's fronds and roughly 2500 shoreline apartments within 20 buildings on the east side of the trunk. Reclamation work on The Palm Jebel Ali commenced in October 2002 and a completion date for infrastructure is set for 2011. This Palm, 50 per cent larger than its Jumeirah equivalent, will be managed by Dubai Waterfront, an even larger development project taking place in the surrounding area (see below). Much groundwork has also been done on The Palm Deira, the largest of the three.

About 90 per cent of reclamation work for the cluster of 303 man-made islands comprising 'The World', costing in the region of Dh3.67 billion (US$1 billion), has been completed. A further Dh27.89 billion (US$7.6 billion) will be spent on developing infrastructure for an estimated 150,000 inhabitants.

Dubai Waterfront and Jebel Ali

Dubai Waterfront will provide homes for 1.2 million residents in ten districts.

Dubai Waterfront, an 81-million-square-metre development under construction on Dubai's last remaining undeveloped coastal strip, will house 1.2 million residents in ten districts. The new city will also feature an arc of man-made islands adjacent to the Palm Jebel Ali. Dubai Waterfront will incorporate a downtown area known as Madinat Al Arab, catering to a wide range of commercial activities and lifestyles. Planning will include a sophisticated transportation network as well as health and education facilities. This development hopes to integrate with other projects such as Dubai World Central on the west side of Dubai. The latter is an independent free zone with several smaller 'cities' catering to the needs of the aviation industry and accommodating up to 750,000 residents and workers which is being built on an 140-square-kilometre site near Jebel Ali (see section on Airports).

Dubailand

Dubailand is designed as a multi-phased global attraction that will be a popular destination for millions of tourists annually.

Projects in Dubailand, categorised into six themed zones known as worlds, include leisure and entertainment facilities, theme parks, shopping malls, hotels and resorts, restaurants and residential units.

Several developments in Dubailand are in operation including The Autodrome and the first phase of the Equestrian and Polo Club project. Others under construction include the Dh4 billion City of Arabia, which will have a high-tech dinosaur theme park, The Restless Planet, and the massive shopping centre, Mall of Arabia, both due to open in the spring of 2008. Groundwork has also commenced on the Snowdome, the Dh3.67 billion dirham (US$1 billion) winter wonderland project, and the first of five overlapped phases of development for Falcon City of Wonders. This Dh5.5 billion (US$ 1.5 billion) development is shaped to represent a falcon, emblematic of the UAE's heritage.

Some of the major projects for Dubailand announced in 2006 include 'Legends', a Dh14 billion (US$ 3.8 billion) mixed-use, family-oriented entertainment project occupying 2.3 million square metres that will be completed in 2013, and The Bawadi project, spread over 13 million square metres featuring a cluster of 31 hotels, including the 6500-room Asia Asia hotel. The first phase of the project, which includes the enormous Asia Asia hotel, will be operational by 2010.

Dubai Marina

Jumeirah

The Jumeirah region has been radically transformed in recent years, both in terms of resorts and residential areas. Major residential projects already in operation or nearing completion include Dubai Marina, a man-made marina with a surrounding development area covering about 5 million square metres. Emirates Living, also known as Emirates Living Community, is a collection of neighbouring developments encompassing Emirates Hills, The Lakes, The Views, The Parklands, The Meadows, The Springs, and The Greens, whilst Jumeirah Beach Residence, close to the north shore of Dubai Marina, is a huge single-phase residential and commercial project costing in the region of Dh6 billion (US$ 1.6 billion).

Major residential projects in Jumeirah include Dubai Marina, Emirates Living Community encompassing Emirates Hills, The Lakes, The Views, The Parklands, The Meadows, The Springs and The Greens, and Jumeirah Beach Residence.

www.uaeinteract.com/urban

MARINA WALK

Dubai is already one of the most impressive young cities in the world. Developments that are currently under way will create one of the world's finest living communities, designed to provide rewarding lifestyles for all its people.

Artists' renderings are based on actual plans and confirmed investments.

Trump Tower Hotel is being built on The Palm Jumeirah.

Towers

Closer to the centre of the city, skyscrapers of record-breaking dimensions have become a feature of the landscape. Work on the world's tallest tower, Burj Dubai, is progressing steadily. The final height of the tower is a well-kept secret but it will certainly be in the region of 200 storeys. The Burj is the centrepiece of 'Downtown Dubai'.

The Burj Al Alam, a recent commercial venture from Fortune Group, will stand at 108-storeys (482 metres). The Dh2.5 billion (US$0.68billion) Executive Towers, Dubai Properties' first project in Business Bay, is also proceeding on schedule. Work is progressing simultaneously on all eleven towers in the complex.

The Creek Waterfront

The second phase of the 6.5-million-square metres Dubai Creek waterfront project 'The Lagoons' went on sale in 2006. Located in Dubai Investment Park near the heart of Dubai, 'The Lagoons' is being built on an extension of Dubai Creek near the Ra's al-Khor Wildlife Sanctuary. Here a series of seven interconnected islands will be created to support a mixed-use project of residential units, shopping centres, office buildings, and marinas.

Another Creek waterfront mixed-use project, this time closer to Garhoud Bridge, Dubai Festival City is already in operation, whilst Arabian culture and heritage will be the theme of a new Dh50 billion, 3.7-million-square-metre leisure and tourist project by the Creek next to Garhoud Bridge.

Malls

Dubai Creek has been extended by 9.8 kilometres as part of the Dubai Properties Business Bay project.

The retail business in Dubai is booming as is evidenced by the huge success of the 223,000-square-metre Mall of the Emirates that opened in September 2005. Completed in spring of 2005, Ibn Battuta Mall is a single level project comprising some 140,000 square metres, and according to developers Nakheel, 'to be doubled in size'. Not to be outdone, the first phase alone of Mall of Arabia, one of the anchor components of Dubailand, is reported to measure 548,000 square metres and another major development, Dubai Mall, situated near Burj Dubai, is scheduled for completion by 2007.

Major new shopping malls such as Mall of the Emirates, Dubai and Marina Mall, Abu Dhabi serve a growing population, providing world-class retail facilities within easy reach of home.

Roads and Public Transport

It is not difficult to appreciate that the pace of development outlined above presents some serious challenges for the transportation network in Dubai. However, efforts being made by Dubai Roads and Transport Authority (RTA) to ease traffic congestion are already bearing fruit. Major road developments to provide access to The Palm Jumeirah have already been completed. The Dh82.5 million (US$22,47 million) expansion of Sheikh Zayed Road to a five-lane highway from Jebel Ali to the Second Interchange was also completed in mid-2006. In addition, traffic should flow more smoothly when Emirates Road and its link roads are widened and the huge new three-level interchange with 13 bridges is completed in 2008 on the roundabout linking Dubailand, the Autodrome and Arabian Ranches.

But perhaps the most significant improvements will ensue when a planned series of new bridges spanning Dubai Creek, a notorious bottleneck, have been completed. Construction of a replacement for the existing Al Garhoud Bridge commenced in 2006. A new

Traffic densities on certain routes are causing long delays. New roads, bridges and a light rail system are being constructed to ease the pressure.

bridge is planned over Dubai Creek between Al Maktoum Bridge and Al Shindagha Tunnel. Another crossing over the Creek at Ra's al-Khor is currently under construction to provide yet another link from Al Rashidiya to Bur Dubai. In the meantime, as one element of a 'quick solution' plan to ease traffic congestion, a Dh81.5 million (US$22.20 million) floating bridge will be built over the Creek between Al Maktoum and Al Garhoud bridges. Construction commenced in September 2006 and the structure will be ready in March 2007. In addition, the long-awaited two-year project to ease traffic congestion on the busy 7.5 kilometre stretch of road between Sharjah and Al Garhoud Bridge commenced in mid-2006.

Dubai's RTA commenced work on two important road projects in 2006: a major upgrade of Interchange One on Sheikh Zayed Road and the construction of a floating bridge over Dubai Creek.

Public transport development and integration is also a major component of Dubai's transport strategy with much hope being pinned on the fully automated Dh15 billion Dubai Light Rail (DLR). Construction work on the 52.1 kilometre DLR Red Line from Rashidiya Station to Jebel Ali Station commenced at 35 sites early in 2006, whilst preparatory work on the 17.6 kilometre Green Line from Dubai Airport Free Zone to Dubai Healthcare City got under way at the end of the year. The two lines and 41 stations (nine underground) will be completed by 2010. Dubai RTA are also studying the possibility of extending the Red Line from Union Square to the Sharjah–Dubai border in the north and from Jebel Ali to the Abu Dhabi border. The Green Line will also be progressively extended from Healthcare City to service developments in the Al Jadaf area.

NORTHERN EMIRATES

Although they are not experiencing quite the same population pressures as Abu Dhabi and Dubai, the emirates of Sharjah, Ajman, Umm al-Qaiwain, Ra's al-Khaimah and Fujairah are all in the throes of developing and expanding their infrastructure to facilitate an escalation in commercial, residential and tourist development. In addition, the Federal Government continues to invest money on infrastructure projects in the Northern Emirates, especially roads, housing, electricity and telecommunications.

Housing in Sharjah

Sharjah

Three new residential areas are planned in the suburbs of Sharjah in order to meet the increasing demand for more homes. Presently, 4000 to 5000 plots are being developed for UAE nationals in Rahmania and Seouh suburban areas, and a new satellite town for expatriates at Al Juwaiza will include 2000 plots for villas, and low-rise residential and commercial buildings. Work at Al Juwaiza, being financed by the government, commenced in 2006 and should be completed by 2008.

The first phase of Emirates Industrial City, one of the largest industrial projects in Sharjah, was completed in 2006. Located in the Saja'a district along the Dubai Ring Road on an area of 7.7 million square metres, Industrial City will have eight sectors accommodating over 3000 medium and light industries, as well as commercial enterprises and residential areas. Al Hanoo Holding Company is also working on the Dh18 billion (US$4.90 billion) Nujoom Islands project, a residential, commercial and tourist venture on 5.58 million square metres near Hamriyah village on the north-eastern coast of Sharjah.

Following the successful completion of the King Faisal Interchange project, Sharjah has embarked on the first phase of an ambitious Dh2.1 billion (US$572 billion) new road scheme. This will not be completed until 2010, but motorists will be able to notice a discernible improvement in traffic flow by 2008, when most of the projects within the city will be finished.

Sharjah Public Transport Corporation (SPTC) intends to provide links with the main Dubai bus routes especially in Al Qusais and Al Nahda areas, which will also have Dubai metro stations. The aim is to provide adequate public transport facilities to people living in Sharjah and ease traffic congestion on roads linking Dubai and Sharjah.

In mid-2006, the Ajman government launched Emirates City, a Dh15 billion (US$4.08 billion) mixed-use development, featuring 72 residential and commercial towers.

Other Emirates

In mid-2006, the Ajman government launched Emirates City, a Dh15 billion (US$4.08 billion) mixed-use development, featuring 72 residential and commercial towers. Located on the Emirates

Road with easy access to the other emirates, the first phase will focus on the construction of 25 towers, while the downtown area will be developed at a later phase.

Umm al-Qaiwain's new marina development will be a vast master-planned waterfront community of villas and apartments located on the shores of Khor al-Beidah.

Expatriates will be allowed to purchase freehold properties in the RAK Properties development, Mina Al Arab, launched in 2006. Spread along a 3-kilometre beach, the Dh10 billion (US$2.72 billion) project is scheduled for completion in 2011 and will include a selection of five-star resort hotels, including two eco-tourism resorts, 3500 residential units, a cluster of 386 villas and six gated communities. RAK Properties is also involved in another landmark master development, Mangrove Islands, at the heart of Ra's al-Khaimah near Manar Mall. The foundation stone for the Dh850 million (US$231.60 million) Wow Rak theme park project on 120 acres in the Khor Qurm region was also laid in August 2006.

Housing in Fujairah

Work on the infrastructure for the Dh2 billion (US$545 billion) Fujairah Paradise project, a concentration of villas, five-star hotel and shopping mall, commenced in 2006. Also under way is the Fujairah Dana (Pearl) development, a complex of villas and hotels being built on a peninsula and group of small islands being reclaimed off the coast near Al Aqah. Projects in the planning stage include a large residential community in one of the more secluded valleys close to the coast, and a smaller community at Ghurfa, just south of Fujairah City.

The Ministry of Public Works has also entered into two contracts valued at Dh328 million in 2006 for road-building in the Northern Emirates. The first, costing Dh230 million, will link three centres in Fujairah with Ra's al-Khaimah, while the second Dh98 million project will connect areas in Sharjah with those in Ra's al-Khaimah. Plans for the more remote regions also include other basic infrastructure projects such as schools, hospitals, mosques, residential complexes, as well as police and civil defence centres. These projects are scheduled for completion by 2008.

ELECTRICITY AND WATER

By mid-2006 the total capacity for electricity production in the UAE was 16,220 MW compared to 9600 MW in 2001 and industry estimates expect the capacity to rise to almost 26,000 MW by 2010.

The escalating scale of urban development outlined above is impacting significantly on the demand for electricity. Annual demand growth peaked in the UAE at 14.1 per cent in 2004, and continued to be strong in 2005 with an increase of more than 12 per cent. In fact, the UAE has the highest projected increase in demand within the AGCC region, which is expected to continue to grow at a minimum rate of 10 per cent per annum until 2010, far outstripping the world average of 3 per cent per annum. Plans are, therefore, being formulated to increase the UAE's electricity generation capacity by as much as 60 per cent by 2010.

By mid-2006 the total capacity for electricity production in the UAE was 16,220 megawatts (MW) compared to 9600 MW in 2001 and industry estimates expect the capacity to rise to almost 26,000 MW by 2010. At present, Abu Dhabi Water & Electricity Authority (ADWEA) accounts for 53 per cent of total capacity, Dubai Electricity & Water Authority (DEWA) is responsible for 29 per cent, Sharjah Electricity & Water Authority (SEWA) for 11 per cent, with the Federal Electricity and Water Authority (FEWA) accounting for 7 per cent.

Approximately 97 per cent of production is fuelled by natural gas and the remaining 3 per cent is produced by diesel generation or steam turbines (primarily in the Northern Emirates). The UAE will commence importing natural gas from Qatar in late 2006. The gas will be transported via Dolphin's 370-kilometre export pipeline to a terminal at Taweelah in Abu Dhabi, from where it will be piped to the centres of use, such as Fujairah's new power and water complex (presently receiving gas from Oman) and Dubai's Jebel Ali complex.

WATER

Historically, all the UAE's water requirements were met from groundwater obtained from shallow, hand-dug wells and the traditional *falaj* system of aquifers. Over the past two decades, rapid economic development, coupled with steep population increases and a push to achieve self-sufficiency in food supplies, have placed ever-increasing pressure on the UAE's precious natural water resources. This is a real challenge for a country with no rivers and little rainfall. Water consumption in Abu Dhabi alone is expected to increase to 5.858 billion cubic metres by 2020. Since the 'transit' labour and tourist population are major consumers of water in the Emirates, the rate of consumption may outpace the actual population growth rate.

Although groundwater still plays a significant role in meeting agricultural demand throughout the Emirates, and more than half of the water distributed by the federal authority (FEWA) in the Northern Emirates is sweet groundwater, a high proportion of the UAE's requirements is being met by an extensive gas-fired desalination programme, with Abu Dhabi accounting for around half of the total desalinated water production in the UAE. Water production, as distinct from capturing groundwater, reached more than 195 billion gallons in 2004. The significant increase in production (up from 130.5 billion gallons in 1996) is primarily a result of the completion of new desalination plants.

In recent years water management initiatives have also included the restoration of the traditional *falaj* irrigation systems, the building of delay and recharge dams, well-drilling and aquifer-testing and exploration. In addition, water conservation measures are being implemented throughout the Emirates, especially in the agricultural and amenity-planting sector where plant suitability, crop replacement and drip irrigation techniques are being promoted to save water (see section on Agriculture in Economic Development). Emirates such as Abu Dhabi are also educating the general public about the importance of water conservation.

Water conservation measures are being implemented throughout the Emirates, especially in the agricultural and amenity-planting sector where plant suitability, crop replacement and drip irrigation techniques are being promoted to save water.

www.uaeinteract.com/elec_h2o

ADWEA has led a re-structuring and privatisation programme of Abu Dhabi's water and electricity sector in a concerted effort to increase capacity and improve efficiency.

ABU DHABI

The electricity and water sector in Abu Dhabi has developed rapidly alongside the emirate's social and economic development. In 1966 when the government's Water and Electricity Department (WED) was formed and the first generation plant installed, Abu Dhabi's installed generation capacity totalled 3 MW. By 2003 the generation capacity had reached 5246 MW. The installed desalination capacity increased from 4 million imperial gallons per day (MIGD) in 1970, when the first desalination plant came on-stream, to 449 MIGD in 2003.

This growth in capacity reflected a rapid rise in demand: peak electricity demand increased from 1766 MW in 1993 to 4134 MW in 2003 and 4680 MW in 2006. Growth in the early years of the sector was exceptionally strong, greater than 30 per cent in some years. By the 1980s the rate had fallen to single digits and continued at this level until 1996 when double-digit growth was again a feature, largely attributable to an increase in the rate of replacement of the housing stock.

Historically water demand has grown at a slightly faster rate than electricity demand. The system-constrained supply of water from generation and desalination plants increased from 97 MIGD in 1993 to 330 MIGD in 2003 and 635 MIGD in 2006.

Privatisation

Since 1997, orchestrated by ADWEA, a wave of re-structuring and privatisation has swept through Abu Dhabi's water and electricity sector in a concerted effort to increase capacity and improve efficiency. As part of this strategy, six independent water and power production plants (IWPPs) have been introduced on a build, own and operate (BOO) basis via joint venture arrangements: ADWEA retains a 60 per cent shareholding in each IWPP, while the remaining 40 per cent is owned by overseas private investors. IWPPs sell water and electricity from their production plant to the single buyer of the sector, Abu Dhabi Water and Electricity Company (ADWEC) under long-term Power and Water Purchase Agreements (PWPAs). ADWEC, in turn, charges the distribution companies (Abu Dhabi Distribution Company (ADDC) and Al Ain

Six independent water and power production plants (IWPPs) have been introduced on a build, own and operate (BOO) basis via joint venture arrangements: ADWEA retains a 60 per cent shareholding in each IWPP, while the remaining 40 per cent is owned by overseas private investors.

www.uaeinteract.com/elec_h2o

Distribution Company (AADC)) for water and electricity, delivered via the TRANSCO networks under a bulk supply tariff (BST).

The sixth IWPP was formalised in 2006 when ADWEA signed a US$1.35 billion (Dh4.95 billion) water and power purchase agreement with top-bidder Sembcorp of Singapore for the privatisation of the Fujairah-based Union Electricity Water Company (UWEC). ADWEA had received four bids for the 656 MW power and 100 MIGD desalination plant at Qidfa, Fujairah, The new owner will add 225 MW of new power generation capacity.

TAQA will take over the state's interests in IWPPs and it has the overall responsibility for the execution of strategic projects in the fields of power, electricity, water, gas, oil and minerals production, locally and globally.

ADWEA's 60 per cent of UWEC was acquired by Abu Dhabi National Energy Company (TAQA), the recently-formed public joint stock company, which is listed on the ADSM. TAQA will take over the state's interests in IWPPs and it has the overall responsibility for the execution of strategic projects in the fields of power, electricity, water, gas, oil and minerals production, locally and globally.

As well as continuing the process of privatising capacity, ADWEA is also studying plans to outsource administration and the next step will be privatising distribution. It has already signed a Dh300 million (US$81.74 million) contract with Injazat Data Systems awarding it a ten-year Information Technology (IT) outsourcing contract to manage all of ADWEA's IT requirements.

Sewage

Abu Dhabi has also formally embarked on the privatisation of its sewage system. Two separate projects will be privatised: an operation, maintenance and management services agreement (OM&MS) for the sewerage networks of the whole emirate, including Al Ain, and a single build-own-operate and transfer (BOOT) project for the major sewage treatment plants. The functions of Abu Dhabi Sewerage Services Company (ADSSC) will be transferred to a new, private company, with the group continuing to own the hard assets of the sewerage network. ADSSC will second most of its staff in charge of operation and maintenance to the new company. ADWEA will indirectly hold 60 per cent of the new company with the bidder holding the remaining 40 per cent.

Demand Forecasts

By 2006 ADWEA had raised approximately Dh40 billion from its privatisation programme. However, with many of the new industrial, tourist and real estate projects entering construction phase, the emirate is preparing for a major expansion of its installed generating capacity in order to meet the expected surge in demand. This will provide new opportunities for IWPPs. In fact, the economic boom in the emirate has meant that electricity demand projections have had to be completely revised and ADWEC has recently completed a new electricity and water demand forecast up to 2020. Given the uncertainties of the timing and size of some of the massive projects, the number of expatriates that will be living in the developments and the fact that several large-scale projects are pending, it has drawn up three separate demand scenarios, covering a high, low and base forecast, which is judged the most likely.

Under its base electricity demand scenario, ADWEC estimates that the large projects will contribute 1221 MW to peak power demand in 2009, rising to 3989 MW in 2013 and 4370 MW in 2015, before reaching 4644 MW in 2020. Overall, ADWEC forecasts that the system peak demand will reach 7333 MW in 2009, 12,590 MW in 2015 and 14,226 MW in 2020.

The growth in water demand is expected to be less dramatic, the assumption being that these projects will focus on water conservation and re-use. However, Abu Dhabi Water and Electricity Company estimates in its base forecast that peak water demand will rise from 635 MIGD in 2006 to 746 MIGD in 2009, 881 MIGD in 2015 and 957 MIGD in 2020.

Abu Dhabi will have sufficient existing capacity to cover demand up until and including 2008. In 2009 it will be in slight deficit, which will increase in the subsequent years as the large-scale projects are commissioned. ADWEA is looking at various means of covering the increased demand. New capacity will need to be in place by 2009/10. (Predictions are for 239 MW of definite new projects in 2009, and more than 1500 MW of possible new projects from 2010 onwards.)

The economic boom in Abu Dhabi has meant that electricity demand projections have had to be completely revised and ADWEC has recently completed a new electricity and water demand forecast up to 2020.

www.uaeinteract.com/elec_h2o

Renewable Energy

ADWEA is also studying ways of using renewable energy to help satisfy demand. In particular, its research division is investigating whether solar technologies can contribute to meeting the emirate's requirement for added capacity. An initial trial involving the installation of solar panels at selected locations in the capital will assess their susceptibility to harsh climatic conditions, focusing in particular on the feasibility of using solar energy to feed electricity into the power grid. ADWEA, in collaboration with Australia's Commonwealth Scientific and Industrial Research Organisation, is also investigating the feasibility of using solar energy to assist in powering air-conditioning units during times of peak demand (see also section on Alternative Energy in Economic Development).

Well-water

Concerns have risen in recent years over the depletion of groundwater resources. So much so that a new law was brought into force in 2006 (No. 6 for 2006) conferring the responsibility to regulate and license activities such as 'drilling a new well, deepening an existing well, increasing a well's diameter, boosting water recovery by using a pump, replacing an old well, transporting or selling well water' on the Environment Agency – Abu Dhabi (EAD). The law also obliges owners to maintain farm wells, pumps, meters, pipes and irrigation conduits.

A new law passed in 2006 confers responsibility for regulating and licensing well drilling and well modification on the Environment Agency – Abu Dhabi (EAD).

The penalties for contractors who practice well drilling works without a licence to do so are 3 to 12 months imprisonment and/or fines of Dh10,000 (US$2724) to Dh50,000 (US$13,623). The law also specifies penalties for other violations by both contractors and owners and the latter are required to notify EAD of any wells dug before issuance of the law.

In addition, an integrated water resource database for the Emirate of Abu Dhabi will be established following a full-scale survey of wells and reservoirs by EAD. The central database will be accessible to all authorities concerned, including Abu Dhabi Municipality and ADWEA.

DUBAI

Dubai Electricity and Water Authority (DEWA) signed contracts worth Dh7 billion (US$1.90 billion) in 2005 as part of its projected Dh20 billion (US$5.45 billion) investment to expand power generation capacity by 2012 to 10,000 MW of electricity. This increase is vital to keep pace with the demand created by massive development in all sectors. In 2005 peak demand for electricity was 3571 MW per day, while annual daily peak demand for water was 194 MIGD (up from 177 MIGD in 2004). Because of the burgeoning real estate sector, demand forecasting is proving to be extremely difficult. However, it is estimated that peak water demand in 2011 will reach 341 MIGD and electricity demand will reach 8513 MW per day by 2011.

New Projects

In 2006 DEWA commenced construction on phase III of Aweer Power station (expansion of H station). The Dh1.64 billion (US$0.446 billion) project, scheduled for completion in mid-2008, will increase capacity at the station to 1800 MW, bringing DEWA's total production capacity to 7200 MW.

Tender documents were released in 2006 for Dubai's largest co-generation project to date – The Jebel Ali M Power and Desalination Plant. Estimated to cost Dh5.5 billion (US$1.50 billion), M Station will increase power generation by 2000 MW and water desalination capacity by 105 MIGD. When completed in 2008 and commissioned in 2010 it will be instrumental in meeting the anticipated increase in industrial demand for electricity in the area.

DEWA also signed a Dh3.4 billion (US$0.93 billion) contract for phase two of Jebel Ali L Station with a consortium of Hyundai Engineering and Fisia Italim-pianti. This phase, will add 1333 MW capacity of electricity and 55 MIGD of desalinated water.

CONSERVING ENERGY

Dubai, like the other emirates, is also investigating ways of conserving energy through improved technology and renewable energy sources. For example Emirates Central Cooling Systems

www.uaeinteract.com/elec_h2o

The UAE is investigating use of alternative energy options including solar generation of electricity.

Corporation (Empower) was formed in December 2003 as a joint venture between Dubai Technology and Media Free Zone and the Dubai Electricity and Water Authority (DEWA). Several large projects in Dubai, including International Media Production Zone (IMPZ), Jumeirah Beach Residence, Dubai Health Care City, Dubai International Financial Centre and Business Bay are using Empower's environmentally-friendly, centralised, cost-effective district-cooling systems.

Wind farms to provide part of the city's electricity could become a familiar sight if DEWA's pilot scheme on renewable energy is successful. Wind conditions are being monitored and suitable mountain, coastal and desert locations are being investigated. However, offshore wind turbines are not an option as maintenance and connection to the grid is too expensive. Although costly to establish, land-based wind turbines could eventually prove to be a cost-effective, supplement for conventional energy sources.

NORTHERN EMIRATES

Sharjah Electricity and Water Authority's (SEWA) construction of its gas-fuelled Dh1 billion (US$272 billion) power generation and water desalination plant in Al Hamriyah is well under way, involving the supply and installation of four gas turbine units at a total capacity of 380 MW. This project is being fast-tracked and once completed (the new gas turbines will enter commercial service between June of 2006 and March of 2007), the power generation unit will be able to produce 2000 MW and the desalination plant will produce more than 80 MIGD day, meeting the demand for power and water in Sharjah City and Hamriyah.

The Fujairah-based Union Electricity Water Company (UWEC), privatisation of which is discussed above, supplies 656 MW of power and 100 MIGD of desalinated water at Qidfa, Fujairah. An additional 225 MW of power generation capacity will be provided by the new owner. UWEC has constructed a 179-kilometre dual pipeline capable of transporting up to 200 MIGD of desalinated water from the plant to Al Ain in Abu Dhabi. An 18-kilometre branch pipeline has also been built to supply the Northern Emirates through Dhaid in Sharjah.

EMIRATES NATIONAL GRID

Dubai and Abu Dhabi's power grids were connected in mid-2006, allowing the two emirates to share energy resources, taking the country one step closer to the November 2006 deadline for execution of the planned Emirates National Grid. The seven contracts for the construction of the Emirates National Grid, including overhead lines, sub-stations and control centre were signed in mid-2004, with different implementation durations varying from 24 to 30 months. Emirates National Grid will amalgamate the power generation, transmission and distribution networks of the seven emirates into a single national grid, combining the backup reserves of each emirate and giving greater flexibility and stability to the network. Eventually, the Dh850 million (US$231.60 million) Emirates National Grid is expected to link up with the US$1.1 billion GCC grid, the first phase of which is scheduled to be operational by 2008. The GCC grid will significantly impact the distribution and rising demand issues of power generation in the entire region.

Dubai and Abu Dhabi's power grids were connected in mid-2006, allowing the two emirates to share energy resources, taking the country one step closer to the November 2006 deadline for execution of the planned Emirates National Grid (ENG).

www.uaeinteract.com/elec_h2o

The majority of telecommunications now utilise wireless or satellite connections.

TELECOMMUNICATIONS

Telecommunications in the UAE entered a new phase in 2006 with the release of the General Policy for the Telecommunication Sector (GTP) by the Supreme Committee for the Supervision of the Telecom Sector (SCSTS). The goal of the GTP, among other things, is to encourage competition between operating companies, foster innovation through research and development, develop state-of-the-art telecommunications infrastructure, increase the involvement of UAE nationals in the process of economic development and contribute to economic diversification by promoting the UAE as an ICT hub.

ETISALAT

Emirates Telecommunications Corporation (Etisalat) was the sole telecom operator in the UAE from 1976 to 2006, when the market was liberalised. The corporation's reign to date has been a very successful one as indicated by the fact that it earned a net profit of Dh4.3 billion (US$1.17 billion) in 2005 on revenues totalling Dh12.9 billion (US$3.51 billion), a 25 per cent growth in profits and 23 per cent jump in revenues over 2004. A similar performance is expected for 2006. Certainly its results for the first half of 2006 are impressive: net profits increased to Dh2.813 billion (US$0.766 billion), a rise of 33 per cent over the same period in 2005. However, the full impact of the recent liberalisation of and subsequent competition in the telecom market will not be felt until 2007.

Etisalat is a major contributor to federal and emirate social development programmes.

In 2006, with a market value of US$25.32 billion, Etisalat was ranked the sixth largest corporation in the Middle East and two hundred and seventy-eighth among the world's top 500 companies.

In its thirtieth year of operations, Etisalat has made the UAE one of the most wired nations in the region and the penetration figures of key services are comparable to the most developed markets worldwide. Mobile penetration, with 5.26 million customers, has exceeded the 100 per cent mark (125 per cent), a first in the region; 630,000 internet subscribers have access to the internet and fixed lines subscribers number 1.3 million.

Etisalat has also regularly cemented its pioneering role in the region by being the first to launch services and applications, such as pre-GSM mobile services in 1982, 3G in 2003 and BlackBerry in 2006. The corporation has also been following an aggressive international expansion strategy that has seen Etisalat forging partnerships to enter many regional markets.

Headquarters of Etisalat in Abu Dhabi

International Acquisitions

Etisalat's first significant international acquisition was of the second GSM network licence in Saudi Arabia. This was quickly followed by acquisition of the licence to operate the second fixed-line network in Sudan. Etisalat then purchased a 50 per cent stake in Atlantique Telecom, a company that operates mobile phone networks in Benin, Burkina Faso, Central African Republic, Gabon, Niger, Togo and Cote D'Ivoire (Ivory Coast). Shortly afterwards, Etisalat placed the winning bid to purchase a 26 per cent stake in Pakistan Telecom Company Limited (PTCL). Etisalat is now represented on the board and in senior management of PTCL. Etisalat has also purchased a licence to offer GSM services in Afghanistan's emerging market and it plans to take part in the partial privatisation of Algerie Telecom to expand its presence in North Africa. In addition, a consortium led by Etisalat has won the bid for the third Egyptian mobile network licence and negotiations are under way to acquire purchase shares in telecommunications companies or acquire licences in Syria, Yemen, Mauritania, Russia, Greece, Uzbekistan and Tajikistan.

Etisalat was ranked the sixth largest corporation in the Middle East and two hundred and seventy-eighth among the world's top 500 companies.

Licence Agreements

To date Etisalat has been a major contributor to government funds as 50 per cent of Etisalat's net profits have been paid in royalties to the Federal Government. Under the new re-structuring programme, Etisalat was required to sign a 20-year full-service licence agreement with the UAE Telecom Regulatory Authority (TRA) which, in consultation with the SCSTS, is responsible for developing the necessary regulatory framework for an orderly transit to free market principles. The corporation will continue to pay royalties;

sector. The board includes representatives from the TRA, Abu Dhabi National Exhibition Company, Etisalat, du, Intel Middle East, UAE University, Etisalat College of Engineering, UAE Higher Colleges of Technology and Mubadala Development Company. Financing for the fund, which will promote research and development in the sector, will come from a levy of 1 per cent on Etisalat's and du's annual revenues, as well as government and private grants.

Etisalat was the sole telecom operator in the UAE up until 2006.

TELECOMMUNICATIONS CONFERENCES

One of the functions of the Telecom Regulatory Authority is to represent the UAE telecommunications industry at international fora. In this context the TRA attended the World Telecommunication Development Conference (WTDC) held in Doha, Qatar in March 2006 where it participated in strategy formulation on key social issues in telecommunications development.

The TRA also represented the UAE at the ITU Regional Radio Communication Conference, which was held in Geneva in May and June 2006. The conference organised channel allocation among participating countries, based on a newly formulated digital terrestrial TV broadcasting plan. The UAE team acquired the rights to 225 digital channels and the TRA will regulate the distribution of licences for these channels (see also Media in Media and Culture).

THURAYA

Thuraya Satellite Telecommunications Company, the Abu Dhabi-based satellite telecom service provider, was founded in the UAE in 1997 by a consortium of leading national telecommunications operators and international investment houses, with Etisalat as a majority shareholder and service provider in the UAE. The company offers cost-effective, satellite-based mobile telephone services to nearly one-third of the globe through dual-mode handsets and satellite payphones. Through partnership with leading national telecom and mobile communications companies, Thuraya provides blanket coverage in urban and remote areas to over 120 countries in Europe, the Middle East, North and Central Africa, the CIS countries as well as Central and South Asia.

Thuraya-1, the first satellite initiated from the Middle East and the heaviest satellite launched to date, was successfully deployed in 2000. A second satellite, Thuraya 2, was launched in 2003. The company has also taken delivery of its third satellite, Thuraya 3, which will be deployed in January 2007. The 113-foot-long, 5250-kilogram satellite is a clone of Thuraya 2 and has high speed alerting capabilities with position-based services. Essentially, Thuraya 3 will replace Thuraya 1, which is currently covering south-east Asia, including Korea and Indonesia. Thuraya 2 will continue to serve the Middle East, Europe, North Africa, India and some Asian markets. Once Thuraya 3 is in orbit, coverage will be from the tip of Iceland to Japan. Thuraya is in discussions with Boeing Satellite Systems for a fourth satellite.

Thuraya provides satellite-based mobile telephone services through dual-mode handsets.

Thuraya has also begun rolling out its PCOs (public call offices) in African markets and the company will have installed 4500 PCOs by the end of 2006. Thuraya is also positioning itself as a satellite telecom provider for the aeronautical industry and has signed a Memorandum of Understanding (MoU) with the UAE Air Force to develop and install a satellite network for the Air Force fleet comprising fighter jets, military helicopters and surveillance planes. This new project is expected to open up new commercial venues for the company not only within the UAE, but also within Thuraya's vast coverage area. In addition, contracts have been signed with Hughes Network Systems for the development and supply of a high-speed mobile data system, including a gateway and 2000 mobile/transportable terminals to Thuraya. This will enable the company to offer its customers broadband data services of up to 384 kilobytes per second through an IP-based network. Hughes will also supply a secondary gateway to act as a redundant gateway and perform load-sharing functions for Thuraya's existing primary gateway in the UAE.

Once Thuraya 3 is in orbit, coverage will be from the tip of Iceland to Japan. Thuraya is in discussions with Boeing Satellite Systems for a fourth satellite.

EMIRATES POST

Emirates Postal Corporation (EPC) was formed in 2001 following re-structuring of the UAE General Postal Authority. Since then the introduction of integrated IT systems, automated sorting centres

Post offices offer a wide range of services in the UAE.

and agreements with international postal authorities has effected a remarkable turnaround in postal and related services in the UAE. Alliances with world giants such as Western Union and DHL facilitated the introduction of money transfer services and cross-branded products.

Emirates Post has not only continued to improve its value-added services, harnessing technology to increase efficiency, but it has also added a host of non-postal services and made moves towards further diversification.

This business strategy is already reaping rewards: Emirates Post recorded a net profit of Dh133 million (US$36.2 million) in 2005, an increase of 6 per cent over the previous year. However, a 59 per cent increase in profits (up from Dh40.5 million to Dh64.5 million) and 31 per cent in revenues (up from Dh89.6 million to Dh117.7 million) was posted for the first four months of 2006.

DIVERSIFICATION

Emirates Post is focused on improving efficiency of existing services while also introducing new ones such as money transfer and marketing operations.

Among the major highlights in 2005 was the Dh48 million (US$13.07 million) acquisition of a 60 per cent majority stake in Wall Street Exchange, a leading money transfer company with international operations. This marks a major diversification for Emirates Post, following amendments to Federal Law No. 8 by the UAE Government permitting Emirates Post to enter the field of financial services.

Another area of diversification was the launch of Emirates Marketing & Promotions (EMP), a new subsidiary dedicated to providing integrated solutions in direct marketing and promotions.

This does not mean that Emirates Post's core business is neglected: the year 2005 witnessed record mail volumes with the Ramoul Sorting Centre breaking its all-time record. Indications are that this will be surpassed in 2006 due to the new advanced sorting machines installed at the facility. Similarly, the Dubai Airport Mail Transit Hub handled record volumes of mail.

In pursuance of its 'one-stop-shop' initiative, whereby post offices can provide a number of services ranging from postal to banking and other governmental transactions, Emirates Post introduced several new services at post offices in 2005, including sale of eDirham (required for government transactions online), Department of Economic Development licence registration, applications for driving licences, DEWA bill payments at all post offices, banking services at 21 post offices in association with Union National Bank, traffic fines payment and attestation of educational certificates in association with the Ministry of Labour and IntegraScreen.

These initiatives continued in 2006 funded by a budget of more than Dh109 million (US$29.70 million) for new projects: one of the most successful being the launch of 'Direct2Door', a speedy parcel and document service to India, Pakistan, Bangladesh, Sri Lanka and Nepal, in collaboration with major courier companies in the respective countries, backed by a money-back guarantee and track-and-trace facility.

Emirates Post also continues to expand its international courier operations into new markets with its recent entry into Europe, positioning itself as a quality provider of customised courier services through its network of more than 80 outlets. This is in line with the company's international expansion plan that started with the Far East and the Indian subcontinent.

To facilitate its expanded business activities, Emirates Post is engaged in the construction of new post office and related buildings worth more than Dh190 million (US$51.77 million), including the Dh100 million (US$27.25 million) postal operations hub next to the existing mail sorting centre at Ramoul, as well as the construction of new post offices and rebuilding of already established ones in urban and rural areas. A number of these projects will be fully operational by the end of 2007.

Several courier companies have main distribution and service centres in the UAE. This picture shows the ARAMEX centre in Jebel Ali.

INTERNATIONAL RECOGNITION

International recognition of Emirates Post's achievements in recent years came with the award for the 'Best New Service' (Training and Development Centre) at the 2005 Stevie Business Awards. The company's chief executive was also a finalist in the 'Best Turnaround Executive' category (Abdulla Al Daboos). Emirates Post also succeeded in raising its international profile through a

Over 110 airlines operate from Dubai International Airport, flying to over 160 destinations. Annual growth in passengers is running at 14 per cent, while cargo is increasing by around 20 per cent per annum.

number of initiatives. One of the most significant was the hosting of the Universal Postal Union's (UPU) Strategy Conference in Dubai in November 2006. Approximately 1000 delegates from 130 countries attended the three-day event.

Emiratisation at Emirates Post has reached 100 per cent in higher management and 57 per cent in all other categories.

AIRPORTS

Not surprisingly, the significant increase in economic, business and tourist activity in the country has led to a corresponding expansion in airport and related infrastructure in the UAE, where the total investment on airport development over the coming 20 years will exceed Dh75 billion (US$20.43 billion). This figure includes redevelopment of Abu Dhabi International Airport at a cost of Dh30 billion (US$8.17 billion), Dh15 billion (US$4.08 billion) being spent on the ongoing expansion of Dubai

International Airport, and Dh30 billion (US$8.17 billion) estimated for the new Dubai World Central development, which will house the UAE's seventh international airport.

In addition, Sharjah International Airport intends to spend Dh227 million (US$61 million) on redevelopment, Ajman is committing another Dh2.9 billion (US$800 million) to build its new airport and Fujairah has pledged Dh183 million (US$49 million) investment for the expansion of its terminal and associated structures. Al Ain International Airport is undergoing a Dh75 million (US$20.43 million) redevelopment, while the Ra's al-Khaimah government is investing Dh1billion (US$272 million) in expansion of its airport. The sum total of these projects ensures that the UAE has become the largest investor in airport development in the Middle East.

ABU DHABI

In 2005, 5.5 million passengers passed through Abu Dhabi International Airport (ADIA), compared to 5.2 million the previous year and a 20 per cent increase on 2005 is expected in 2006. However, the major new expansion plan for ADIA, which got under way in mid-2005, will significantly increase these figures.

Abu Dhabi is in a position to deliver the massive growth of its airport thanks to the emirate's foresight three decades ago in choosing a site within easy reach of the growing city of Abu Dhabi, and yet with sufficient space to allow for its future expansion. Costing an estimated Dh30 billion (US$8.17 billion), the ADIA master plan involves the construction of a new 220,000 square-metre, mid-field passenger terminal, a second runway, 4100 metres in length, and 2000 metres from the existing runway, as well as maintenance facilities and other commercial development on land immediately adjacent to, and north of, the existing airport. Work commenced on the new category 111 all-weather runway in 2006 following the signing of a Dh1 billion (US$272 million) contract between Abu Dhabi Airport Company (ADAC) and Odebrecht Al Jaber, a UAE-Brazilian joint venture. Completion is scheduled for November 2007, which should be in

Inside the Duty Free shop at Abu Dhabi International Airport

www.uaeinteract.com/airports

time to receive the first of the giant Airbus A380s scheduled to join the fleet of the national carrier Etihad Airways, commencing in 2008.

Another key part of the project is the provision of a substantial increase in cargo facilities, with an ultimate handling capacity of around 2 million tonnes of freight a year. Etihad has identified airfreight, in particular transit cargo, as one of the key growth areas and will be a major user of this facility, although the other 20 or so airlines using Abu Dhabi International Airport will also benefit.

The multi-phase project is being overseen by the Supervision Committee for Expansion of Abu Dhabi International Airport (SCADIA) with the mandate to oversee its execution up to the stage of the delivery of a fully-functional facility. Overall, the project will see a doubling of the existing airport land area to 3400 hectares, with dedicated buffer zones to the north and south. The new facilities will be designed for an initial handling capacity of 20 million passengers a year by 2010 and an ultimate capacity of 50 million passengers a year. This multi-billion dirham project will provide the capital city with an ultra-modern gateway to the world. It represents a major part of the long-term strategy for Abu Dhabi to become one of the leading aviation, tourism and business centres of the region.

In the meantime, a number of immediate remedies had to be applied to deal with the spiralling growth in both passengers and air traffic at the airport, triggered by the success of Etihad Airways. A major renovation of the main terminal was undertaken and two new interim terminals, Terminals 1A and Terminal 2, became fully operational in late 2005, having been delivered by SCADIA in a record six months. The new terminals have increased the airport's capacity by three million passengers per year to 6.5 million and are designed to relieve pressure on the existing terminal until the new complex situated between the two runways is completed. The 12,000-square-metre Terminal 2, which services 12 airlines, delivers enhanced passenger comfort from arrival to departure. Terminal 1A, at 5000 square metres, has been dedicated to Gulf Traveller.

Abu Dhabi's new airport is designed for an initial handling capacity of 20 million passengers a year by 2010 and ultimate capacity of 50 million passengers a year.

Scadia is currently working on a four million passenger-capacity concourse that is being built for Etihad Airways. The concourse, boasting eight gates capable of handling wide-bodied aircraft, will accommodate the airline's growth until 2010, when the new midfield terminal comes on line.

The new developments will see a vast increase in the space allocated for Abu Dhabi Duty Free (ADDF) enabling the retailer to tailor its stock to the new passenger profile that is emerging at the airport. ADDF posted an 8 per cent increase in total revenue for 2005 with average spending per departing passenger increasing to US$46 from US$44 in 2004, one of the highest in the industry.

A dedicated concourse is being built for Etihad Airways at Abu Dhabi airport.

Abu Dhabi Airports Company

Abu Dhabi Airports Company (ADAC), which replaced the Department of Civil Aviation early in 2006 and became a formal commercial entity in September 2006, is now responsible for all airport operations and is focusing on core activities at the airport. The company intends to outsource non-core facilities, like ground handling, catering, air traffic control tower, IT services, facility management etc, to specialists. ADAC also plans to create an Airport Free Zone and is considering taking on a strategic partner as shareholder.

DUBAI

Dubai's strategy is also focused on investing billions of dollars in continually developing aviation infrastructure. In particular, it is planning for a large increase in passenger throughput as it equips its facilities with the capability to rival major transit hubs such as Heathrow and Atlanta. Again Emirates airline, which is based at Dubai International Airport (DIA) in the centre of Dubai, has been a major catalyst for growth at the airport.

Passenger traffic at DIA has increased by 247.8 per cent from 7.1 million in 1995 to 24.7 million in 2005. Currently, 113 airlines operate from the airport, flying to over 160 destinations. Dubai recorded an air traffic growth of 14 per cent in 2005, when 24.7 million people passed through the airport compared to 21.7 million in 2004. Cargo at Dubai airport's cargo village registered a 20

Dubai Duty Free area at Dubai International Airport

per cent growth in 2005 with a total volume of 1.3 million tonnes compared to 1.1 million tonnes in 2004. This exponential growth continued in 2006 as flights (at 116,543) in the first half of that year increased by 10.31 per cent over the same period in 2005 (105,646 flights). Passenger traffic increased by 6.24 per cent to 13.75 million during the first half of 2006. Dubai Cargo Village handled 690,775 tonnes of cargo compared to 627,704 tonnes in the first half of 2005, an increase of 10 per cent. Dubai's Department of Civil Aviation (DCA) expects to see 29 million passengers pass through the airport by the end of 2006, with cargo touching 1.4 million tonnes.

To facilitate this growth, the second phase of DIA's Dh15 billion (US$4.1 billion) development plan is well under way. This includes construction of the new Terminal 3, Concourse 2 and Concourse 3 (a dedicated facility for Emirates airline), a giant cargo terminal, and an upgrade and expansion of Terminal 2. Terminal 3 (a multi-level underground structure featuring lounges, restaurants, a hotel and 10,000 square metres of commercial space, including Dubai Duty Free outlets) and Concourse 2 are scheduled to be operational by the first quarter of 2007. When the project is completed, Dubai airport will be able to handle 70 million passengers a year.

Dubai Duty Free

Dubai Duty Free (DDF) is also constantly enlarging the scale and scope of its services as sales continue their upward trend. By mid-2006 half-year sales at DDF had reached Dh1.18 billion (US$323 million), representing a 15 per cent increase over 2005's totals and placing the operation on track for another record-breaking year. The airport retailer is currently ranked No. 3 in the world in terms of turnover and this position is reflected in the latest batch of awards presented to DDF, including the Raven Fox 'Middle East Travel Retailer of the Year' for the sixth consecutive year and the Business Traveller Middle East Award for 'Best Duty Free'.

Dubai World Central

Dubai World Central Airport (JXB) is a key component of Dubai World Central development, the massive Dh30 billion multi-phase aviation project situated at Jebel Ali 40 kilometres south of

Dubai city-centre. When completed, the new airport, with six parallel runways and a passenger handling capacity of over 120 million will be ten times the size of Dubai International Airport. This will be bigger than Atlanta, the world's busiest airport, which in 2004 handled 83.5 million. The airport will also have a cargo capacity of 12 million tonnes, more than enough to serve the emirate's transportation needs until 2050 and beyond.

Dubai Civil Aviation Authority (DCA) awarded 37 bids for the new airport in 2006. Al Naboodah Contracting has already commenced work on a runway at the airport, which is on target for completion in the last quarter of 2007, and the UK's National Air Traffic Services (NATS) is designing its airspace.

SHARJAH

Sharjah International Airport (SIA) will have the capacity to handle 8 million passengers by early 2007 on completion of a Dh227 million (US$61.8 million) expansion currently under way. The development will add new departure, arrival and transit areas, in addition to more restaurants, coffee shops and car parking. The new arrival hall was inaugurated in August 2006. As part of the expansion programme, additional warehouses will be added to the cargo division, which already has five terminals with an area of 7200 square metres each. SIA has been awarded EN ISO 14001:2004 certificate in environmental management procedures from RWTUV, a German Certification Body.

Both Sharjah and Ra's al-Khaimah are expanding their international airports.

SIA reported a 37.26 per cent jump in passenger traffic in the first half of 2006, representing 1,423,007 passengers compared to 1,036,709 in the first half of 2005. Aircraft movement increased by 10.56 per cent, up from 18,755 flights in the first half of 2005 to 20,735 flights in the first half of 2006. The airport also experienced a 16.17 per cent increase in cargo operations. As with Abu Dhabi and Dubai, a national airline, in this case the budget Air Arabia, is a key factor in the growth of SIA.

RA'S AL-KHAIMAH

Over Dh1billion (US$272 million) will be spent by 2008 on the first phase of expansion at Ra's al-Khaimah (RAK) International

Mina (Port) Zayed in Abu Dhabi City is the emirate's main general cargo port.

Airport. The master plan prepared by the French company Aeroport de Paris will include a cargo warehouse, arrival and departure halls, a hotel, and, at a later stage, a business free zone. The emirate expects a quantum leap in tourism in the coming years, and is also setting up the region's first 'space-port'. By 2020, at least five more terminals will be added to the airport. RAK Airways, which has the contract to operate and develop the international airport, came into operation at the end of 2006.

PORTS

Considering its strategic geographical position between East and West, the UAE's ports, like its airports are an essential tool for driving economic growth, particularly economic diversification.

ABU DHABI

Mina (Port) Zayed in Abu Dhabi City is the emirate's main general cargo port, whilst the terminals at Jebel Dhanna/Ruwais, Umm al-Nar, Das Island, Zirku and Mubarraz islands handle the vast bulk of the UAE's significant crude oil and gas exports. In addition the recently formed Abu Dhabi Ports Company (ADPC) is building a major new port, Khalifa Port, with adjacent industrial zone, at Al Taweelah, the first phase of which will cost in the region of Dh8 billion (US$2.18 billion). Work on the project has already begun. Feasibility studies are also being carried out by the Higher Corporation for Specialised Economic Zones (ZonesCorp), which is responsible for developing and regulating the industrial free zones in the emirate, for a port at Mussafah that will have the capacity to handle industrial cargoes to the tune of 5 to 9 million tonnes per annum. This new port is expected to commence operating in 2009.

Operations at Mina Zayed (the port currently handles over 3.8 million tonnes of cargo) will be relocated to Khalifa Port by 2011, when the first phase is complete. As Abu Dhabi continues to focus on privatisation, a subsidiary of ADPC, Abu Dhabi Terminals, will manage day-to-day port operations in Abu Dhabi, including those at Khalifa Port. Abu Dhabi Terminals will itself be managed by DP World. The latter was created in 2005 by the amalgamation of

The UAE's ports, like its airports, are an essential tool for driving economic growth, particularly economic diversification.

Dubai Ports Authority (DPA) and DPI Terminals. Abu Dhabi's ports will be integrated into DP World's global network and marketed jointly with other ports such as Dubai's Jebel Ali and Port Rashid.

DUBAI

Dubai's ports play a pivotal role in trade in the UAE.

Dubai's ports at Port Rashid in Dubai City and Jebel Ali south of the city play a pivotal role in trade in the UAE. In particular, Jebel Ali, which primarily handles bulk cargo and industrial material for Jebel Ali Free Zone, is the largest port in the country and the largest man-made port in the world. In addition, Dubai's Al Hamriyah Port, which is currently undergoing modernisation, caters to small and medium vessels involved in the Gulf's significant re-export trade.

All of Dubai's ports have experienced a steep rise in business in recent years. This is set to rise even further when the first phase of the four-phase, Dh4.6 billion (US$1.25 billion) expansion at Jebel Ali comes on-stream in the first quarter of 2007, which will result in a 20 per cent increase in trans-shipment handling and a 16 per cent rise in imports and exports. On completion in 2020, Jebel Ali will have 82 berths with 125 quayside cranes and supporting yard equipment, and will be able to handle 21.8 million containers a year.

Adjacent developments taking place at Jadaf Dubai, Dubai Dry Docks and Dubai Maritime City in 2006 will also be a tremendous boost to the emirate's maritime industry (see section on Shipping and Shipbuilding in Economic Development).

Since 1999 DP World (or Dubai Ports International (DPI) as it was formerly known) has applied the expertise it had acquired at Jebel Ali to managing ports worldwide (see panel in Economic Development). DP World now has 52 terminals spanning 30 countries and five continents. DP World's UAE operations handled 7.62 million TEUs (twenty-foot equivalent container units) in 2005, a 19 per cent increase over 2004. In 2005, DP World joined the Container Security Initiative, which saw US Customs officers stationed at its terminals.

SHARJAH

Sharjah's ports are Mina (Port) Khalid in Sharjah City and Khor Fakkan on the East Coast. Port Khalid's original depth was dredged in the early 1980s to deal with deeper draft vessels, and today the berth and quay configuration is designed to accept most types of vessels. The port handles a wide variety of tonnage, ranging from tankers, container vessels, and ro-ro ships, to a multitude of smaller vessels such as coasters, supply boats, tugs, barges and crew boats.

Location plays an important role in Port Khalid's development plans for future growth, especially as Sharjah's industrial base has expanded in recent years, encouraged in no small part by the establishment of Sharjah Airport Free Zone and Hamriyah Free Zone.

Sharjah has also spent Dh200 million on Hamriyah Port's development. With a draft of 16 metres, the port can accommodate large cargo vessels. Hamriyah primarily handles non-containerised break bulk cargo, liquid petroleum gas and petrochemical vessels, although it is also designed to handle containers.

Sharjah is the only emirate with a port on both UAE coasts. Its East Coast port, Khor Fakkan Container Terminal (KCT), the only natural deep-water port in the region, is a dedicated container port. KCT has a strategic geographical position in the context of today's huge deep-sea container trade, being close to the main east-west shipping lanes and outside the sensitive Straits of Hormuz. A modern highway connects KCT with industrial and urban centres on the UAE's Gulf coast.

Already one of the top container trans-shipment hub ports in the country, KCT is being significantly expanded at a total cost of Dh300 million (US$81.75 million). As part of the recently completed first-phase, KCT's surface area has increased by 50 per cent, its container storage capacity has risen from the current 23,000 units to 35,000, four new super post-Panamax gantry cranes have been installed and the quay length has been increased by 400 metres to 1500 metres. As a result, KCTs container handling capacity has risen to 3 million TEUs a year. The project was scheduled to be ready at the end of 2005, but faced delays due to changes in the original plan. The new 16-metre deep quay, protected by an 800 metre breakwater, is designed to give maximum protection to the new berth, while at the same time providing the easiest possible access for the latest

Quayside adjacent to Sharjah souq

Sharjah is the only emirate with a port on both UAE coasts. Its East Coast port, Khor Fakkan Container Terminal (KCT), the only natural deep-water port in the region, is a dedicated container port.

generation of 8000 plus TEU capacity ships. This is significant since the rising trade between Asia and Europe is helping the port of Khor Fakkan position itself as a regional trans-shipment hub able to handle giant container ships on this strategic sea route.

AJMAN

Ajman Port, which also services Ajman Free Zone situated in the port, has eight berths designed to handle both container and general cargo. The port had a depth of 5 metres when it was first built, but this has been dredged to 8 metres. Plans are under way to deepen the port to 10.5 metres, enabling visits by 40,000–50,000 dwt (dead weight tonnage) ships up to 175 metres long. Incoming cargo is stored in large purpose-built warehouses covering an area of 43,200 square metres. There are also special facilities to handle cargoes of chemicals, waste paper and fodder.

The Port Authority has also set up two dry docks to provide maintenance and repair services. One berth is allocated for wooden boats and launches. Maintenance services are provided by firms such as Arab Heavy Industries Company, experts in the field of structural steel fabrication, tank and shipbuilding and marine services.

RA'S AL-KHAIMAH

Approval was given in 2006 for Ra's al-Khaimah's fourth port at Al Jeer, north of the emirate at a total cost of Dh30 million (US$8.17). The new port will have a 270-metre quay and will be dredged to 6 metres.

Ra's al-Khaimah's Port Saqr is located in the Khor Khuwair industrial arca 25 kilometres north of Ra's al-Khaimah City. Cement, marble and gravel from the nearby quarries and factories are shipped from the port, which is responsible for almost 90 per cent of the UAE's cement exports.

Kuwaiti firm KGL was awarded a Dh165.15 million (US$45 million) contract to build, operate and manage the container terminal at Port Saqr. The contract, which expires in 2025, involves investment of Dh55.05 million (US$15 million) to build berths 8 and 9, Dh14.68 million (US$4 million) to reconstruct berths 1, 2 and 3, and Dh11.01 million (US$3 million) to build additional facilities for the port. Another Dh84.41 million (US$23 million) will be spent on equipment. Future plans involve creating an additional 500,000 TEU bulk handling capacity in the ports, the

10-million-tonne container handling capacity will be raised to about 30 million tonnes.

Ra's al-Khaimah Customs and Ports Department has already spent Dh30 million (US$8.17 million) to build a new 303-metre quay at Ra's al-Khaimah Port. The second phase will see construction of a 400-metre berth at a cost of Dh28 million (US$7.62 million). Work has also begun on 16 warehouses, including two cold storage facilities and an accommodation block for port employees. A Dh50 million contract has been awarded to UAE-based company Haif to build the warehouses and staff units.

Approval was given in 2006 for construction of Ra's al Khaimah's fourth port at Al Jeer, north of the emirate at a total cost of Dh30 million (US$8.17). The new port will have a 270-metre quay and will be dredged to 6 metres. It should be completed by the middle of 2007 and will include a hotel, administrative buildings and warehouses, along with berths to accommodate 120 vessels.

FUJAIRAH

Fujairah Port commissioned an additional 150,000 cubic metres of onshore bunker storage facilities early in 2005, ensuring that it now ranks as the second largest bunkering centre in the world, supplying 12 million tonnes of fuel oil a year, worth US$2.5 billion (Dh9.17 billion). Singapore remains the world's largest bunkering centre with a capacity of 19 million tonnes of fuel oil a year and Rotterdam is in third position with 10 million tonnes.

The Port of Fujairah

www.uaeinteract.com/ship_ports

Dubai Ports World (DPW) took charge of the Port of Fujairah's container terminal in 2005. Under a 30-year concession, DPW will spend more than Dh568 million (US$155 million) to develop and operate the terminal.

Fujairah's deep-water facility has more than 1.3 kilometres of quay. Upgrades to the Fujairah terminal will include new super-post Panamax ship-to-shore gantry cranes and yard-handling equipment that will lift annual capacity to an eventual 1.7 million TEUs. While DPW will operate the container terminal, all non-containerised cargo, such as general cargo, oil, aggregate and project cargo, will continue to be handled by the Port of Fujairah. The agreement between the Fujairah Port Authority and DPW also includes an option to mutually extend the concession by a further 20 years, potentially taking the contract through to 2055.

INTERNET LINKS

Air traffic agreements:	www.uaeinteract.com/airtraffic
Airports:	www.uaeinteract.com/airports
Aviation agreements:	www.uaeinteract.com/aviationagr
Aviation and airlines:	www.uaeinteract.com/air
Dubai Aerospace Enterprise:	www.uaeinteract.com/dae
Electricity and water:	www.uaeinteract.com/elec_h2o
Free Zones:	www.uaeinteract.com/freezones
Infrastructural development:	www.uaeinteract.com/infrastructure
Internet:	www.uaeinteract.com/internet
Parks:	www.uaeinteract.com/parks
Ports and shipping:	www.uaeinteract.com/ship_ports
Postal service:	www.uaeinteract.com/post
Roads, tunnels and bridges:	www.uaeinteract.com/roads
Shipbuilding:	www.uaeinteract.com/shipbuilding
Shopping:	www.uaeinteract.com/uaeshopping
Stamps:	www.uaeinteract.com/stamps
Telecommunications:	www.uaeinteract.com/telecomms
The Palms:	www.uaeinteract.com/palms
Thuraya and satellite communications:	www.uaeinteract.com/satcomms
Transportation:	www.uaeinteract.com/transport
Urban development:	www.uaeinteract.com/urban

Investment in its people as 'the wealth of the nation' has been a primary focus of the UAE Government since the inception of the state.

Ninety-five per cent of all females and 80 per cent of all males who complete secondary school apply for admission to a higher level institution in the UAE or study abroad.

SOCIAL DEVELOPMENT

INVESTMENT IN ITS PEOPLE as the 'wealth of the nation' has been a primary focus of the UAE Government since the inception of the state. The population is now reaping the benefits of a high standard of education and a sophisticated health service. Efforts are being made to develop human resources, effect the empowerment of women, and provide social welfare to the more vulnerable in society. Nevertheless, the impact of social change has been significant, in particular the demographic imbalances brought about by urbanisation and immigration. Despite this, the UAE continues to be a tolerant, open, caring society that cherishes its traditional roots.

As a result of its remarkable progress in social development, the UAE was ranked forty-first in the Human Development Index (HDI) compiled by the UN Human Development Report for 2005, compared to its forty-ninth position in 2004. This progress was reflected in many aspects of development in the country, including rising income per capita, an increase in government expenditure on education and health services, a higher percentage of women participating in the work force, a low rate of postpartum and infant mortality, and the elimination of dangerous diseases.

The UAE moved up eight positions in the UN Human Development Index.

POPULATION

The UAE population was estimated to be 4.32 million at the end of 2004. However, more precise figures were gathered by 'Tedad 2005', the fifth census in the UAE's history and a major initiative on the part of the Government to accumulate accurate information on population structure in order to better target its resources. Fieldwork, initially involving 1000 enumerators counting and marking buildings and gathering all related data, began on 3 September 2005, culminating in a head-count on 6 December. Census-taking was based on a UN-recognised method known as *de jure* population, i.e. counting people according to their permanent residence in the UAE, regardless of where they were staying during the census period.

www.uaeinteract.com/population

Preliminary results of the census released in mid-2006 revealed that the total UAE population counted on census night was 3,769,080.

Preliminary results of the census released in mid-2006 revealed that the total UAE population counted on census night was 3,769,080. This figure includes nationals and non-nationals, but does not take into account a group of non-nationals numbering 335,615 who have residence visas but were not in the UAE on the night, including members of non-national households that live in neighbouring countries, people with invalid residency visas, non-nationals working on national vessels in regional and international waters who don't have families residing in UAE, and all members of households that refused to cooperate. When both figures are added together, the actual total is 4,104,695. This is an increase of 74.8 per cent compared to the last census conducted in 1995 when the population was 2,411,041.

Obviously, since the detailed demographic structure of excluded groups is not available, the population census breakdown covers only those counted (3,769,080) during the reference period of the census. On that basis, 2,547,043 or 67.6 per cent of the population are male and 1,222,037 or 32.4 per cent are female. Nationals at 824,921 constitute 21.9 per cent of the total counted population, with national males at 418,057, forming 50.7 per cent, and national females at 406,864, constituting 49.3 per cent of the total nationals. The total number of non-nationals counted in the census is 2,944,159, which is 78.1 per cent of the total counted population and 79.9 per cent (3,279,774) of the total UAE population. Non-national males at 2,128,986 constitute 72 per cent and the total number of non-national females is 815,173, or 27.7 per cent.

Based on the census data, 38.1 per cent of nationals are less than 14 years old, 51.1 per cent are less than 20 years old, and 48.8 per cent of non-nationals belong to the age group 25 to 40 years. Overall 52.9 per cent of the total population are between 20 and 39 years old.

The census also confirmed that the illiteracy rate in the country is 9 per cent, (approximately the same for nationals and non-nationals), 31.5 per cent of nationals have high school certificates only and 11 per cent have university degrees (Bachelor and above), whereas 18.4 per cent of non-nationals are university graduates.

Book fairs are held in each of the emirates and attract large numbers of visitors. The Abu Dhabi Book Fair is one of the largest regional book fairs.

According to the census, there are 336,815 buildings in the country and 34.9 per cent (117,469) of them are in the Emirate of Abu Dhabi. The total number of housing units in the country is 863,860, 60.8 per cent of which are in the emirates of Abu Dhabi and Dubai. The total number of establishments in the country is 192,247, 38.1 per cent (73,294) of which are in the Emirate of Dubai.

ID CARDS

Another fundamental information-gathering drive initiated by the Government was that entrusted to Emirates Identity Authority (EIA), a Federal Government organisation. EIA is developing and implementing a modern and integrated population register and identity management system for both citizens and residents of the UAE. The hope is that the Population Register and ID Card Project (PRNIDC) will help to establish an accurate database on the economic, demographic and social characteristics of the country. Amongst other things, this will facilitate the identification of common needs in fields such as education, health and housing and will positively impact on the future of the country with faster and more efficient services being offered to the public. Enabling legislation governing this project is contained in Federal Law No. 9 of 2006 comprising 32 articles, including safeguards for individual security and privacy.

The third phase of the Population Register and Identity Card Project will begin in 2007 and include the whole UAE population, both nationals and expatriates.

ID cards were issued in mid-2006 to 60,000 employees from 16 chosen ministries and federal institutions who had been registered in the first phase of the project. Registration of employees and their families from 16 ministries and governmental institutions with less than 500 employees was completed in the second half of 2006. Registration at 14 PRNIDC centres will be open to all citizens and expatriates from early 2007 and the registration process, during which an individual's photograph, fingerprint and e-signature are entered into the system, is expected to be completed in three years. The new card is a multipurpose smart card, replacing the labour card, health card and driving licence. Plans are also being formulated to bundle e-dirham and e-gate facilities.

LABOUR AND SOCIAL AFFAIRS

At present the majority of the national workforce (88 per cent) is working in a public sector that has reached saturation point and is, therefore, incapable of absorbing the 16,187 nationals entering the job market in 2006. This figure will rise to 19,610 in 2010 and 40,000 by 2020. At present, UAE nationals account for a very small percentage of the total workforce in the private sector, while private sector employment accounts for 52.1 per cent of the jobs in the UAE. Therefore, the creation of job opportunities for national graduates in the private sector is a situation that the Federal Government is anxious to address. One strategy put in place was the establishment in 2001 of the National Human Resource Development and Employment Authority (Tanmia), an independent body whose main objectives are to create job opportunities for UAE nationals, especially in the private sector, reduce the unemployment ratio, enhance the skills and productivity of the national workforce through relevant training, undertake policy-oriented research on a multiplicity of labour-market issues and make recommendations to the Government.

The UAE has drafted a set of laws and regulations ensuring that guest workers are temporary and not permanent immigrants. The laws protect the rights of foreign workers in accordance with national laws and international treaties on labour and human rights.

Tanmia registered 33,503 UAE nationals as applicants for public and private sector jobs between the end of 2001 and December 2005. Abu Dhabi had the highest number of national jobseekers at 11,727, while Dubai accounted for 7714 applicants. Tanmia placed 2208 nationals in various organisations during this period. Of the successful jobseekers, 33 per cent were employed in the trading sector, 25 per cent in the public sector and 17 per cent in banking. Tanmia also undertook an intensive re-training programme for national jobseekers and released a comprehensive 92-page guide for UAE nationals that will assist them in finding suitable jobs and ensure high levels of performance in the workplace.

A detailed review of human resources in the UAE in 2004 is outlined in *UAE Human Resources Report 2005* compiled by Tanmia. The report highlights the fact that three important factors have shaped the nation's workforce: a demand for skills in the face of fast economic growth; a working age population that is increasingly made up of young people (as confirmed by

www.uaeinteract.com/employment

the census results) and a growing reliance on foreign labour as a source of skilled and unskilled workers. Generally, UAE nationals' share of the total labour force increased marginally from 9.1 per cent in 1995 to 9.3 in 2004. However, the contribution of national women to economic activity increased significantly from 5.4 per cent in 1995 to 16.1 per cent in 2004.

Previous reports by Tanmia have highlighted the fact that the UAE is, perhaps, one of the very few countries in the world where foreigners dominate the private sector, both as employers and employees, and in almost all countries that allow immigration the norm is that foreigners are only allowed to take up jobs when suitably qualified nationals are not available. This provision is also part of the UAE labour law. However, in a country where foreign workers are the rule, not the exception, implementing the law is not easy. Tanmia recommended strong Government intervention simply because there is unequal competition in the job market between national workers and a trained and experienced expatriate workforce. However, although urging a more aggressive approach towards the private sector, it clearly recognises that expatriate workers will continue to play a 'vital role' in the country's economy. Nevertheless, Tanmia feels that the growth of the private sector and employment of non-nationals must be regulated and that choosing the 'carrot policy' as opposed to the 'stick' will simply not work.

The UAE is, perhaps, one of the very few countries in the world where foreigners dominate the private sector, both as employers and employees.

EMIRATISATION IN THE BANKING SECTOR

No discussion of the UAE's human resources would be complete without an examination of the quota system. UAE HR 2005 concludes with an examination of the application of employment quotas in the UAE banking sector. From 1999 to 2004 there was an increase of approximately 282 per cent in the number of Emiratis working in banks. This is nearly 3500 new workers and a total workforce representation, according to Tanmia, of 26.4 per cent in this sector at the end of 2004. These developments were the result of positive changes in working conditions and the introduction of career development, and the report invites other sectors, such as insurance and trade, to address these issues in order to attract more nationals.

Banks in the UAE are continuing to make progress towards emiratisation according to data released by the Emirates Institute of Banking and Financial Services, Sharjah. Overall in 2005 emiratisation in this sector increased by 2.21 per cent: only 22 of 47 local and foreign banks maintained the stipulated annual percentage growth of 4 per cent. Whilst 2977 UAE nationals were recruited in 2005 and 1302 nationals resigned, the total number of UAE nationals engaged in banking increased to 6975, constituting 29.83 per cent of the total in 2005, up from 27.62 per cent in 2004.

Although there has been a 47 per cent increase in the number of bank branches, from 353 in 1997 to 520 in 2005, there has not been any significant progress in the emiratisation of branch managers. So far, only nine banks have achieved the target of appointing UAE nationals as branch managers at all their branches. Nevertheless, the percentage of UAE nationals holding such positions has risen from 53.9 per cent in 2004 to 57.4 per cent in 2005.

From 1999 to 2004 there was an increase of about 282 per cent in the number of Emiratis working in banks. This was the result of positive changes in working conditions and the introduction of career development.

THE INSURANCE SECTOR

Insurance has been identified as a growing sector with insufficient national representation in its workforce. In 2006 an agreement was signed between the Higher Insurance Committee of the UAE and the Higher Colleges of Technology (HCT) to fund the enrolment of UAE nationals in an insurance diploma programme at HCT. The Committee will facilitate placement of students within relevant organisations as a co-requisite to study in the programme and develop employment and career advancement opportunities for UAE graduates of the programme.

The agreement provides for cooperation with industry professional societies, such as the Chartered Insurance Institute, an international professional body that promotes education and training of insurance professionals.

HUMAN RESOURCES MANAGERS

Having successfully replaced around 1300 of 3000 foreign government personnel officers with UAE nationals, the Government is now targeting human resources in the private sector. To this end, the private sector (excluding businesses in free zones) has

@ www.uaeinteract.com/emiritisation

been given a grace period of 18 months from mid-2006 to replace foreign human resources managers with UAE nationals. In addition, no more work permits for non-national secretaries will be issued with immediate effect.

The ministerial resolutions, which were issued by the Ministry of Labour in June 2006, instructed the firms to coordinate with Tanmia in the training of UAE nationals to enable them carry out the required duties. Training programmes are also being conducted in cooperation with local training providers in Dubai and Sharjah, including Emirates National Development Programme (ENDP) in Dubai and the Department for Human Resources Development in Sharjah. Current holders of secretarial positions who have valid labour cards under service contracts approved by the Ministry may continue in their job until the end of their contract, or expiration of their labour card. Alternatively, they may move to another position in the company. The resolution also specifies minimum salary levels for UAE applicants, contravention of which will negate the mandatory quota requirement.

The private sector (excluding businesses in free zones) has been given a grace period of 18 months from mid-2006 to replace foreign human resources managers with UAE nationals.

It is hoped that emiratisation of human resources managers and secretarial posts will create thousands of jobs for UAE nationals. It is also envisaged that the decision will pave the way for further emiratisation in the private sector, since companies that have had nationals working in their human resources departments have been able to meet emiratisation targets more effectively.

CAREERS FAIR 2006

Careers fairs also assist in the process of job creation for nationals. It was estimated that exhibitors at Careers UAE, a successful recruitment, training and education exhibition which took place in April 2006, will place around 5000 UAE nationals in jobs in the near future. Over half of the participating exhibitors come from the private sector, an indication of the increasing priority being accorded to emiratisation as a growth strategy across all sectors.

Dubai government departments participated in the fair through a common platform provided by Dubai eGovernment. This made it easier for job-seekers to search for vacancies in various government departments from a centralised location, thereby facilitating the government's efforts to achieve targets for emiratisation. Prospects in the aviation industry are particularly promising: the Dubai Civil Aviation Department alone wants to fill more than 2000 vacancies by 2007 and Gamco has a strategic plan in place to raise the number of nationals in non-technical departments to 40 per cent.

Attendees at a Careers Fair in Abu Dhabi

LABOUR STANDARDS

Reports issued by the International Labour Organisation (ILO) during 2006 praised the positive steps made by the UAE in implementing the international labour conventions to which it has acceded, particularly international labour standards relating to the minimum age convention and the success achieved by the UAE in resolving the use of underage camel jockeys.

The UAE has not acceded to ILO conventions governing the rights of workers to freedom of association and collective bargaining and to date does not have any legislation regulating the establishment of trade unions. However, in 2006 a proposed amendment to the Labour Law authorising the Labour Ministry to issue the necessary regulations facilitating the establishment of trade unions was submitted to a ministerial advisory council. The memorandum suggested that membership of trade unions should be open to UAE nationals and expatriates, 'but there should be full membership for citizens and associate membership for expatriates'.

The Labour Ministry has also used the 'carrot and stick' approach here, including preferential status, immediate processing of visas and cancelling of bank guarantees, to remedy difficulties over the prompt payment of workers salaries, working and living conditions, and the regulation of labour agencies that recruit construction and other temporary workers, especially those that illegally charge for visa applications, workers thereby incurring crippling loans.

Use of innovative technology, including high-resolution satellite imagery to monitor building sites for health and safety violations and conditions at labour accommodation camps, will help fill a big gap in the needs of an under-staffed inspection department.

www.uaeinteract.com/emiritisation

Moves are also in place to construct specialised 'workers cities' for temporary workers. The first phase of the Worker's Residential Complex was opened at Industrial City of Abu Dhabi (ICAD) in April 2006. Five more residential complexes are planned, three of which are to be in ICAD while two others will be in Al Ain. These residential complexes will be the model for future dwellings for workers in the UAE, part of a wider and long-term plan to improve the living conditions of workers.

PENSIONS

Those entitled to monthly social benefits include widowed and divorced national women, the disabled and the handicapped, the aged, orphans, single women, married students, relatives of jailed dependants, estranged wives and insolvents.

The Abu Dhabi Retirement Pensions and Benefits Fund has launched a new website to provide a wide range of useful information and services to its members comprising insured individuals, pensioners and beneficiaries in the government, semi-government and the private sectors, throughout Abu Dhabi.

SOCIAL WELFARE

Despite the UAE's economic success there are, inevitably, individuals who are not in a position to benefit directly from the country's good fortune. Therefore, an extensive social welfare network exists to assist these vulnerable members of society. This takes the form of social security benefits administered by the Ministry of Labour and Social Affairs, in addition to the practical help offered by the network of Ministry-supported social centres run by the General Women's Union (see section on Women), and the government-supported social welfare and rehabilitation centres providing assistance to the disabled. UAE citizens are also eligible for free or subsidised housing.

Those entitled to monthly social benefits include widowed national and divorced women, the disabled and the handicapped, the aged, orphans, single women, married students, relatives of jailed dependants, estranged wives and insolvents. Also eligible for financial assistance are widowed and divorced national women previously married to foreigners and the expatriate husbands of UAE women. While the number of those receiving assistance has dropped between 1980 and 2005, the cost to the Government has risen, reflecting a steep rise in the cost of living.

Effective from 1 October 2005, President HH Sheikh Khalifa ordered a 75 per cent increase in the value of social support assistance given to UAE nationals, following a study of GCC countries presented by the Ministry of Labour and Social Affairs' Studies and Research Unit that reported a 25 per cent increase based on increases in the prices of basic foodstuff since 2001, the year when the country adopted the last increase in social aid. The generous 75 per cent increase granted by the President raised annual social welfare allocations to Dh1.135 billion from Dh658 million. Social welfare beneficiaries numbered 67,102 in 2005.

In June 2006, 3217 plots of land for housing were given to citizens of Abu Dhabi and Al Ain.

HOUSING

Access to modern comfortable housing is considered to be the right of every citizen. The rapid rise in population coupled with the demands of modern living has necessitated Government intervention at federal and emirate level to ensure that the housing needs of nationals are met throughout the Federation. Programmes coordinated by municipalities in each emirate include the free distribution of houses and land to UAE nationals. Between 2000 and 2005, 6050 houses were distributed by the Zayed Housing Programme (ZHP). In 2005, ZHP approved 50 per cent of the applications submitted for housing and loan assistance by the various housing committees from all over the country. A total of 1280 UAE nationals received Dh655 million, including non-refundable housing grants and loans. ZHP's budget for 2006 was Dh65.6 million (US$17.87 million).

Access to modern comfortable housing is considered to be the right of every citizen.

Early in 2006 Sheikh Khalifa, in his capacity as Ruler of Abu Dhabi, ordered the distribution of a new batch of houses and sites to UAE nationals. This distribution included 3217 plots of land, 2573 in Abu Dhabi and 644 in Al Ain, in addition to 359 low-cost houses, 141 in Abu Dhabi, 193 in Al Ain and 25 in the Western Region of Abu Dhabi Emirate. ZHP is also building 30 houses in the Khatt area of Ra's al-Khaimah and 50 in the Raefa, Rashidiya and Bayata areas of Umm al-Qaiwain.

Dubai Municipality is undertaking eight government housing projects for low-income UAE nationals comprising a total of 824 houses in various parts of the emirate. The Municipality is also

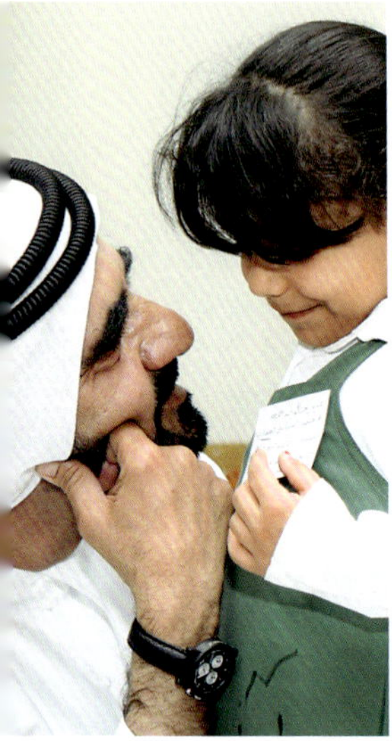

The UAE Government is carefully monitoring progress and performance of its social development programme.

engaged in maintenance work on existing government housing projects and a number of special teams have been set up to conduct a survey of the Al Rashidiya neighbourhood in Dubai, the intention being to provide suitable new houses to the residents on vacant plots of land. Maintenance and preservation work on existing houses will also be carried out.

SOCIAL WELFARE ASSOCIATIONS

Volunteer work represents the embodiment of Islamic and social values in UAE society and the importance of volunteerism in enhancing social solidarity and contributing to the process of social development is widely recognised. To that end, the Government has encouraged and promoted volunteer work by supporting volunteer and humanitarian organisations and has implemented legislation to regulate their services to the public. For their part, volunteer and charitable organisations in the UAE, among which the UAE Red Crescent is most prominent, have contributed generously to social welfare services and development programmes covering such areas as medical aid, student sponsorship, disability, special care, health care, the welfare of prisoners and lump-sum aid programmes.

The UAE Red Crescent (RCS) is the largest charitable organisation in the country and a major international relief agency (see Foreign Aid in the section on Government for an account of international aid provided by the RCS). Approximately Dh115 million (US$31.34 million) was spent by RCS on local assistance programmes in a five-year period up to 2003, involving the provision of services to needy families and the establishment of orphanages, clinics, special schools and homes for the elderly, whilst Dh16.4 million (US$4.47 million) was spent on projects during the first quarter of 2006, benefiting approximately 15,000 needy families.

The UAE Red Crescent (RCS) is the largest charitable organisation in the country and a major international relief agency

The RCS works closely with the Zakat Fund, distributing money donated by Muslims fulfilling their religious duties. The RCS and the Fund has distributed Dh23.8 million to 24,680 families over three years.

The Sheikh Zayed bin Sultan Al Nahyan Charitable and Humanitarian Foundation finances projects to benefit large communities both within the UAE and overseas. It does not distribute financial resources to individuals or groups. The Abu Dhabi-based Zayed Higher Foundation for Humanitarian Welfare of Special Needs People and Minors in Abu Dhabi was formed in 2004. Bodies under its auspices include the Authority for Social Welfare and Minors' Affairs, Zayed House for Comprehensive Welfare, Abu Dhabi Elderly Welfare Centre, Centre for Rehabilitation of Special Needs People, and Al Ain Centre and Club for Handicapped.

Children painting to raise money for Lebanon.

Eighty per cent of the Mohammed bin Rashid Al Maktoum Charitable and Humanitarian Foundation's budget is normally allocated to projects within the UAE. The Foundation's domestic programmes concentrate on education, medical treatment, monthly or one-time assistance, food coupons, training courses and housing.

The Bait Al Khair Charity Society, established in 1989, was recently awarded ISO 9001:2000 certification, the second charitable and humanitarian society to receive this award in the Middle East, the first being the Zayed Charitable Foundation. The Society provides assistance to poor students and emergency aid to those who have been hit by catastrophes. It also works with other charity organisations to ensure that the needy get the best of help.

Other organisations include the women's associations in each emirate, charity associations in Sharjah and Fujairah and Dubai, Ajman Care Society, Sharjah City for Humanitarian Services, the Handicapped Guardians Association and Taryam Omran Establishment for Cultural and Humanitarian Services.

RIGHTS OF THE DISABLED

Believing that handicapped persons possess skills and capabilities that could be utilised in economic and social development, the Government has established care centres for persons with special needs. It has also expanded and enhanced vocational training programmes for the handicapped so that they can acquire professional skills, build their self-confidence and facilitate their integration into society. There are currently 32 centres for 3229 children with a variety of special needs. Accurate statistics for

www.uaeinteract.com/welfare

people with special needs or their disabilities will not be available until the full results of the 2005 UAE census are released. Media reports, however, put the figure at around 5500.

Provisions contained within the law include guaranteeing a job quota in the public and private sectors, increasing accessibility to public buildings and residences and integrating people with special needs into public and private schools.

The draft of a ten-page law enshrining the rights of the disabled was referred to Cabinet for approval in June 2006, years after it was initially drafted. One of the major reasons for the delay was the impact the law will have on a wide range of legislation, organisations and services. The law primarily governs UAE nationals, although it sets out general principles on the rights of all persons with special needs. Provisions contained within the law include guaranteeing a job quota in the public and private sectors, increasing accessibility to public buildings and residences and integrating people with special needs into public and private schools. The law also provides for retirement considerations, allowing people with special needs to retire with full benefits earlier than usual. Penalties for non-compliance have also been included in the legislation, which was issued by Sheikh Khalifa..

The Zayed Foundation, which has established a number of rehabilitation centres for people with special needs, has also launched a national campaign to provide employment for the disabled. Other programmes, like Tamkeen, based at Knowledge Village, tries to raise the professional skills of blind and partially sighted people in the UAE and has taken the lead in designing and delivering effective English courses for the visually impaired in collaboration with the British Council. In addition, organisations such as the DTCM has a Special Needs Tourism Task Force that works round the year to understand the sensitivities related to special needs tourism and constantly works towards achieving those goals.

YOUTH

Recognising that the youth of today are the future of the country, the UAE has implemented child-centred programmes, enacted laws and acceded to regional and international conventions protecting children's rights, including the UN Convention on the Rights of the Child.

Some of the most significant child-centred measures undertaken by the Government include the establishment of specialised health care and medical centres for mothers and children, and the introduction of compulsory education for both sexes at primary level and free education for all stages from kindergarten to university (See Health and Education). New laws were also enacted to ensure the safety and protection of children within the family or in national institutions that are concerned with providing care to orphans and abandoned children and to protect children from all forms of exploitation, the latest of which is the law that specifies a minimum age of 18 years for jockeys in camel races. Establishment of the Supreme Council for Mother and Child also advances standards of care and attention given to mothers and children, especially in areas targeting their educational, cultural, health and social well being. In addition, the establishment of care centres for handicapped children and children with special needs provides them with the medical, psychological, social and educational services they require. The Government has also established special centres for the treatment and rehabilitation of juveniles and troubled youth under the supervision of specialised psychologists and social workers and set up training programmes to prepare them for their return to society.

In addition, the Government has placed particular emphasis on the promotion of youth activities, through social, scientific, sporting and cultural clubs. Scouts' and Guides' packs have been established across the country and they organise cultural, religious, social, scientific and educational programmes for their members.

But the Government's child-centred focus is not confined to domestic concerns: convinced that international cooperation is instrumental to the achievement of development, the UAE is keen to participate in international efforts aimed at realising this objective. To this end, the UAE has made significant contributions in cash and in kind to the UN agencies concerned with children, and extended direct assistance to developing countries and countries affected by natural disasters and armed conflicts, where children suffer from poverty, illiteracy, violence, displacement,

650,000 pupils were studying at 1256 public and private schools during the 2006/07 academic year: 280,000 attended 756 public schools and there were 370,000 students at 500 private schools.

sexual exploitation, trafficking and recruitment in wars, in order to assist these countries in improving their social and economic conditions and creating a world fit for children.

EDUCATION

Educational opportunities in the UAE have blossomed since the establishment of the Federation when only a tiny minority of the urban population had access to formal education. Today, the UAE offers a comprehensive education to all male and female students from kindergarten to university, with education for the country's citizens being provided free at all levels. There is also an extensive private education sector, while several thousand students, of both sexes, pursue courses of higher education abroad at Government expense.

Now that the infrastructure is in place, the educational focus is on devising and implementing a strategy that will ensure the youth of the country are ready to meet the challenges of the twenty-first century workplace.

A major practical shift in timetabling took place in 2006 following the Federal Government's announcement that from 1 September 2006 the weekend schedule would be changed to make Friday and Saturday the official weekend for all public sector establishments as well as government schools and universities.

PRIMARY AND SECONDARY EDUCATION

Education at primary and secondary level is universal and compulsory up to ninth grade. This takes place in a four-tier process over 14 years: 4 to 5 year-olds attend kindergarten, 6 to 11 year-olds attend primary schools, the preparatory stage caters for children aged between 12 to 14 years, and 15 to 17 year-olds attend secondary schools. The emiratisation of teaching staff in government schools is scheduled to reach 90 per cent by 2020, in order to ensure that the Islamic principles and traditions of the UAE are maintained.

Over 40 per cent of pupils attend private schools. Some of these offer foreign language education geared towards expatriate communities, usually preserving the culture and following the curriculum of the students' countries of origin.

A Cabinet decision issued in 2001 excluding expatriate students from government schools, was rescinded in mid-2006. Commencing in the academic year 2006/07, admission for expatriate students will be based on merit and fees will be levied.

Abu Dhabi Education Council (ADEC), an independent Abu Dhabi-based corporate body which was established by Sheikh Khalifa in 2005, has been entrusted with the task of developing education and educational institutions in the emirate. The council will work closely with the Ministry of Education in formulating the emirate's education plan within the framework of the UAE's general education policy.

ADEC has already announced a new initiative to improve the quality of public education. The project entitled 'Public-Private Partnership for Public School Management' enables leading local and regional private education providers to manage selected public schools in the Emirate of Abu Dhabi in conjunction with ADEC. Launched as a three-year pilot programme commencing in September 2006, selected Abu Dhabi schools, including kindergarten and primary schools for boys and girls in the three educational zones of Abu Dhabi, Al Ain and the Western Region, will be involved in the project. It is hoped that participating schools and their students will enjoy a richer educational environment, including better school facilities, efficient and less bureaucratic school administration systems, modern teaching and assessment methods, up-to-date curricula, more intensive use of information technology and additional extra-curricular activities. Principals and teachers, including national staff, will experience improved working conditions and professional development opportunities.

ADEC issued a decree in 2006 abolishing fees at model schools in Abu Dhabi. ADEC will be responsible for all costs at the model schools, which will be directly involved in the development and evaluation of the educational process. ADEC and the Model Schools Committee are setting new standards for admission of students.

ADEC has also entered into an agreement in which Zayed University will assist in developing the English language skills of

The 'Public-Private Partnership for Public School Management' enables leading local and regional private education providers to manage selected public schools in the Emirate of Abu Dhabi in conjunction with ADEC.

One of the goals is to provide a computer for every ten children in kindergarten, every five pupils in primary schools, every two students in preparatory schools and one computer per student in universities.

elementary level students at four model schools. Thirty faculty members from ZU will work with the first and fourth grade students at these schools, observing and evaluating English language teaching methods, and designing modern academic programmes. The initiative will be extended to all schools at a later stage.

IT EDUCATION

The Ministry of Education is constantly honing its educational strategy to ensure that the programmes developed in its schools comply with international standards, with particular focus on introducing the latest IT resources at all levels. For example, one of the goals is to provide a computer for every ten children in kindergarten, every five pupils in primary schools, every two students in preparatory schools and one computer per student in universities.

That IT education in the formative years has become a major priority for the UAE is underlined by the success of the Sheikh Mohammed bin Rashid IT Education Project (ITEP), which was launched in 2000. As well as installing computer labs in all participating schools, and creating a comprehensive cutting-edge curriculum, ITEP also provides an invaluable online educational resource at www.itep.ae. ITEP now provides courses in 40 high schools in the UAE (20 in Dubai, 20 in Abu Dhabi) and over 13,000 students pass through the programme every year. ITEP's trainee pupils achieved 97 per cent success rate in courses in the 2005/06 academic year.

HIGHER EDUCATION

The UAE has established an excellent and diversified system of higher education in a very short period of time. Nationals can attend government institutions free of charge, and a wide range of private institutions, many with international accreditation, supplement the public sector. The country now has one of the highest application participation rates in the world. Ninety-five per cent of all females and 80 per cent of all males who are enrolled in the final year of secondary school apply for admission to a higher education institution or to study abroad.

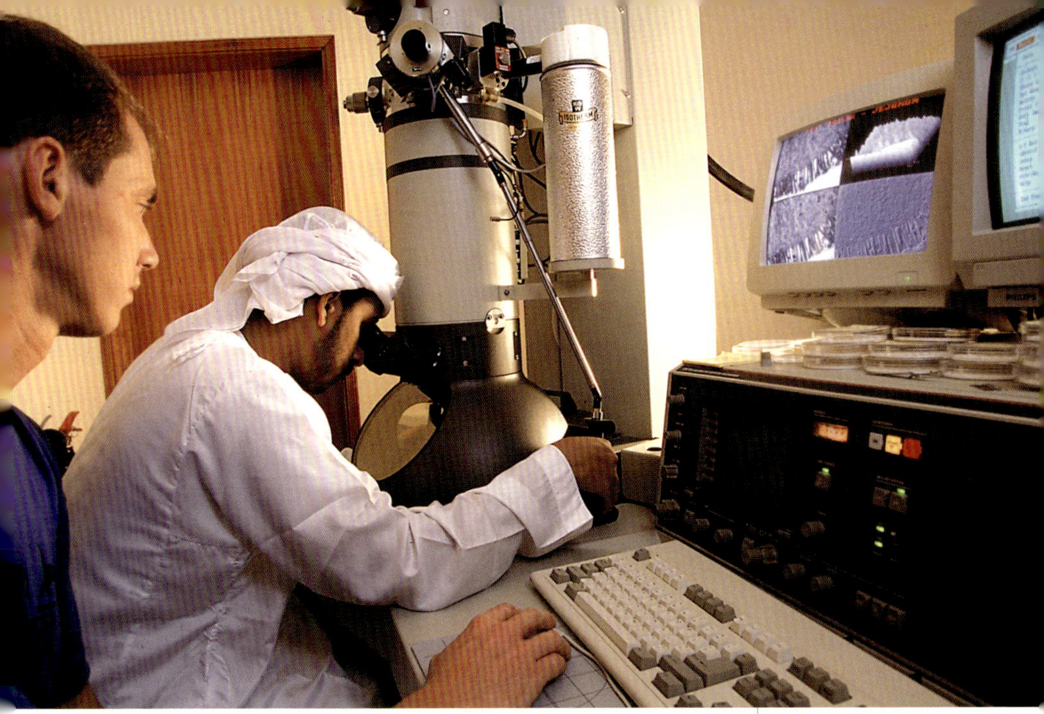

UAEU

The Al Ain-based United Arab Emirates University (UAEU), which opened in the academic year 1977/78, continues to be the country's flagship national institution of higher education and is committed to its role as the leading teaching and research institution in the UAE. UAEU offers over 70 undergraduate bachelor degrees and a number of graduate programmes in a wide range of disciplines. International accreditation has been awarded to the professional academic programmes and the non-professional programmes undergo periodic external evaluation by international experts to ensure that they meet international standards. Collaboration with international institutions also opens up new opportunities for UAEU's students.

UAEU is focusing on research and graduate studies and is moving from an open enrolment to a more restricted policy. The number of students enrolled at UAEU has increased from 502 in 1977/78 to 14,741 in the first semester of the academic year 2006/07. Enrolled male students represent 21 per cent of the total, while female students constitute 79 per cent. The total number of faculty members in the University was 700. This growth has necessitated the building of a new campus at Al Maqam, Al Ain that will provide 280,000 square metres of additional educational

and residential facilities. In line with the UAE's focus on constructive public-private partnerships in education, UAEU and Mubadala Development Company (see Economic Development) executed a 30-year concession agreement in 2004 that will enable the development of the new facilities on a BOOT basis (Build Own Operate and Transfer).

Zayed University

Zayed University (ZU) was established in 1998 by the Federal Government to educate UAE national women. Both ZU campuses in Abu Dhabi and Dubai are governed by a single administration and offer similar programmes. ZU's Dubai campus relocated to the Academic City complex in the Al Ruwayyah area in 2006. This Dh370 million facility encompasses a total area of 711,000 square metres comprising six colleges, departments and laboratories.

ZU is organised academically into five colleges: Arts and Sciences, Business Sciences, Communication and Media Sciences, Education, and Information Systems. The primary language of instruction is English, but the University expects its graduates to be fully bilingual in English and Arabic, proficient in the use of information technology, and strong in quantitative and research skills. ZU is currently engaged in cooperative relationships with a number of leading institutions throughout the world.

ZU is organised academically into five colleges: Arts and Sciences, Business Sciences, Communication and Media Sciences, Education, and Information Systems.

The reason for ZU's success lies partly in innovativeness. Smart Square, located in Dubai Internet City (DIC), is an example of the ZU approach. This cooperative venture between ZU and IBM, which was inaugurated in early 2003, established a new business partner in the UAE for private and public institutions to create and enhance their e-business and communication activities. Tanmia sponsors a section of the graduate on-the-job training for projects undertaken by Smart Square as part of its policy of equipping nationals with the necessary skills for today's demanding work environment.

The 'Women as Global Leaders' conference organised by ZU at Emirates Palace Hotel in Abu Dhabi in 2006 (see section on Women) is but one of a number of programmes run by the University to ensure that their students are well-prepared to actively participate in society.

Higher Colleges of Technology

A system of UAE colleges offering a more technically oriented education was devised in 1988. The four founding Higher Colleges of Technology (HCTs) began the new experiment with an enrolment of 239 students. Today, 12 men's and women's colleges in Abu Dhabi, Al Ain, Madinat Zayed, Dubai, Ra's al-Khaimah, Sharjah and Fujairah provide a diversity of programmes to over 15,000 students in modern, technologically equipped campuses. New colleges and facilities are being added to the list on a regular basis. Built on a total area of 43,000 square metres and costing around Dh200 million, the new campus of the Dubai Men's College at Academic City in Al Ruwayyah, which was inaugurated in 2005, provides a truly digital environment. Everything from assignments and mark sheets to missed classes and the library is online and can be accessed by each of the 2000 students and 300 faculty members at any point in time.

The new HCT Madinat Zayed campus, serving the needs of students in Abu Dhabi's Western Region, welcomed its first class of students in September 2006.

The HCT and its commercial arm, The Centre of Excellence for Applied Research and Training (CERT), through a number of strategic alliances with multinational business organisations and prestigious international training institutions, pride themselves on responding quickly and effectively to current needs in the regional and international work place, providing professional development and lifelong learning opportunities for the UAE, the Gulf region, and – through online training courses – to many other parts of the business world.

CERT, which was founded in 1997 and is now the largest private education provider in the region, has also been at the forefront of providing specialised customised training, promoting entrepreneurship and creativity, and facilitating technological advance through its technology park. CERT is collaborating in applied research with industry leaders such as Intel, Microsoft and IBM, and in 2006 it will become the first organisation in the region to offer supercomputing power through its acquisition of

Twelve men's and women's colleges in Abu Dhabi, Al Ain, Dubai, Ra's al-Khaimah, Sharjah and Fujairah serve over 15,000 students in modern, technologically equipped campuses.

the IBM Blue Gene, the fastest computing platform in the world. CERT's clients are large public and private sector organisations in the region, including the UAE Military, and the Presidential Court.

Having been converted into a joint stock company in 2005, CERT is now primed for the next stage in its development. Plans are in place to raise Dh1 billion (US$272 million) and offer 55 per cent of its share capital to the public through the first education and technology IPO in the Middle East. In addition to the lure of good financial returns, investors will be able to participate in a project that has significant socioeconomic benefits for the country and its people.

CERT is planning a unique 'CERT City' concept, based on the creation of a fully integrated community of research, innovation and entrepreneurship. Included in this world of 'learning, living and leisure', will be early-learning centres for pre-schoolers, world class primary and secondary educational institutions, the CERT College of Arts and Applied Science, CERT University (for undergraduate studies), the CERT Open University dedicated to postgraduates, the Emirates Centre for Entrepreneurship and the Jumeirah Institute for Executive Leadership. Supporting these centres of excellence will be a well-equipped convention centre, five-star hotel facilities, housing estates, shopping malls and sports, recreation and leisure facilities.

CERT, which was founded in 1997 and is now the largest private education provider in the region, has also been at the forefront of providing specialised customised training, promoting entrepreneurship and creativity, and facilitating technological advance through its technology park.

The first CERT Education and Research City is being established in Abu Dhabi on a site of over 1 million square metres, to be followed by similar ventures in Dubai and Sharjah, some of the other emirates, and eventually throughout the region.

Private Institutions

Many excellent private institutions offer a wide range of tertiary-level opportunities. Notable institutions include the American Universities of Sharjah and Dubai, Sharjah University and the Ajman University of Science and Technology. The Ministry of Higher Education and Scientific Research is responsible for the accreditation of institutes and degrees and its website, www.uae.gov.ae/mohe/, provides a comprehensive list of recognised institutes and programmes.

Abu Dhabi University (ADU), which opened its doors in 2003, is in a process of continued development. It has campuses both in Abu Dhabi and Al Ain and has unveiled plans for a 4-million-square-metre campus in Khalifa City, with provisions for flexible future expansion. The first phase includes 70 classrooms and laboratories, administrative headquarters and accommodation. Plans are in place for a medical teaching facility, a graduate centre, a student centre and sports facilities. ADU, which has direct access from the Al Ain highway and is very conveniently located for students from Khalifa City, Abu Dhabi and Al Ain, accepted its first students for the academic year beginning in September 2006.

Al Hosn University in Abu Dhabi opened in 2005. This new private university, which is supported by Abu Dhabi Holding Company (ADHC), will initially be operating from two separate premises for men and women near Mussala Al Eid along the airport road in Abu Dhabi. Starting with three faculties – Engineering, Business and Arts and Social Sciences – Al Hosn University will offer a unique set of disciplines, some of which are being introduced for

the first time in the UAE. A large plot of land in Madinat Khalifa has been earmarked by the Abu Dhabi government for the construction of a permanent campus.

An Abu Dhabi chapter of the Sorbonne University was also established in 2006. This chapter is wholly owned by ADEC and although headquartered in Abu Dhabi it is authorised to establish branches of the University in the rest of the UAE and in the region. The University will award qualifications under French regulations and in accordance with academic standards set by the Sorbonne in Paris. Instruction will be in French and all subjects will be taught by tutors from the Sorbonne. Credits accumulated by students at the UAE chapter can be transferred to any European university. The new University, which is open to students of both sexes and of all nationalities, will initially operate from an interim campus, but will move to a permanent home by early 2008.

Knowledge Village (KV), established in 2003 in the Dubai Free Zone for Technology and Media, houses more than 200 companies and institutes for training and education. Over 6000 students come to the campus every day. Some 25 per cent of them are from countries in the Middle East, whilst other students from Arab and foreign communities residing in Dubai. KV offers undergraduate, postgraduate, MBA and PhD programmes in fields such as computing, technology, business management, life science, fashion and media.

Dubai Knowledge Universities (DKU) is being established as a multi-university complex on 2.33 million square metres in the heart of Academic City in Dubai. DKU is targeting students from the region who are unable to go abroad to study for various reasons. On completion DKU will be able to accommodate 20 to 30 universities and house between 30,000 and 40,000 students and will be designed to provide a quality of student life and services that is international, culturally diverse and dynamic. The giant campus will have two wings, a west campus for undergraduates and an east campus for graduates.

Dubai Academic City (DAC), marketed as 'a new global fully integrated academic destination', was officially launched in 2006. Investment in this phased project, which is being built on a 12-million-square-metres campus, is forecast to exceed Dh12 billion (US$3.27 billion). A completion date is set for 2012.

Other Institutions

In addition to the higher level institutions outlined above, the UAE also has several vocational and technical educational centres for those seeking practical training in their chosen careers. These include the Emirates Institute for Banking and Finance, the Abu Dhabi National Oil Company Career Development Centre, the Dubai School of Government, and The Emirates Aviation College for Aerospace and Academic Studies.

EMIRATES FOUNDATION

The Abu Dhabi-based Emirates Foundation is a public- and private-sector, nation-wide initiative to support creativity and innovation in science, education, technology, art, sports, environment and health. Continuing the late Sheikh Zayed's philanthropic legacy, the Foundation recognises that in an increasingly global economy where the transfer of technology is a prerequisite for development, research is no longer a luxury but a necessity requiring funding and a sound infrastructure. The Foundation will, therefore, manage a variety of endowment funds to foster, enhance and maintain a diverse range of innovative centres of excellence and educational institutions in the UAE. The Technology and Research Endowment Fund is the first to be launched. Ultimately, it is hoped that the Foundation will stimulate increased social consciousness and act as a forum for active participation between the private and public sectors for the benefit of the community.

The Foundation is a public- and private-sector, nation-wide initiative to support creativity and innovation in science, education, technology, art, sports, environment and health.

LITERACY

As well as providing for the educational needs of the youth of the country, the Government has undertaken an adult literacy programme in cooperation with the UAE General Women's Union. In 1975, the rate of adult literacy was 54.2 per cent amongst men,

www.uaeinteract.com/uaeeducation

and 30.9 per cent amongst women. Today, the illiteracy rate in the country is in the region of 9 per cent (census figures) and the UAE is on its way towards achieving its target of full literacy. The UAE also provides free primary and secondary education for those adults who missed out on education during their childhood.

WOMEN

Economic prosperity has brought vastly improved health care, extended life expectancy and significant educational opportunities for all the citizens of the UAE. But there was a danger that as the country began to develop and as its men moved to take advantage of newly provided opportunities, that the UAE's women might be left behind. Fortunately, government-backing and their own anxiety to play their part in the development of the country has ensured that this has not happened. In particular, women have embraced education with particular fervour and are outperforming males at every educational level. This enthusiasm for education ensures that women can exercise their right to participate in the labour market and in the decision-making process.

THE LEGAL FRAMEWORK

Women constitute 18 per cent of the appointed members of the Electoral College, which will form the basis for the December 2006 elections to the Federal National Council.

The belief that women are entitled to take their place in society is grounded in the UAE Constitution which guarantees the principles of social justice for all, in accordance with the precepts of Islam. Under the Constitution, women enjoy the same legal status, claim to titles, access to education, health care and social welfare and the same right to practice professions as men.

The Constitution stipulates that:

The family is the basis of society, which shall be responsible for protecting childhood and motherhood. Laws shall be formulated in all fields to observe this protection and care, in a way which safeguards the dignity of women, preserves their identity and secures for them the conditions appropriate for a prosperous life and suitable work which is in accordance with their nature and capabilities as mothers and wives and as workers.

Women play a key role in the UAE education system. The Government continues with its efforts to promote a culture of gender equality and justice in all government institutions, especially in schools and in the media.

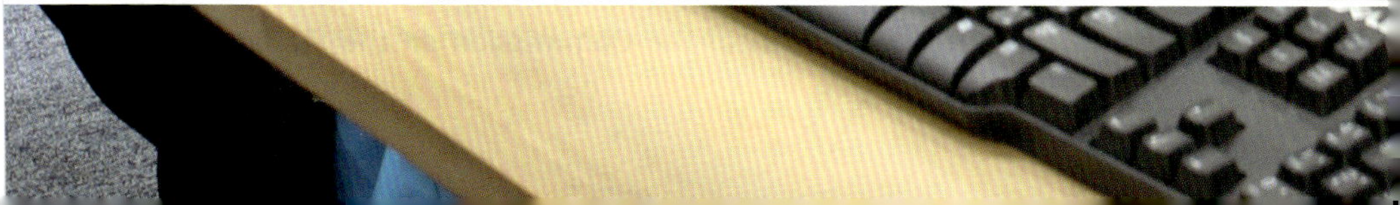

and is affiliated to the Arab Women's Federation, the International Women's Federation and the International Family Organisation.

The GWU maintains strong links with Arab and international women's organisations.

The GWU has participated in all of the UN-sponsored world conferences on women over the last few decades, culminating in Beijing in 1995, the largest conference in the history of the United Nations. As a result of its dedicated work in this area, GWU is now focusing on the necessary measures at a national level to activate CEDAW and to implement the recommendations of the Beijing Declaration.

In this context, The GWU is intimately involved in The National Strategy for the Advancement of Women, a joint initiative with UNDP, the United Nations Development Fund for Women (UNIFEM), local government agencies and NGOs. The strategy's purpose is 'to activate the role of women and their positive participation in eight major and significant fields, including education, economy, information, social work, health, legislature and environment, in addition to political and executive fields'. The effect of the strategy is to raise the debate on female participation to a new level with a rhetoric that unapologetically assumes gender equality and focuses on the removal of obstacles to that participation.

This focus also extends beyond the UAE's borders. The UAE Government, along with UAE-based NGOs, led by the UAE Red Crescent, have contributed financially and in kind, to assist many developing countries and regions affected by natural disasters, armed conflicts and foreign occupation where women suffer from poverty, dangerous diseases, violence, displacement and violation of human rights. Contributions were directed to the implementation of social development programmes and advancement of women in these countries.

The UAE was re-elected to membership of the Women's Committee of the UN Economic and Social Council from 2006 to 2010.

The UAE was re-elected to membership of the Women's Committee of the UN Economic and Social Council from 2006 to 2010.

WOMEN IN POLITICS

Considering the pivotal role that the GWU plays in political affairs in the UAE, it is not surprising that the organisation is actively pursuing greater participation for women in national politics. This aim may be realised in the near future since 1189 members of the 6689-strong Electoral College, the basis for the December 2006 Federal National Council elections, are women. Much progress has been made, including the appointment of the first female ministers to the Federal Government (to the Ministry of Economy and the Ministry of Social Affairs) and a considerable amount of groundwork is being done at grassroots level to ensure that political decision-making will be open to all women.

Sheikha Fatima has commented that 'What has been achieved by UAE women, notably in education and positive participation in the national development and construction, make us look forward with confidence for their entry into the political scene.

We are looking forward to the engagement of women in political life, building on the unstinting support of (the late) H.H. President Sheikh Zayed bin Sultan Al Nahyan for women's aspirations . . . Engagement of women in national action is part and parcel of their basic rights guaranteed by Islamic faith and valuable Arab traditions'. Sheikha Fatima stresses that strengthening the role of the GCC women's organisations with the aim of serving local communities is an important way of improving the participation of women in all aspects of national life, including politics.

Under the national strategy for the development of women, GWU and UNIFEM are conducting a training programme to assist UAE women to positively engage in decision-making and parliamentary life in the future. The programme features three key areas: establishing Arab women MPs' forums, increasing awareness of social gender issues in Arab parliaments, and launching of national incubators for future Arab women leaders. Under the programme around 200 UAE women leaders, specialists in political, economic and social sciences and human resource development, deliver lectures on leadership and management skills, decision-making, strategic planning, creative thinking, the electoral process, protocol and ethics.

LEADERSHIP CONFERENCE

The 'Women as Global Leaders' conference, organised by Zayed University at Emirates Palace Hotel in Abu Dhabi in 2006 under

Sheikha Lubna Al Qasimi is Minister of Economy and a role model for Arab women.

the patronage of Sheikha Fatima, is another facet of the efforts being made to encourage women to take their rightful place in society. Attended by over 1200 female student delegates from 75 countries, keynote speakers at the conference included Queen Rania of Jordan, Cherie Blair, human rights lawyer and wife of British Premier Tony Blair, Sheikha Lubna Al Qasimi, Minister of Economy, Mary Robinson, former President of Ireland and former High Commissioner for Human Rights (UNHCHR), and several global women leaders.

The conference not only provided an opportunity for students and educators from all over the globe to meet and share ideas but also to learn about leadership and its role in community transformation from internationally renowned speakers. In addition, the theme 'Communities In Transition' provided a unique opportunity to explore and understand perspectives on the empowerment of women in Arab and Islamic societies.

WOMEN AND EMPLOYMENT

The UAE is singular in registering the highest rate of females in higher education in the entire world [77 per cent].

Recent reports (by PricewaterhouseCoopers which quotes a study by AlMishkat Centre for Research and Training, Egypt) have concluded that 'The UAE is singular in registering the highest rate of females in higher education in the entire world [77 per cent].' The report continues: 'Indeed four of the Gulf countries (UAE, Qatar, Bahrain and Kuwait) surpass even the United States in percentage of female students in higher education'. However, the challenge is to translate these educational accomplishments into employment.

According to the *UAE Human Resources Report 2005*, the contribution of UAE national women to economic activity increased significantly from a mere 5.4 per cent in 1995 to 16.1 per cent in 2004. This positive development was due not only to the substantial enrolment by women in education, particularly higher education, mentioned above, but also to relaxed social restrictions on female employment and the fact that work was increasingly being seen not merely as a source of income but as establishing personal identity.

Abu Dhabi recruits almost half of all females from the national workers' pool and it has a large percentage of educated women who are part of the labour force. The Northern Emirates have proportionally less working national women.

Although the participation rate of economically active female nationals went up by 11 per cent between 1995 and 2004, their relatively small share of the total labour force underscores the importance of current efforts to target women for jobs. As it is, the unemployment rate among national women is at a high of 19.7 per cent or 14,000 job seekers compared to 8.2 per cent for males, despite the fact that women graduates greatly outnumber male graduates. In 2004 alone, over 66 per cent of the nationals who applied to Tanmia for jobs were women, 76 per cent of the applicants had completed secondary education or above, and women constituted 79 per cent in this category.

There are several reasons why the ratio of female to male participation in the workforce is relatively low. Firstly, the number of males between 15 and 65 years (2.12 million in 2005) far exceeds the female figure (838,941), mainly because foreign workers are predominantly male; secondly, some companies restrict the numbers of females employed; thirdly, UAE society is patriarchal and the changing of traditional views concerning a woman's place in the family is a slow process; fourthly, although women are well-represented at every educational level, it is no longer enough for women to gain a qualification – it is vital that what women choose to do in tertiary education should be relevant to the needs of the ever more technologically challenging workplace. This is where organisations such as Tanmia can make a big difference. In addition, many UAE women cease working after marriage and bearing children, partly because of an insufficiency of childcare centres and partly because maternal care is considered to be more beneficial for their children.

On the positive side, females constitute 66 per cent of the workforce in the government sector, of which 30 per cent are in decision-making positions. In particular, UAE women comprise over 40 per cent of all employees in education, at least 35 per cent

Females constitute 66 per cent of the workforce in the government sector, of which 30 per cent are in decision-making positions. In particular, UAE women comprise over 40 per cent of all employees in education, at least 35 per cent work in the health sector and approximately 20 per cent in social affairs.

work in the health sector and approximately 20 per cent in social affairs. In 2004 female participation in the private sector was 18 per cent. Women are now working in all areas of the private sector, including a significant 37.5 per cent in financial services. This is set to increase with emiratisation of human resources managers and secretarial positions in the private sector (see Labour and Social Affairs), coupled with a gradual shift in attitudes. Nowadays, according to Tanmia, women, especially college and university graduates, realise the changing requirements of the job market and are less likely to restrict their horizons to the government sector or to companies where they would not be required to work with men.

The consensus is that national women stand an equal if not greater chance of employment in the private sector, compared to men. 'These women are qualified, have effective communication skills, and are extremely confident'.

There is no doubt that role models for women in all walks of life are multiplying rapidly in the UAE, encouraging women to break away from traditional areas of employment.

Role Models

There is no doubt that role models for women in all walks of life are multiplying rapidly in the UAE, encouraging women to break away from traditional areas of employment. Whether her skills lie in finance, IT, the arts, medicine, engineering, the army, police work or the social sciences, the contemporary UAE woman is assured of finding herself following in the footsteps of pioneering predecessors. The formerly unprecedented is gradually becoming the norm.

New appointments in Government have already been mentioned; a woman holds the rank of Brigadier in the UAE Army; the first female chief executive officer has been appointed to JAFZA; and Dubai Technology and Media Free Zone Authority has appointed a female Executive Director of its Media Sector. Female police officers throughout the Emirates are working in all aspects of police work from administration and IT to traffic regulation and prison work. Women with full training in cargo and passenger control have graduated from Dubai Civil Aviation Centre's airport security course. A unit of female fire-fighters, initially trained for the Dubai Shopping Festival, has become a permanent feature of the Civil Defence. Dubai Municipality has its first female director; several women have been appointed as administration directors and section heads in Dubai Public Prosecution; three women have been appointed to the board of the Dubai Chamber of Commerce and Industry; a national woman is Vice-President of Distribution at Dubai Bank, another heads the Social Service at the Primary Heath Centre of the Department of Health and Medical Services and the first national endocrinologist and the regional director of Harvard Medical School are women. A young UAE woman has started working in the engineering hangars at Emirates airline headquarters; two UAE women feature in the top ten most powerful Arabian businesswomen, according to an in-depth *Forbes Arabia* survey; a UAE national woman has been appointed to the Administrative Review Board of the UN; and four UAE women have been elected to the executive council of the Islamic Federation of Women's Sports. If that is not enough, the UAE has hosted the first women's international car rally and an Emirati woman is making a bid to become the UAE's first ever Formula One racing driver.

Two UAE women feature in the top ten most powerful Arabian businesswomen, according to an in-depth Forbes Arabia survey.

Nevertheless, gender inequality remains an issue requiring renewed focus to ensure that individual success stories are no longer exceptional. In particular, there is a need to conduct increasingly targeted and direct interventions to influence policy-makers and legislators and to encourage skilled groups of capable individuals to lend support to and act as advocates for the strategy.

Businesswomen's Councils

A key recommendation of the National Strategy for the Advancement of Women was for businesswomen's councils to be attached to each of the Chambers of Commerce and Industry throughout the UAE in order to assist women in business and to provide a link with public policy makers. This has been implemented in the larger emirates.

The UAE Businesswomen's Council, a nationwide network of business, professional and academic women, was set-up in 2002,

The UAE Businesswomen's Council, a nationwide network of business, professional and academic women, was set-up in 2002, supported by the Federation of Chambers of Commerce and Industry.

supported by the Federation of Chambers of Commerce and Industry. One of its first initiatives was to issue the first-ever commercial directory for businesswomen in the UAE. as part of the council's determined efforts to offer services to businesswomen in various sectors and strengthen links between them and clients and consumers. The Businesswomen Council has over 10,000 members, running investments worth more than Dh12 billion (US$3.27 billion).

Abu Dhabi Businesswomen Group (ADBW) is implementing a number of major projects in cooperation with trading and educational partners. One is the education and training of potential female entrepreneurs in collaboration with ZU and the HCT. A second – 'Employment Passport' – provides an opportunity for graduates to gain work experience in companies and businesses run by the members of the ADBW. In 2006 ADBW organised the Third National Businesswomen's Campaign to help national businesswomen as well as graduates start private business enterprises. An award for the best project idea has been launched. About 3000 national women are engaged in small and medium businesses in Abu Dhabi, some of them in partnership with their husbands.

'We are living in a world calling for empowerment and emancipation of women and we believe the first step to support women should start from improvement of women's economic and living conditions. Women should be backed to set up their own businesses to achieve their dreams for independence and emancipation,' Sheikha Fatima told the opening session of the first forum for businesswomen and women investors organised by Abu Dhabi Chamber of Commerce and Industry (ADCCI) in conjunction with Abu Dhabi Businesswomen Council and Arab Women Investors Association. The two-day forum was held under the theme 'Towards a Promising Arab Strategic, Investment Partnership'.

Dubai Business Women Council (DBWC) is providing women entrepreneurs in the UAE with assistance for small and medium ventures, from compiling feasibility studies to consultancy in all areas, from setting up business to availability of finance.

Other organisations are also recognising that given the right conditions, targeting women can be a valuable marketing strategy. In 2004, a special floor for business transactions for women was opened at the Abu Dhabi Securities Market (ADSM) with the objective of encouraging UAE national women to participate actively in the business activities at the ADSM. As a result, the number of UAE women engaged in transactions at ADSM is on the rise.

NEW AWARD

Sheikha Fatima established a new award in 2006 entitled 'The Sheikha Fatima Bint Mubarak Award for the Distinguished Woman in the Arab Family'. The award is intended to highlight the distinctive role of the Arab woman in the family, society and nation and to honour distinguished pioneers, as an incentive to young women, the architects of the future at the side of their male partner. The award coincides with and marks the Arab Woman's Day, celebrated on 1 February every year.

'We are living in a world calling for empowerment and emancipation of women and we believe the first step to support women should start from improvement of women's economic and living conditions.' (Sheikha Fatima)

HEALTH

As already mentioned the UAE was ranked forty-first in the 2005 *UN Human Development Report*, having risen from forty-ninth place in 2004. HDI focuses on three measurable dimensions of human development: living a long and healthy life, being educated and having a decent standard of living. Thus it combines measures of life expectancy, school enrolment, literacy and income, providing a broader view of a country's development than income alone. The 2007 *Yearbook* has already highlighted the country's achievements in education and the Government's continuing efforts to provide a high standard of living for its people. This section, therefore, explores the success of the UAE's efforts to provide a world-class health service for its population.

The Federal Government spent Dh1.6 billion (US$436 million) during the period from 1996 to 2003 on the health sector. Growth percentages have shown a steady increase in recent years, at 4.4 per cent in 2000, 6.5 per cent in 2001, 2.0 per cent in 2002 and

www.uaeinteract.com/women

5.5 per cent in 2003. Between 1989 and 1995 the health sector experienced a 5.8 per cent steady annual growth, culminating in an expenditure of Dh 4.40 billion (US$1.2 billion) during the year 1995, 1 per cent of GDP revenues.

At 78 years, life expectancy at birth in the UAE has reached levels similar to those in Europe and North America.

A sophisticated physical infrastructure of well-equipped hospitals, clinics and primary care centres has been instrumental in delivering a high standard of health care to the population. Most of the infectious diseases like malaria, measles and poliomyelitis that were once prevalent in the UAE have been eradicated, while pre-natal and post-natal care is on a par with the world's most developed countries. In fact, infant mortality and maternal mortality rates have dropped remarkably and, according to the Arab Human Development Report (AHDR), the UAE is one of two countries from the Arab Gulf Cooperation Council (GCC) that have successfully maintained maternal mortality rates at levels considered low by international standards. The new-born (neonate) mortality rate has been reduced to 5.54 per 1000 and infant mortality to 7.7 per 1000. Maternal mortality rates have dropped to 0.01 for every 100,000 in 2004, primarily due to the fact that almost all deliveries in the country take place in hospitals under direct medical supervision.

As a consequence of this high standard of care at all stages of the healthcare system, life expectancy at birth in the UAE, at 78 years, has reached levels similar to those in Europe and North America.

CHALLENGES AHEAD

Despite these major strides, there is an ever-increasing pressure on the country's healthcare services. This is primarily due to the unprecedented growth in population, but other factors come into play, such as the burgeoning cost of technology and the limited role, to date, played by the private sector. The reason for this is that free high-quality care and medicines have been readily available at government hospitals and pharmacies. Expatriates were also entitled to use MoH facilities for minimal fees on production of a health card which cost as little as Dh300 (US$82) per year. Not only did this put a heavy burden on public health care but it also prevented the development of private facilities. There has been a fundamental shift away from government subsidies in recent years. Since 2001 visitors to the UAE and residents without health cards or with expired ones have had to pay full fees for hospital beds and surgical operations and free medicines are no longer issued to expatriate cardholders. But the most radical development in the system has been the introduction of compulsory health insurance, ultimately leading to more cost-effective and efficient services. Residents of Abu Dhabi will be covered by a comprehensive insurance scheme introduced by Abu Dhabi's General Authority for Health Services (GAHS) in 2006 under the terms of Law No. 23 for 2005. The new scheme, covering treatment in public and private hospitals, will phase out health cards, which will not be renewed once they expire.

Under the terms of the new law, all foreign residents and their family members must participate in the scheme. The law obliges employers to enrol all employees, spouses and three children under the age of 18 and pay the cost of the policies. Employees are obliged to secure health insurance for persons sponsored by them, who are not covered by the employer. Participation in the scheme is, however, optional for UAE citizens. Initially, the National Health Insurance Company (Dhaman) will handle policies for the government sector, while the private sector scheme will be handled by a number of private companies.

The first phase of healthcare insurance cover was enacted for all expatriate employees working for Abu Dhabi-based ministries, federal and local organisations and private companies with more than 1000 employees. Fees are being introduced in Abu Dhabi government hospitals and private providers must obtain permission from GAHS to offer their services under the scheme. The hospital will bill the insurance company directly and GAHS has set prices for all operations and medical services in line with the costs of medical services offered in GCC countries.

The Ministry of Health has also been re-structured and streamlined, both at administrative and technical levels, to keep abreast with international developments and reinforce the private health sector so as to enable it to play a more significant

Most of the infectious diseases like malaria, measles and poliomyelitis that were once prevalent in the UAE have been eradicated while pre-natal and post-natal care is on a par with the world's most developed countries.

Sheikh Khalifa Medical City

role in providing health services. Hospital boards are being revitalised, regular hospital visits are being initiated and a UAE council for medical specialists is being put in place to upgrade the training of UAE medical personnel. In addition, training programmes are being conducted in conjunction with international universities.

Nursing schools have been set up across the country, from Ra's al-Khaimah to Abu Dhabi. The UAE's first nursing association, Emirates Nursing Association, has been formed.

To date, the healthcare services are primarily staffed by foreign nationals. Nursing schools have been set up across the country, from Ra's al-Khaimah to Abu Dhabi, to remedy this situation, although UAE nationals are under-represented at these schools. The UAE's first nursing association, Emirates Nursing Association, has been formed in an attempt to rectify the situation. Nursing salary scales are under review and the profession's first nursing journal, *Abu Dhabi Nurse*, has been launched by GAHS.

Approximately, 10 per cent of doctors in the country are UAE citizens. However, medical training at UAEU's Faculty of Medicine and Health Sciences and other centres, including new postgraduate facilities at Dubai Healthcare City (see below), will ensure that a qualified local workforce is nurtured.

Recognising that reference libraries are an essential aspect of health education, the Zayed Foundation for Humanitarian and Charitable Works has provided funds and state-of the art electronic equipment to the Zayed Medical Library at the headquarters of the Emirates Medical Association and to medical libraries in Abu Dhabi hospitals.

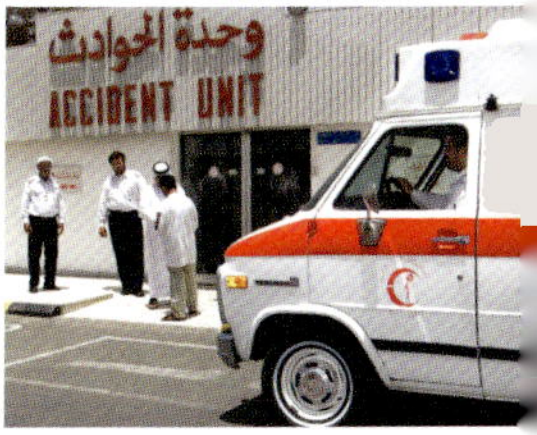

Emergency medical services in the UAE operate with efficient equipment that enables rapid response rates.

HOSPITALS

There is a renewed focus on improving facilities across the board and new hospitals and clinics are constantly being opened in both the public and private sector. For example, GAHS in Abu Dhabi has been developing the area known as Sheikh Khalifa Medical City (SKMC) as a top-class medical cluster. Facilities recently established there include a Dh300 million obstetrics and gynaecological unit with 320 beds, a ten-bed, C4 intermediate care and reconstructive unit and a specialised diabetes centre.

Services have also been improved in other parts of the emirate, including a new 180-bed unit at the public hospital in Al Ain and a new Dh135 million complex for the Oasis Hospital, which was established in November 1960 and is, therefore, the oldest medical facility in the emirate.

New urban areas are springing up at an increased rate in Dubai and a new private hospital, Jebel Ali Hospital, was opened in 2006 to cater for the medical needs of the rising population in that area. Developments under way at Dubai Healthcare City (see below) will also revolutionise the delivery of health care in that emirate.

Sharjah's Dh100 million Kalba Hospital opened at the beginning of 2005, and another new Sharjah-based development, the Dh180 million, well-equipped Royal Hospital, opened its doors to patients in September 2006. A health resort is to be launched within the hospital, with hotel services, swimming pools and a fully equipped spa.

SPECIALISED SERVICES

The UAE provides a high level of specialised health care at its many hospitals and clinics, including open-heart surgery and organ transplantation. Comprehensive diagnostic and therapeutic

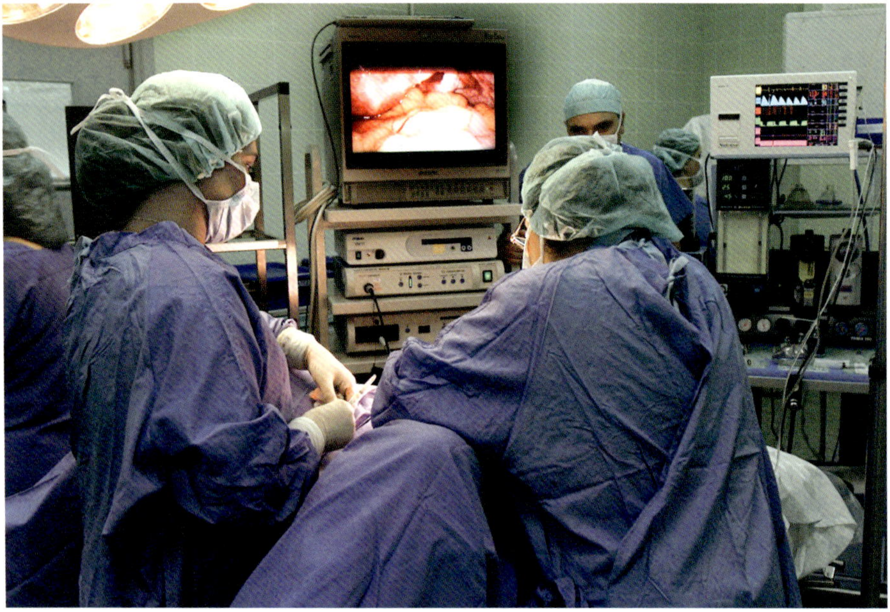

radiological facilities, along with surgical treatment, are offered at oncology departments in Tawam Hospital in Al Ain and Al Mafraq Hospital in Abu Dhabi. Gastrointestinal, renal and ENT units are also available in many general hospitals. Efforts are constantly being made to upgrade these services.

John Hopkins Medicine will oversee the management and operation of Tawam Hospital up to 2016 and will also supervise the building of the Middle East's largest cancer treatment centre.

Early in 2006 agreements were signed between GAHS and John Hopkins Medicine, part of the world-renowned John Hopkins University, sealing a partnership between the two and ensuring that Tawam Hospital will benefit from the medical expertise of one of the United States' top medical institutions. Under the terms of the agreements, John Hopkins Medicine will oversee the management and operation of Tawam Hospital up to 2016 and will also supervise the building of the Middle East's largest cancer treatment centre, the Tawam and John Hopkins Cancer Centre, based at the Al Ain Hospital. The centre will be completed in 2010.

In 2006 construction was completed in Abu Dhabi on a private cancer diagnosis and treatment centre, the Emirates International Cancer Centre (EICC). A joint venture between

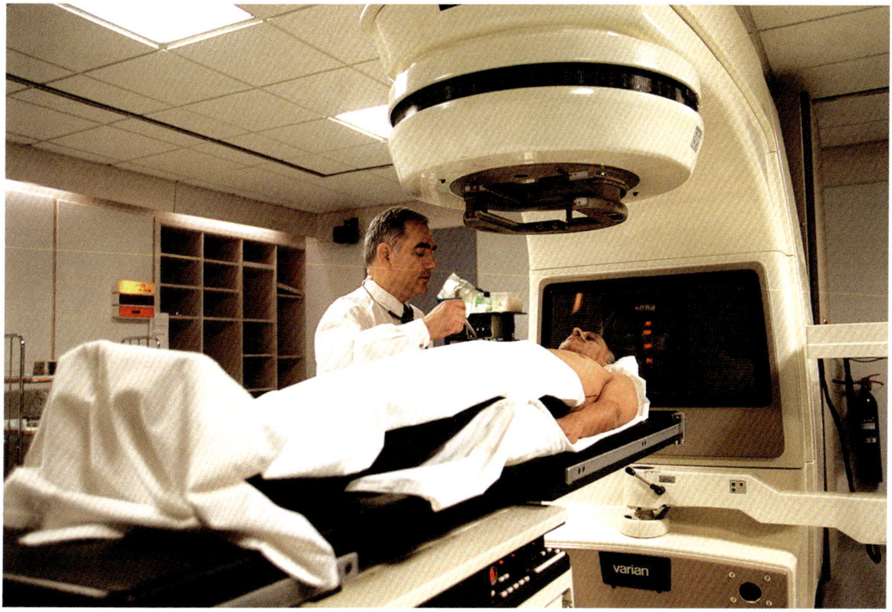

Emirates American Medical Services and Abu Dhabi International Medical Services (ADI), a supplier of medical equipment in the UAE, the private centre will be affiliated to St Luke's Hospital of Baylor University in Houston, Texas, and will offer cancer treatment for patients of all ages.

Many of the new hospitals, public and private, also offer advanced techniques such as 'keyhole' or minimally invasive surgery and interventional radiology. Up until recently, these procedures were only available abroad. As with cancer treatment, obviously it is not only more cost-effective and convenient to treat people in their own environment, it is also a better solution for the patient.

In 2003 Dubai's Welcare Hospital became the first private hospital to offer open-heart surgery in the UAE. In 2005 the American Hospital joined 'Emirates World Heart Foundation', a non-profit organisation based in the UAE that has a panel of eminent international heart surgeons who are on-call to carry out complicated heart surgery, free of cost, on underprivileged patients in any corner of the world. Established by Dr Adel Al

The UAE provides a high level of specialised health care at its many hospitals and clinics, including open-heart surgery and organ transplantation.

Shamry, Consultant Cardio-Thoracic Surgeon at Sheikh Zayed Military Hospital, the Foundation also works with local and international medical staff under the umbrella of the UAE Red Crescent to provide surgical training, assistance with diagnostic procedures and consultations, as well as to provide educational programmes in the medical field. It also donates equipment and medicines to needy hospitals. The Foundation, which started with 20 doctors, now boasts 100 surgeons who set aside one month of the year to handle the Foundation's projects.

DUBAI HEALTHCARE CITY

The UK's Great Ormond Street Hospital has announced plans to open a regional centre at DHCC.

DHCC is destined to be a major player in the provision of health care, medical education and research, not only in the UAE but in the entire region. Scheduled for completion in 2010 but likely to be finished sooner, DHCC is being built on the former site of the Global Village in the vicinity of existing hospitals Al Wasl, Rashid, the American Hospital and Welcare. Investment in DHCC's first two phases has been projected at Dh11 billion (US$3 billion). Phase one includes a 300-bed university hospital, a medical college, a nursing school, a life sciences research centre, 40 fully equipped, ready-to-go clinics (to be offered on both leasehold and freehold terms) and specialised laboratories. Phase two, four times the size of phase one, both in terms of area and investment, was unveiled in 2006 and will include centres for rehabilitation, nursing, obesity and nutrition and alternative medicine, as well as facilities for pharmaceutical companies.

The Dubai Harvard Foundation for Medical Research will be headquartered at the Harvard Medical School Dubai Centre's Institute for Postgraduate Education and Research (HMSDC), which has its premises at the DHCC. Programmes will be implemented through HMSDC, which will also develop collaborative scientific and medical research between regional laboratories and Harvard Medical School. One of the world's best-known hospitals specialising in child health care, the UK's Great Ormond Street Hospital, has announced plans to open a regional centre at DHCC and Eleva, a new Dh100 million (US$27.24 million) seven-storey medical, healthcare centre strictly for women is scheduled to open at DHCC in 2008.

MEDICINES

The UAE is the highest consumer of medicines in the Gulf region. Average per head consumption amounts to Dh293.6 (US$80) annually, while the average in other Gulf and Arab countries is US$52 and US$20.3 respectively.

Online access to all pharmaceutical products registered by the Ministry of Health is part of an e-pharma project that aims to ensure availability of vital information concerning approved pharmaceutical products to the public. It is hoped that the move will greatly reduce health hazards resulting from unregistered drugs, as well as bring to an end unlicensed promotion of certain types of drugs. The available data will cover warnings, side effects, labelling, active ingredients, first aid (in case of poisoning or serious adverse side effects) and the actual price of the drugs. The e-project will also facilitate registration of medicines for import and the licensing of private pharmacies.

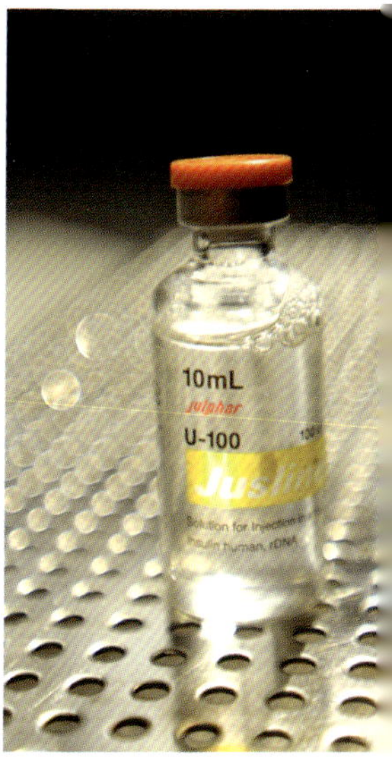

The leading pharmaceutical manufacturer in the UAE is Gulf Pharmaceutical Industries, known as Julphar, which is based in Ra's al-Khaimah.

HEALTH EDUCATION

The Ministry of Health has paid particular attention to health education as an effective method for changing unfavourable attitudes and behaviour that negatively influence the health and well-being of individuals and the community at large. To meet this challenge, the Ministry has established a Department of Health Education in the preventive health sector with representation in all medical districts. The Department's responsibility is to develop and implement national plans to raise public awareness. The Department has also organised conferences in collaboration with WHO on cancer prevention, nutrition and chronic diseases, in addition to studies on health topics, including the prevalence of diabetes in the community.

WORLD HEALTH AWARD

The UAE's commitment to the objectives of the WHO are underscored by the initiation of the World Health Award by the late Sheikh Zayed bin Sultan Al Nahyan. The UAE's desire to reinforce the WHO worldwide has become even stronger with the support of President HH Sheikh Khalifa bin Zayed Al Nahyan.

www.uaeinteract.com/health

DISEASE CONTROL

Thirty-six infectious diseases are included in the control programmes that are jointly organised by the Ministry of Health with other relevant ministries and agencies in order to effectively coordinate suitable intervention methods, including vaccination, vector control, health education and chemoprophylaxis. The elimination of polio, measles and neonatal tetanus are examples of the successes achieved in this area.

The National TB Programme in the UAE was launched as a result of an initiative by WHO in coordination with the Executive Office of the Council of Health Ministers of the GCC countries, taking into consideration the epidemiological factors of the disease and the healthcare system in the country. The death rate resulting from TB decreased from 0.60 per 100,000 population in 1990 to 0.13 in 1995, a reduction of 78.3 per cent. With the re-emergence of the disease worldwide, the death rate increased again in the UAE to reach 0.32 per 100,000 population in 1996 and 0.42 per 100,000 population in 1997. However, due to the country's TB control strategy, including DOTS (Directly Observed Treatment Short Course) and the TB Programme, incidence decreased to 0.1 in 2001 and 2002 consecutively, a reduction of 76.2 per cent since 1997. The objective is to reduce the incidence rate to less than 1 per 100,000 population by 2010.

The National Strategy for Malaria Control has succeeded in eliminating indigenous transmission of malaria and the last locally transmitted cases of malaria in the UAE were recorded in July 1997.

The National Strategy for Malaria Control has succeeded in eliminating indigenous transmission of malaria and the last locally transmitted cases of malaria in the UAE were recorded in July 1997. However, due to its multinational population who frequently travel abroad, the country has been recording imported cases of infection. It is expected, nevertheless, that the UAE will be declared malaria-free by the World Health Organisation following studies done by WHO.

IMMUNISATIONS

The National Immunisation Programme (NIP), launched in 1980, has made significant progress over the last 20 years. The vaccination schedule started with the six immunisable childhood diseases

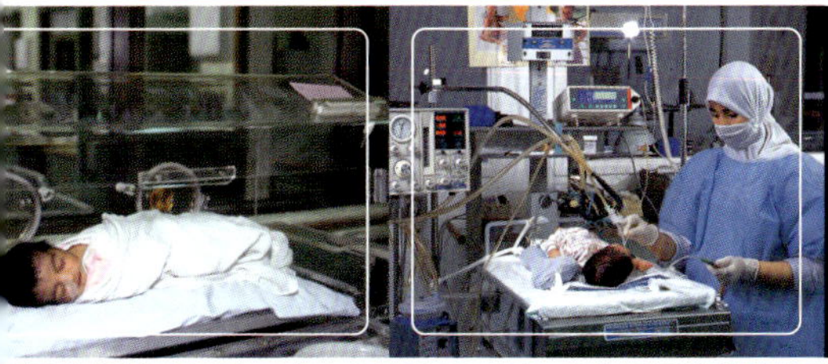

Pre-natal and post-natal care in the UAE is on a par with the world's most developed countries.

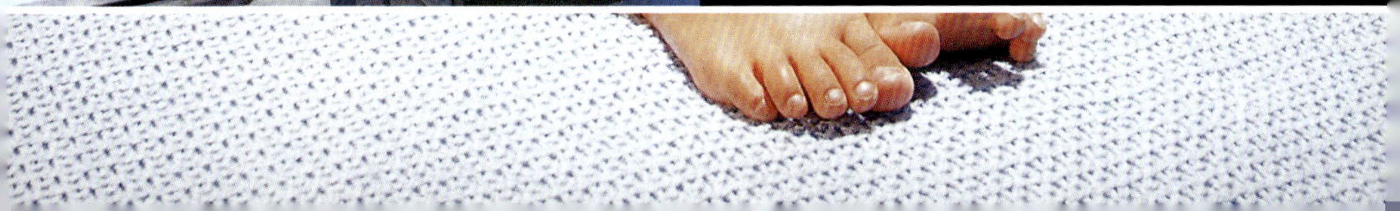

(polio, measles, tetanus, pertusis, diphtheria and tuberculosis) recommended by WHO. MMR (measles, mumps and rubella) vaccination was added to the programme in 1985, hepatitis in 1990 and the Haemophilus influenza B (Hib) vaccine in 1999. In addition to regulating vaccination practices, national strategies have been focusing on sustaining high coverage, ascertaining the effectiveness and safety of vaccines, as well as on adequate and rational utilisation of new biotechnology.

A comprehensive review of NIP was made in 2002, taking into account the recommendations of the First Emirates International Conference on Vaccination held during the same year. Based on this review, the NIP was revised and updated to introduce multivalent combined vaccines, beginning in January 2005.

Pentavalent vaccines, offering protection against five diseases (hepatitis B, Hib and DPT – diphtheria, polio and tetanus) is currently administered at two, four and six months; quadravalent vaccine (Hib and DPT) booster at 18 months and MMR at 12 months. An additional dose of hepatitis B vaccine is also given at birth. All children born after January 2005 will be covered under the updated NIP.

According to World Health Organisation statistics, the UAE is one of the countries with the lowest number of reported HIV/AIDS cases in the world. Cultural, social and behavioural Islamic norms have contributed to keeping infection at these very low levels.

NACP

In a conservative society like the UAE, AIDS is a rare disease. According to World Health Organisation statistics, the UAE is one of the countries with the lowest number of reported HIV/AIDS cases in the world. Cultural, social and behavioural Islamic norms have contributed to keeping infection at these very low levels.

The National AIDS Control and Prevention programme (NACP), established in 1985, has the ultimate objective of preventing transmission of the disease and the control of its entry into the country, through primary prevention, early detection and effective management. Prevention is accomplished through early detection and screening, including screening of blood, blood products, organs and tissues before transfusion or transplants and screening of population groups. Budgets have been allocated for testing all expatriates at the time of issuing or of renewing residence visas.

Free treatment is provided to cases, if detected, and the Government provides financial, psychological and social support to patients and their families.

No cases of transmission through blood or blood products provided in UAE facilities have been recorded since 1985, when the AIDS programme was first implemented. This and the very low prevalence of HIV/AIDS in the country indicate the success of the programme. However, as with any programme, it is continually being updated in order to meet the threat that new global patterns of infection may pose to the UAE within the context of the changing social dynamics of the country. The Ministry of Health, in coordination with WHO and the Executive Office of the GCC, is engaged in continuous follow-up of developments in this field.

The National Disaster Life Support (NDLS) training programme addresses approaches to natural disasters, explosions, fires and public health emergencies resulting from disease outbreaks.

DISASTER TRAINING

The new National Disaster Life Support (NDLS) training programme features a comprehensive approach to dealing with natural disasters, explosions, fires and public health emergencies, resulting from disease outbreaks. The national programme in cooperation with the Emirates Centre for Strategic Studies and Research, Georgia University, and the American Medical Association (AMA) will train up to 3000 disaster managers, physicians, nurses, assistants, paramedics, emergency medical technicians, fire-fighters, police, and hospital administrators nationwide over a three-year period.

BLOOD TRANSFUSION SERVICES

An important factor in the control of disease and the long-term health of the population has been the creation of a reliable blood transfusion service. The UAE ceased importing blood in 1983 and has relied on local donors ever since. New laboratories costing Dh15 million have been established at the Department of Blood Transfusion and Research Services (DBTRS) based in Sharjah. The Department has the capacity to take blood from 20 donors every five minutes – a rate of extraction which can be increased to 40 in an emergency situation – and provides blood to public and private health institutions in the UAE. It collects in the region of 40,000 units in the UAE annually.

The UAE ceased importing blood in 1983 and has relied on local donors ever since.

www.uaeinteract.com/health

The Sharjah facility is one of only ten in the world to utilise gamma radiation for blood sterilisation procedures and it was the first in the Arab region to use the NAT procedure to screen for Aids and Hepatitis A, B and C. Meanwhile the UAE's first bone marrow transplant centre is being set up at DBTRS, following the establishment of the first umbilical chord blood bank in the region in 2005. The services are available to both private and public sector hospitals in the country. A human genome map of the Arab population is also on the cards, with the region's first DNA bank at DBTRS commencing collection of gene samples from September 2006.

The UAE's first bone marrow transplant centre is being set up at DBTRS, following the establishment of the first umbilical chord blood bank in the region in 2005.

It is not surprising given the innovative services available at the Sharjah-based department and branches that in 2006 the World Health Organisation (WHO) chose the UAE as the regional centre for blood transfusion services in the Middle East. The Director of the Blood Transfusion and Research Services Department was also elected as Director for the East Mediterranean region, for 2006/10. The blood transfusion centre will be responsible for coordinating all activities, seminars and workshops for other bank centres in 26 countries in the region, including Iran, Pakistan, Afghanistan, Turkey and Cyprus.

ALTERNATIVE MEDICINE

A federal law was passed in 1995 to regulate the sale and use of herbal medicines. But with the rapid increase in popularity of herbal remedies in the UAE comprehensive regulation in the field of alternative medicine and the establishment of regional harmonisation of regulations and standards is of prime importance. To achieve this objective, the MoH has set up an Office of Complementary and Alternative Medicine (OCAM) to draw up rules and conditions governing the licensing of complementary and alternative practitioners, and to evaluate alternative medicine degrees. Under new regulations, herbal mixtures being sold at herbal medical centres must be prescribed by doctors and registered by the MoH. Pharmacists and assistant pharmacists working in such centres must be licensed to practice by the Ministry.

The Zayed Complex for Herbal Research and Traditional Medicine was created in 1996. In addition to conducting research on herbs and plants (many of which occur in the UAE), the Complex treats patients suffering from chronic illnesses. In recognition of its success in producing, on a small scale, internationally standardised herbal medicines for the treatment of chronic diseases such as diabetes, hypertension, joint inflammation, and ulcers, WHO recognised the Complex as a regional centre for alternative medicine in the Middle East.

The Zayed Complex for Herbal Research and Traditional Medicines has been named by WHO as a regional centre for alternative medicine in the Middle East.

INTERNET LINKS

Amnesty for Illegal Immigrants:	www.uaeinteract.com/amnesty
Children:	www.uaeinteract.com/children
Civil defence:	www.uaeinteract.com/civildefence
Consumer protection:	www.uaeinteract.com/consumer
Crisis management:	www.uaeinteract.com/crisis
Disabled:	www.uaeinteract.com/disabled
Drugs:	www.uaeinteract.com/drugs
Education:	www.uaeinteract.com/uaeeducation
Elderly:	www.uaeinteract.com/elderly
Emirates Foundation:	www.uaeinteract.com/emiratesfoundation
Emiritisation:	www.uaeinteract.com/emiritisation
Employment:	www.uaeinteract.com/employment
Health:	www.uaeinteract.com/health
Holidays:	www.uaeinteract.com/holidays
Housing:	www.uaeinteract.com/housing
Human development:	www.uaeinteract.com/hdi
Human rights:	www.uaeinteract.com/humanrights
Immigration:	www.uaeinteract.com/immigration
Laws:	www.uaeinteract.com/laws
Local charities:	www.uaeinteract.com/charity
Marriage Fund:	www.uaeinteract.com/marriagefund
National Health Insurance:	www.uaeinteract.com/nhi
National Identity Card:	www.uaeinteract.com/idcard
Pension and social security:	www.uaeinteract.com/pension
Police Force:	www.uaeinteract.com/police
Population:	www.uaeinteract.com/population
Real estate:	www.uaeinteract.com/realestate
Religion:	www.uaeinteract.com/religion
Social studies:	www.uaeinteract.com/socialstudies
Social welfare:	www.uaeinteract.com/welfare
Students:	www.uaeinteract.com/students
Trade Unions:	www.uaeinteract.com/tradeunions
Traffic and licensing:	www.uaeinteract.com/traffic
Women:	www.uaeinteract.com/women
Youth:	www.uaeinteract.com/youth

Reorganisation of ministries in 2006 led to the closure of the Ministry of Information and Culture and establishment of a National Media Council and a new Ministry of Culture, Youth and Community Development.

The UAE printing industry is growing at 15 to 20 per cent annually with total worth estimated between Dh8 to Dh10 billion.

MEDIA AND CULTURE

MEDIA

A reorganisation of government ministries in 2006 led to the closure of the Ministry of Information and Culture and to establishment of a National Media Council and a new Ministry of Culture, Youth and Community Development. The core media bodies of the old Ministry of Information and Culture, in the form of the Press and Publications Department, the External Information Department, Emirates News Agency (WAM) were placed under the authority of the National Media Council. The aim of these moves was to streamline the different and varied functions that previously fell under the remit of a single ministry. The Government was also of the opinion that the culture and media fields are both in the process of rapid development and it was necessary to take a fresh look at how government support could be most effectively structured.

NATIONAL MEDIA COUNCIL

The National Media Council has been established to oversee media development in the UAE and to support certain media initiatives. It has the power to cancel or suspend media licences if there are violations of conditions attached to these. All jurisdictions and responsibilities concerning media affairs that previously fell under the Ministry of Information and Culture were transferred to the Media Council. In July 2006 the Council of Ministers appointed Sheikh Abdullah bin Zayed Al Nahyan, Minister of Foreign Affairs, as Chairman of the Council and Mohammed Abdullah Al Gergawi, Minister of State for Cabinet Affairs, as his deputy.

The National Media Council has been established to oversee media development in the UAE and to support certain media initiatives.

EMIRATES MEDIA

Emirates Media Inc. (EMI) is a multimedia pioneer in the Arab region. Its origins in television, radio and press go back as far as 1969 with the establishment of *Al Ittihad* newspaper, UAE

Television from Abu Dhabi and Abu Dhabi Radio. Television and radio were incorporated under Emirates Broadcasting Corporation (EBC) in 1996 and three years later EBC was reincorporated as EMI, with its television and radio services expanded to include *Al Ittihad* newspaper, *Zahrat Al Khaleej* and *Majed* magazines. Today, EMI's diversity provides a unique advantage as it continues to reach millions of Arabs from around the world. The broadcasting group's coverage extends from the Middle East to Europe as well as North America, whilst its operations currently include three satellite television channels (Abu Dhabi TV, Abu Dhabi Sports Channel and the Emirates Channel); six radio channels (Abu Dhabi Radio, Emirates FM, Holy Qur'an; Sound of Music, English FM1 and FM2) as well as the above mentioned publications. Additionally, EMI's electronic services include a number of internet websites with more planned. Its *Al Ittihad* newspaper website (www.alittihad.ae) as well as its main corporate website (www.emi.ae) were among the first Arabic websites in the region and EMI's new media division has considerable in-house capabilities in the IT field.

Emirates Media's operations currently include three satellite television channels (Abu Dhabi TV, Abu Dhabi Sports Channel and the Emirates Channel); and six radio channels (Abu Dhabi Radio, Emirates FM, Holy Qur'an, Sound of Music, English FM1 and FM2).

EMI's satellite coverage of the latest events around the world attracts international recognition and acclaim. Since its inauguration, EMI has been the recipient of many prestigious accolades for all sectors of their operations.

With so many people commuting between work and home in their cars, radio is a very important element of the UAE's media mix. Emirates Radio Network, owned by EMI, recently assigned the running of ERN's existing English-language channels Radio 1 and Radio 2 to Al Nisr Publishing LLC, which has also been engaged in launching a new English-language station. The management deal covers the editorial and advertising operations of Radio 1, Radio 2 and the new station, to be called Radio 3. Radio 1 and Radio 2 will be revamped as part of the agreement, which does not cover ERN's Arabic stations.

DUBAI MEDIA INC.

Dubai Media Inc. (DMI) is a semi-government company that owns and runs the major TV and radio stations in the Emirate of Dubai.

Formed in 2003 to replace the Dubai Department of Media, DMI currently runs four TV channels including Dubai TV, ONE TV, Sama Dubai and Dubai Sports. Keen to support excellence, quality and reliability in the UAE's emerging media sector, DMI recently introduced a media ethics charter as a step towards corporate commitment to achieve the highest standards of transparency, credibility and objectivity. Speaking at the launch of the charter, DMI's chief executive commented that the ethics criteria are focused on the customer both in terms of understanding their needs and in building a larger customer base. This is being achieved through high quality programming and marketing and the charter provides a framework to promote innovation and development of new services across all media platforms. The charter also calls on all DMI employees to conduct DMI business with honesty, integrity and in a professional manner and to avoid actual or potential conflicts of interest in transactions on behalf of DMI.

Emirates News Agency transmits news on national, regional and Arab affairs and is a widely respected source for international media.

EMIRATES NEWS AGENCY

The Emirates News Agency (WAM or Wakalat Anba'a al-Emarat) has been in operation since 1976. It transmits news on national, regional and Arab affairs and is a widely respected source for international media. WAM is a member of the Group of Arab Gulf Cooperation Council news agencies, the Federation of Arab News Agencies (FANA), the Islamic News Agencies Union, the Pool of Non-Aligned News Agencies and of the Organisation of Asia-Pacific News Agencies (OANA). Its headquarters is in the UAE capital, Abu Dhabi, with other offices in Dubai, Sharjah, Ajman, Umm al-Qaiwain, Ra's al-Khaimah, Fujairah, Al Ain and Madinat Zayed. Since mid-2006 the news agency is under the authority of the National Media Council.

WAM maintains a team of around 25 reporters outside the UAE, with offices in the Arab cities of Cairo, Beirut, Rabat, Riyadh, Damascus, Sanaa, Algiers, Jerusalem, Gaza, Khartoum, Amman, Baghdad and Tunis. Other offices and reporters are located in London, Paris, Brussels, Geneva, Moscow, Washington, New York, Tehran, Islamabad, New Delhi, Istanbul and Canberra. The Agency also operates a website (www.wam.ae) with services in both Arabic and English.

www.uaeinteract.com/wam

Since it was established, WAM has kept abreast of changes in technology and now distributes its news and picture services by satellite and internet, both locally and internationally. Over 90 per cent of its photographs are available in digital format, which has helped both to expedite performance and to cut costs.

WAM provides daily news coverage of official and other events throughout the country and is one of the key sources of information for all media establishments in the Emirates. It provides coverage of around 85 to 90 per cent of official activities, as well as the activities of official delegations abroad. WAM also plays an important role in documenting development in the country, and in providing information to researchers and others.

WAM receives the transmissions of 30 Arab, Gulf and international news agencies and has co-operation and news exchange agreements with 20 Arab, Asian and international news agencies.

WAM receives transmissions from 30 Arab, Gulf and international news agencies and has cooperation and news exchange agreements with 20 Arab, Asian and international news agencies, part of an effort to strengthen collaboration between the media of the UAE and other countries.

Meanwhile WAM presently transmits its daily news service to more than 3000 newspapers, TV and radio broadcast stations around the world via a central news portal run by IPS. The portal relays WAM news in English, Spanish, French, Portuguese and Swahili languages to over 1000 newspapers and 2000 broadcast stations worldwide. A weekly UAE news digest in Japanese has recently been added to the agency's news services. The IPS news portal is www.ipsnews.net, while WAM's daily English news as well as selected news service in Spanish, Portuguese, Swahili and Japanese languages are relayed over the internet.

ANALOGUE TO DIGITAL

The Telecommunications Regulatory Authority (TRA) acquired rights to 225 digital channels at the 2006 ITU Regional Radio Communication Conference (RRC) held in Geneva from 15 May to 16 June 2006. The Conference was focused on establishing the technical foundation for the planning of digital terrestrial broadcasting of television and radio services for Europe, Africa, the Middle East and Islamic Republic of Iran. The 2006 conference rescheduled digital broadcasting channels in the 174–230 MHz and 470–862 MHz frequency bands to pave the way for digital channel growth.

Digital broadcasting is roughly six times more efficient than analogue, allowing more channels to be carried across fewer airwaves. Digital terrestrial television broadcasting offers the advantage of better signal quality with higher throughput resulting in more channels. In conjunction with the scheduled worldwide transition to digital broadcasting in 2009, the Authority is aiming to further its scope of service delivery by utilising the opportunities offered by the new paradigm.

RADIO STATIONS

The UAE has over 20 radio stations – more than any other country in the Arab world. In addition to the channels mentioned above, owned by EMI, some of which are operated in cooperation with Al Nisr, there are radio stations based in Dubai, Umm al-Qaiwain and Ajman. And not all of the UAE's radio stations are aimed at national listeners.

Channel 4 Radio Network, headquartered in Ajman, commenced transmissions in mid-2006 from the first Arabic music-based radio station in Iraq, 98.8 FM Channel 4 Radio Network, which is part of a joint venture that obtained an Iraqi broadcasting licence. The UAE company will manage the operations of the radio station, which will initially cover a population of 8 million within a 100-kilometre radius of Baghdad. In time, the promoters expect to cover the whole of Iraq. A similar station, concentrating on music for Arab audiences, was also opened in Khartoum, Sudan.

Competition among radio broadcasters is very healthy and quality has improved as a result of this. Emirates Media broadcasts seven channels and is the biggest radio broadcaster in the UAE, but other stations are also making an impact on the air waves. Arabian Radio Network (ARN) is a 'young kid on the block', but one that is proving to be a fast learner. Like Emirates Media, ARN addresses the interests of various audiences, communities and cultures, through genre-specific programming.

Competition among radio broadcasters is very healthy and quality has improved as a result of this. Emirates Media broadcasts seven channels and is the biggest radio broadcaster in the UAE, but other stations are also making an impact on the air waves.

www.uaeinteract.com/radio_tv

More than 40 television stations broadcast from the UAE.

ARN started Al Arabiya 98.9 FM, a round-the clock Arabic music and news station, in 2001. Soon afterwards, the network launched an English Radio Service, Free FM (96.7 FM) and City FM (101.6). In January 2003 the network launched Al Khaleejiya, thus creating a new platform for Khaleeji (Arabian Gulf) music and giving it a wider reach reflective of the UAE's inherent roots and traditions. HIT 96.7 FM followed and was designed to serve the interest of the largest expatriate community in the Gulf, the Malyalees.

The broadcasting field is one where technologies are constantly changing and improving. Various strategic alliances ensure that UAE stations keep abreast of these developments. ARN recently created a strategic tie-up with KLOTZ, the leading Radio System, to enhance ARN's hardware solutions.

TELEVISION STATIONS

More than 40 television stations broadcast from the UAE (see panel). Once again Emirates Media is a dominant force in the country's broadcasting profile with three major satellite channels in operation.

Dubai's well known CH33 was closed down at the end of 2004 and was replaced by 'One TV', a new channel with a new look and a new line-up of Western-style programming. With 27 movies a week and some of the biggest box office titles, such as Harry Potter, The Matrix, Lord of the Rings, Austin Powers, Rush Hour and The X-Men, One TV is unashamedly popular in its approach and is focused on providing entertainment.

The international news channel CNN has offices in Dubai Media City where it is equipped to produce local reports and to provide services for its regional reporters. CNN also produces its Arabic website (www.cnnarabic.com) at its DMC offices.

PRINTING, PUBLISHING AND ADVERTISING

The UAE printing industry is growing at 15 to 20 per cent annually with total worth estimated between Dh8 to Dh10 billion. Approximately 500 printing presses are operating in the country, many of which are expanding due to the high proliferation of local and foreign publications. The UAE is the regional hub for the publishing, printing and advertising industries and is expected to receive the largest single share of the estimated US$1.7 trillion worth of business that is predicted will be generated in this sector in the Middle East by 2008.

Dubai Media City has attracted many major international media companies and the number of partners in DMC increased by 20 per cent from 880 in 2004 to approximately 1077 in 2005, with a considerable number of companies on the waiting list to enter the zone. There are currently eight media segments in the DMC, of which marketing, broadcasting and publishing have been experiencing the most rapid development.

Over US$900 million was spent on advertising in the UAE in 2005, up from just under US$700 million in 2004. Advertising spend in the UAE's print media rose by 70.43 per cent to reach Dh2.15 billon (US$588 million) in 2005, compared to Dh1.26 billion (US$345 million) the previous year. The main advertising groups were the car trade, banking, telecommunications and real estate sectors. Mobile handset maker Nokia and real estate major Emaar Properties jointly topped the list in 2005 with nearly US$8 million in annual advertisement spending, followed by Dubai Shopping Festival and Damas Group, which spent about US$6.7 million and US$5.8 million annually respectively.

Advertising expenditure in the Gulf has been growing at 15 per cent per year and is expected to reach US$5 billion in 2006. The UAE has about 400 advertising agencies, but 90 per cent of the business is controlled by the top 20 companies, including the world's leading names.

The UAE is the regional hub for the publishing, printing and advertising industries.

INTELLECTUAL PROPERTY RIGHTS

According to the Business Software Alliance (BSA), software piracy levels in the Middle East declined in 2005, and the UAE led the way with the lowest piracy rate in the region. In fact, the UAE has posted the lowest piracy rate in the region for the past ten years, and is the only Middle East entry in the worldwide list of 20 nations with the lowest piracy rates. At 34 per cent, the UAE's piracy level is lower than that of several European countries, such as France, Italy, Spain, Portugal, Greece and Ireland, and is comparable to the piracy rates of the United Kingdom (27 per cent), the Netherlands (30 per cent) and Australia (31 per cent).

www.uaeinteract.com/copyright

Not satisfied with this situation, the UAE authorities have stepped up efforts to further reduce software piracy levels in the country and have reinforced their association with BSA. Proposed measures include organising more awareness campaigns to create better understanding of the detrimental impact of software piracy, and ensuring rigorous enforcement of IPR and copyright laws.

A study on this subject pointed out that by bringing piracy down in the UAE by ten percentage points, the country could generate more than 667 new jobs and result in an additional US$357 million in contributions to the UAE's GDP. With the help of a ten-point reduction in its 34 per cent software piracy rate, the IT sector could grow to nearly US$2.3 billion by 2009, creating new business opportunities for entrepreneurs and new jobs possibilities for employees.

MEDIA ZONES

The UAE's first media zones were Internet City and Media City in Dubai. They have been a resounding success, so much so that demand for space in the free zones exceeds the available places. Construction has begun on the International Media Production Zone (IMPZ) in which investment in the first phase will touch Dh1 billion (US$272 million). The 4-million-square-metre area will cater to the printing, packaging and publishing sectors and is due to be completed in 2007. Investment in the second phase, which comprises mainly offices, will approach Dh700 million (US$190 million). Printing and packaging companies within the zone are expected to invest Dh1.5 billion (US$408 billion) in IMPZ as they prepare to move in.

PUBLICATIONS

The UAE Government supports the production of a number of special books each year. In addition to publications prepared by individual ministries, dealing with matters of special interest, the *UAE Yearbook* is an annual publication that is now produced in cooperation with the National Media Council. This unique series, of which the present volume forms a part, is published in Arabic, English, and French. The book covers a wide range of topics on the United Arab Emirates and seeks to focus attention on developments over the previous 12 months. The *UAE Yearbook* is accompanied by a DVD-rom containing a range of media resources on the country, in addition to several e-books.

UAEINTERACT

The website www.uaeinteract.com provides daily updates of news on the United Arab Emirates in English and provides links to many other information sources on the UAE. In operation since the dawn of the 'Internet Age' in 1997, the website stores all news stories, photographs and other data in an archive that is freely available to users and which offers several search options. It is of particular help to researchers following any particular aspect of the UAE's recent development. The user base of UAEINTERACT has been steadily increasing year by year. Preliminary results indicate that the 2006 figures were 2.6 million visitors creating 64.8 million hits compared to 1.9 million visitors and 51 million hits in 2005, a growth rate of 37 per cent for visitors and 27 per cent for hits. The number of page views also climbed in 2006, to reach around 8.4 million compared with 6.7 million in 2005, a growth rate of approximately 25 per cent. This *Yearbook* identifies web pages on UAEINTERACT where regular updates can be found throughout the year and the two media products are thus linked.

UAE Interact is one of the top websites on the country with over 2.6 million individual visitors per year making over 64 million 'hits' on the site.

www.uaeinteract.com/uaeinteract

CULTURE

Culture and heritage are crucially important aspects on the UAE Government's list of development priorities. Since it is a relatively young country with a burgeoning youthful population, its older generation is deeply concerned that the strengths of character and identity that were nurtured by the lifestyle, customs and traditions of the past could be lost as a result of a new affluence and the effects of globalisation. There is good cause for this concern, especially with the pervading influence of satellite television and the internet, but there is also considerable cause for optimism: the context may have altered but core values have been preserved. As a visit to a local school or activity group is likely to confirm, cultural ethnicity is alive and well in terms of Emirati music, dance, poetry, story-telling, art and sports such as falconry, camel-racing, and sailing.

Part of the process has involved making sure that physical evidence of the UAE's rich heritage is not lost. Preservation of many of its unique archaeological and architectural sites and its manuscripts has been given top priority. Literature and customs are widely studied in schools, while museum displays, heritage villages and the rebuilding of vanished monuments (based on photographs, local memory and documentary evidence) have helped to create a context and feel for this cultural legacy. Recognising that preservation of culture is not just a social obligation but a commercial necessity, the UAE is also focused on ensuring that its cultural richness is given centre stage in shaping its modern development, particularly with regard to tourism.

More contemporary activities, such as theatre and film, also play important roles in nurturing the cultural side of Emirati society, feeding the soul and enhancing that widespread spirit of well-being that both Emiratis and expatriates enjoy in the UAE.

While much has been achieved in the past, the time was considered right to undergo a root and branch assessment of the Government's role in cultural enrichment. The newly established Ministry of Culture, Youth and Community Development clearly links three key areas of social development that feed into the UAE's cultural climate.

Preservation of many of the UAE's unique archaeological and architectural sites and its manuscripts has been given top priority.

The UAE is committed to safeguarding intangible cultural heritage and continues to sponsor the Sheikh Zayed Prize for Oral and Intangible Heritage of Humanity.

INTANGIBLE CULTURAL HERITAGE

In mid-2006, the UAE was elected as a member of UNESCO's Intergovernmental Committee for the Safeguarding of Intangible Cultural Heritage. The elections for the 18-member committee were held during the general assembly of the Convention for the Safeguarding of Intangible Cultural Heritage (CSICH). The UAE is committed to safeguarding intangible cultural heritage and continues to sponsor the Sheikh Zayed Prize for Oral and Intangible Heritage of Humanity. It has also been working on a bid to register falconry as a world heritage activity that is being practiced in over 70 countries. UNESCO set a series of conditions for registering falconry on the list, including creation of a national authority to put the Convention in place. The UAE met this condition by setting up the Abu Dhabi Culture and Heritage Authority (see below).

ABU DHABI CULTURE AND HERITAGE AUTHORITY

In October 2005 a law was passed in Abu Dhabi establishing Abu Dhabi Culture and Heritage Authority. Based in Abu Dhabi, the new Authority's remit is to sponsor intellectual and artistic activities as well as preserve the cultural heritage of the emirate.

This includes directly promoting Abu Dhabi's cultural heritage; drawing up and implementing cultural policies, plans and programmes; reviewing cultural heritage projects; and organising exhibitions and conferences on cultural heritage.

The Authority's jurisdiction also includes management of lectures, conferences and cultural shows, together with organising symposiums, seminars and intellectual, scientific and art gatherings; publishing studies and research; preserving archaeological and heritage buildings and historic sites; locating and excavating archaeological sites as well as issuing the necessary licences for such activities; restoring archaeological sites and heritage buildings; overseeing scientific and archaeological expeditions; establishing a department to manage, develop and supervise museums and other buildings where cultural artefacts are housed; recommending laws and regulations to protect, promote and preserve cultural heritage; providing support for training and educational activities in the Authority's field of specialisation, as well as developing resources in the fields of documentation, archiving and preservation of cultural heritage; taking legal action, where necessary, against the perpetrators of damage to the cultural heritage and antiquities of the emirate; providing support and assistance to bodies working in the field of the preservation and promotion of cultural heritage; exercising control over heritage and cultural property, whether public or private; managing the National Library so as to enrich and promote intellectual, artistic and scientific activities in Abu Dhabi; and recording national history through the collection of documents, the registering of the heritage of the emirate and through the publication of works in this field. The Authority is run by a Board of Directors, consisting of a chairman, a deputy chairman and seven members, who serve for a renewable term of five years. The Authority has its own budget, which is approved by the Executive Council.

GUGGENHEIM ABU DHABI

Abu Dhabi signed a Memorandum of Understanding (MOU) with the New York-based Guggenheim Foundation to establish a world-class museum devoted to modern and contemporary art. To be

The UAE supports a strong arts movement with a number of its artists gaining international reputations. This painting is by Abdul Qader Al Rayes.

called the Guggenheim Abu Dhabi (GAD), the museum, designed by internationally acclaimed architect Frank Gehry, will position the emirate as a leading international cultural destination. At 30,000 square metres, the Abu Dhabi museum will be the only Guggenheim museum in the region and will be larger than any existing Guggenheim worldwide. It is expected that the museum will be constructed within five years.

The museum will form its own major collection of contemporary art and will also exhibit masterpieces from the Guggenheim Foundation's global collections. It will be built in the Cultural District of Saadiyat Island, a natural island lying 500 metres off the UAE capital, which is being transformed into an international tourism destination. The Cultural District will also be home to a national museum, classical art museum, maritime museum, performing arts centre and an expansive arts centre park.

Abu Dhabi's Tourism Development & Investment Company (TDIC), which manages the Authority's tourism assets, will own the museum. The Guggenheim Foundation will establish and manage the museum's programme, which will include collection development, exhibitions and educational initiatives. Abu Dhabi's museum will join a highly exclusive Guggenheim museum network that currently includes New York and Las Vegas in the USA, Venice in Italy, Bilbao in Spain, and Berlin in Germany.

DUBAI OPERA HOUSE

A decision was finalised in late 2005 to construct an opera house, general museum and arts centre in Dubai. The three cultural landmarks are intended to be state-of-the art facilities for those with an interest in arts, culture and aesthetics. They will reflect the UAE's passion for peace and cultural interaction. The 280,000-square-metres opera house will be built on a man-made island in the middle of the Dubai Creek and it will have a capacity to accommodate 2500 people.

MUSEUMS

In addition to the large number of forts and heritage buildings that house museums, the UAE has a rich selection of purpose-

built, modern museum buildings dedicated to specific subject areas, such as the discovery of petroleum, archaeology, natural history, science, popular medicine, astronomy, numismatics, philately, Islam, traditional jewellery, policing and aviation.

Al Ain Museum, run by the Department of Antiquities and Tourism in Abu Dhabi's Eastern Region, now part of ADACH, has an extensive archaeological and ethnographical collection, including some spectacular second millennium gold pendants and an important coin collection. Finds from excavations at Umm al-Nar and Qattarah are displayed and the museum also houses a reconstruction of the Great Hili Tomb with its distinctive rock engravings. Reconstructions of a traditional *majlis* and other aspects of life in the pre-oil era are also very interesting.

Dubai is constructing an opera house, general museum and arts centre.

Sharjah is well known for its museums, heritage and environment centres, which include a number of world-class displays, not only of local interest but also dealing more broadly with the cultures and science of the Islamic world. Sharjah has now established a special department for museums as part of its ongoing effort to strengthen the emirate's role as a cultural tourism destination. The department's main task is to protect and promote museums in the emirate and foster a fertile environment to consolidate Sharjah's reputation as an attractive cultural heritage venue. The new

Dinosaur display at Sharjah Natural History Museum

department is authorised to initiate cooperation with prominent international museums and research centres and can hire experts and seek assistance from other local bodies to support its administrative and technical mission.

Sharjah's Planetarium specialises in astronomy and celestial navigation. Its Police Museum has a good collection of armaments, riot and combat gear and models of old walls and forts. Its Archaeological Museum is a modern, lively interactive museum tracing the history of Sharjah from ancient times. A gold halter found with a ritually slaughtered horse in a grave near Mleiha is particularly beautiful. The museum's library houses a range of archaeological and historical books, magazines, periodicals and specialised reports. The Science Museum has 50 excellent interactive exhibits covering physics, chemistry, biology and astronomy, whilst the Discovery Centre is the first interactive 'hands-on' children's museum in the UAE and a very popular venue.

Meanwhile the grounds of Sharjah Desert Park, 25 kilometres out of town at Junction 8 on the Sharjah–Dhaid Highway, contain the Natural History Museum, a Children's Farm, the Arabian Wildlife Centre and the Breeding Centre for Endangered Arabian Wildlife. The Natural History Museum opened in 1995 and was immediately very popular because of its state-of-the-art exhibits. Lively with light and sound effects as well as interactive video displays, the exhibits deal with local habitats, plant and animal life, geology and marine life. Outside are wildflower gardens as well as formal gardens. The Arabian Wildlife Centre is an impressive modern zoo that displays local wildlife in replicas of their natural habitats. Most of the displays can be viewed from inside an enormous climate-controlled building. Exhibits include a reptile house, a huge aviary with free-flying birds as well as rock-hopping hyrax, a night house with many desert mammals, an 'Ibex Mountain' overlooked by the restaurant, and a corridor with huge windows looking out onto enclosures for hamadryas baboons and large predators such as wolves, cheetahs and the Arabian leopard.

The Breeding Centre is focusing on the breeding of endangered Arabian species with the hope of re-introducing some of the rarer species into the wild. This is where, for the first time in the UAE,

Arabian leopards, endangered in the wild, have been successfully bred at the Arabian Wildlife Breeding Centre in Sharjah.

captive breeding of the Arabian leopard was achieved. For obvious reasons, this particular centre is not open to the public.

Over on the East Coast, at Kalba, an enclave of Sharjah, the former house of the local ruling family has been carefully restored, as has a rectangular Islamic fort nearby, while work is also under way on the restoration of a larger fortress at Khor Kalba that may rest on the site of a fort build by the Portuguese in the fifteenth century AD.

Dubai Municipality's old house was recently re-opened as a museum offering glimpses of local history. The re-opening took place after a renovation programme using traditional materials and methods. The two-storey building is located near the Deira Old Souk overlooking the Creek and was originally built in the mid-1950s with three shops in the ground floor. Later, another floor was added as a residence for visiting traders. Dubai Municipality, formerly a part of the Customs Department, moved to the building's first floor in 1957.

CULTURAL FOUNDATION

Situated in the centre of Abu Dhabi, the Cultural Foundation, now part of the Abu Dhabi Authority for Culture and Heritage (ADACH), is at the heart of the capital's cultural life, being used by young and

Book cases at the National Library

old, UAE citizens and expatriates alike. Surrounded by gardens and with an open courtyard with fountains, the main building is a dramatic white structure of arches and colonnades, within which are lecture halls, libraries and meeting rooms, as well as ample space on its three floors for displays and exhibitions.

Perhaps the most important part of the Cultural Foundation is the National Library, which has well over a million books, most in Arabic, although there are also collections in a variety of foreign languages. Most of these are available for consultation by the public, once a simple registration process has taken place, although some of the rarer items, including a fine collection of Qur'ans, can only be examined with special permission.

A dedicated children's area is particularly popular, while there are a number of special events arranged for children, especially during the school holidays. An open area occupies much of the ground floor, this being used on a regular basis for exhibitions, which include displays of old photographs of the Emirates, paintings, handicrafts, archaeological artefacts and a wide range of other items. There are also rooms on the first floor suitable for smaller events.

Along the corridors are a number of small cases displaying a range of items reflecting the UAE's culture and history. These include postage stamps, coinage used in the country before the UAE was established, silver bedouin jewellery, small carpets and rugs, highly decorated wooden doors and other items.

The two large theatres are used for a range of cultural activities, including classical music concerts, some staged by the Abu Dhabi Music Foundation, which brings top artists and orchestras from Europe and elsewhere to Abu Dhabi; film shows, including regular film seasons from individual countries or directors; plays and meetings held by external organisations. The Emirates Natural History Group, the UAE's oldest environmental non-governmental organisation, has held its open meetings in the Cultural Foundation on a twice-monthly basis for 20 years. Other voluntary groups also make use of the facilities, including a gardening group and chess enthusiasts, while the Foundation's small and tastefully designed restaurant has become a popular meeting place.

Next to the building, an open area is used each spring for the Abu Dhabi Book Fair. Staged in a large tented compound, this brings dozens of publishers from the UAE and from the rest of the Arab world, as well as from further afield, to promote their titles at specially discounted rates.

EMIRATES HERITAGE CLUB

Established in 1993, Emirates Heritage Club (EHC) has as its core objective the preservation and promotion of the country's heritage to the younger generation that would otherwise be unfamiliar with the customs and traditions of their ancestors. EHC organises heritage exhibitions, oversees heritage centres and collaborates with all other UAE institutions sharing the same interests. Activities organised by the Club for all age groups not only cover traditional sports such as camel racing, boat racing and falconry, and traditional skills like tent-building and coffee-making, but also contemporary sailing, equestrian, shooting and other sports. EHC is instrumental in organising competitive events in these fields, as well as youth camps on the island of Al Sammaliah, north-east of Abu Dhabi City.

Heritage research is conducted through its affiliate, the Zayed Centre for Heritage and History in Al Ain, and environmental research through the Department of Environmental Research (DER) on Al Sammaliah. DER is primarily concerned with coastal biodiversity, conservation and sustainable development of coastal habitats. EHC formed the Amateur Astronomers Group (AAG) in May 1998 to spread astronomy awareness among all categories of society. Another affiliate, Emirates Sailing Academy (ESA-ESS), was set up in July 2000.

THE EMIRATES CENTRE FOR STRATEGIC STUDIES AND RESEARCH

The ECSSR, founded in 1994, is an independent institution dedicated to the promotion of professional research and educational excellence in the UAE and the Gulf area. ECSSR serves as a focal point for scholarship on political, strategic, military, environmental, economic, and social issues pertinent to the UAE,

The main thrust of ECSSR's work lies in identifying and analysing issues of vital significance, predicting future trends and devising management strategies to cope with such issues.

the Gulf, and the greater Middle East through the sponsorship of research and studies conducted by scholars from around the globe. The core of its work lies in identifying and analysing issues of vital significance, predicting future trends and devising management strategies to cope with such issues. As well as maintaining and training its own staff of researchers, it hosts conferences, symposia, workshops and lecture series renowned for the eminence of the participants and the quality of their content and influence. Integral to the success of ECSSR's research programme are the annual *Trend Assessment Reports* prepared in the Centre's various units which, by providing a survey of major international and domestic developments and their possible implications, become a powerful tool in the task of prioritising the goals for the following year.

The ECSSR's publishing activities have made it a major source of specialised scholarly publications in the region. As well as publishing monographs in its *International Studies Series*, it also publishes the proceedings of conferences, symposia and lectures in *Emirates Occasional Papers* (an English series) and *Strategic Studies* (an Arabic series). In addition to these publications, ECSSR translates into Arabic works of importance to the Centre and its audience.

Recent publications include: *The Gulf Oil and Gas Sector: Potential and Constraints; Arab Media in the Information Age; Education Technologies and Their Impact on the Educational Process: A Case Study of the Faculty of Humanities and Social Sciences (FHSC), UAE University; Governance and Globalization: An Economic Perspective; In the Shadow of Just Wars: Violence, Politics and Humanitarian Action; NATO's Growing Role in the Greater Middle East; The Religious Right and US Middle East Policy;* and *The Role of Water Exports in Iranian Foreign Policy Towards the GCC states*.

RESTORED FORTS AND OTHER BUILDINGS

Abu Dhabi

Qasr al-Hosn, (often known as 'the Old Fort' or 'the White Fort.') was founded by Sheikh Shakhbut bin Dhiyab, Ruler of Abu Dhabi, in 1795 and is the oldest building on Abu Dhabi Island, although it has been much enlarged over the last couple of centuries. Residence

of the rulers of Abu Dhabi until the 1960s, it served for many years as the home of the government's Centre for Documentation and Research. Surrounded by palm trees, and with old cannon outside its well-fortified door, the Qasr al-Hosn is now scheduled to become a national museum.

Qasr al-Hosn, Abu Dhabi

Al Ain has more than its complement of impressive forts and heritage structures, including the Eastern Fort, located within the compound of Al Ain Museum; Murabba Fort, which used to be the police headquarters and a prison; and Jahili Fort, a large restored fort in the city centre that has a distinctive corner turret with four levels or terraces. Going back much further in time is a superb renovation of an important Umm al-Nar tomb from the third millennium BC at Hili Archaeological Park in Al Ain.

A recent agreement between UNESCO and Al Ain Economic Development and Tourism Promotion Authority, now replaced by the Abu Dhabi Tourism Authority (ADTA), has initiated a cooperative effort to protect the cultural and historical wealth of the city. The end-result, launched at a conference in Abu Dhabi in late 2005, is a cultural heritage strategy for the whole emirate, which is being implemented by ADACH and incorporates all

The restored Al Fahidi Fort in Dubai was originally the ruler's residence; it subsequently became an arsenal, then a jail, and is now a thriving interactive museum with a wide range of archaeological and ethnographic exhibits.

aspects of the emirate's rich heritage, both man-made and natural, with a view to sustainable development of its assets in harmony with the growing value of cultural tourism.

Dubai

At least three of Dubai's major historical sites, Shindagha, Bastakia and Hatta Heritage Village, are already under consideration by UNESCO.

Dubai announced plans to restore over 300 historic buildings in the emirate by 2010 as part of the government's architectural conservation plans. Where appropriate, buildings will be submitted for inclusion to UNESCO's approved list of heritage sites. At least three of Dubai's major historical sites, Shindagha, Bastakia and Hatta Heritage Village, are already under consideration by UNESCO. The Shindagha Heritage Area alone contains around 65 heritage sites. Al Bastakia Quarter has around 55 heritage sites, about half of which were restored by 2005. Amongst these buildings are Sheikh Saeed house – an elegant late nineteenth century, two-storey building of Arabic design, complete with four wind towers, housing a unique collection of rare coins, photographs, stamps and documents; Bait Al Wakeel – Dubai's first office building dating back to 1934 and now housing a museum devoted to Dubai's fishing and maritime traditions; and Al Ahmadiya School, Dubai's first regular school, established in 1912 and now a museum of education.

The restored Al Fahidi Fort in Dubai was originally the ruler's residence; it subsequently became an arsenal, then a jail, and is now a thriving interactive museum with a wide range of archaeological and ethnographic exhibits. The underground section of the museum houses lifelike exhibits of an ancient souq, a Qur'an school, typical Arabic households and an oasis. There is also a display of the desert by night with interesting local wildlife.

Historical buildings are major tourist attractions in Dubai and are also used for commercial purposes to generate some income and support the restoration work. A hotel is being run in one of the restored buildings, while others are used for restaurants and coffee shops. Some of the restored buildings have also been rented out for residential purposes.

SHARJAH

Sharjah's renovation and restoration of architecturally significant heritage buildings and an old souq in the Sharjah Arts Area and Sharjah Heritage Area have earned it international acclaim. Many of these fine buildings house art, Islamic and ethnographic museums, including the country's first national art gallery, and one is also home to The Emirates' Fine Arts Society. Nearby is Sharjah Fort or Al Husn. Built by Sheikh Sultan bin Saqr Al Qasimi in 1820, this carefully renovated fort was the residence of the ruling family for many years. It was torn down in 1969, but the present ruler, himself a prominent local historian, has restored it with the help of old photographs and documents, his own notes and the assistance of elderly residents. It now houses a museum with exhibits on pearl fishing, education, and trade, as well as jewellery, weapons and old photographs. Al Mahatah Fort at the old airport site right in the centre of Sharjah houses aviation memorabilia relating to the 1930s, 1940s and 1950s.

Sharjah's renovation and restoration of architecturally significant heritage buildings and an old souq in the Sharjah Arts Area and Sharjah Heritage Area have earned it international acclaim.

NORTHERN EMIRATES

The eighteenth century fort in Ajman switched in 1970 from being the ruler's palace and office to housing the local police force. In 1981, it changed function once again to become a museum housing an interesting collection of archaeological artefacts, manuscripts, old weapons and reconstructions of traditional life.

Another fort which reinvented itself as a police headquarters was that of Umm al-Qaiwain. This is one of the most atmospheric forts in the UAE, situated alongside Umm al-Qaiwain's creek, its main gates flanked by two impressive old cannons. Subsequently restored as a museum, the upper floor includes a high-ceilinged *majlis* (a meeting room and a place to receive guests) elegantly decorated with carved wooden balconies. The lower level is occupied by a cooking area and store rooms.

Situated behind the Police Headquarters on Al Hosn Road in the old town, the beautifully renovated Ra's al-Khaimah Fort, residence of the ruling family until the early 1960s, houses an intriguing collection of archaeological and ethnological artefacts, although plans are being drawn up for the construction of a purpose-built museum. An important series of surveys has been undertaken in Ra's al-Khaimah Emirate over the years, documenting mountain villages, towers, mosques, the old houses of the palm gardens of Al Nakheel and Shamal, and now the traditional buildings of Ra's al-Khaimah City. Archaeologists from the Ra's al-Khaimah National Museum are researching and cataloguing all traditional structures and the more important ones are being earmarked for restoration. Already, the museum has begun restoration of the atmospheric old souq area.

FUJAIRAH

The Emirate of Fujairah also has its fair share of historical buildings, particularly impressive forts and other defensive structures on the coast and traditional routes through the major wadis. Work by the Department of Archaeology and Heritage on restoration of Fujairah Castle, begun in the late 1990s, was completed in 2000, while many of the adjacent buildings, including walled courtyard-houses once occupied by members of the ruling family, have also been restored. The whole area is to be surrounded by a new wall, within which a number of new buildings will be constructed to act as a focus for the heritage of Fujairah. These new buildings are expected to include a three-storey museum, an amphitheatre, a souq, a mosque, a restaurant and a children's play area.

The Emirate of Fujairah has a wide range of historical buildings, particularly impressive forts and other defensive structures on the coast and traditional routes through the major wadis.

The Department recently completed the renovation of another major site at Awhala in southern Fujairah, where a Late Islamic fort sits on top of the foundations of a much larger Iron Age fortress. Work also commenced on restoration of the Late Islamic palace and adjacent buildings in Wadi Hayl, around 13 kilometres west of Fujairah City. Once the residence of a junior branch of the ruling family, this is one of the best-preserved sites of its type in the whole of the UAE.

INTERNET LINKS

Abu Dhabi Dramatic Society:	www.the-club.com
Advertising:	www.uaeinteract.com/advertising
Arts:	www.uaeinteract.com/arts
Breaking news:	www.uaeinteract.com/breakingnews
Copyright:	www.uaeinteract.com/copyright
Culture:	www.uaeinteract.com/uaeculture
Cultural Foundation, Abu Dhabi:	www.cultural.org.ae
Dubai Community Theatre & Arts Centre:	www.dubaitheatre.org
Dubai Drama Group:	www.dubaidramagroup.org
ECSSR:	www.ecssr.net.ae
Emirates Heritage Club	www.emirates-heritageclub.com
Emirates News Agency:	www.uaeinteract.com/wam
Falconry:	www.uaeinteract.com/falconry
Films:	www.uaeinteract.com/films
Media:	www.uaeinteract.com/media
Monuments:	www.uaeinteract.com/monuments
Public libraries:	www.uaeinteract.com/libraries
Publications:	www.uaeinteract.com/publications
Radio and television:	www.uaeinteract.com/radio_tv
Theatre:	www.uaeinteract.com/theatre
UAE Interact:	www.uaeinteract.com/uaeinteract

ENVIRONMENT & WILDLIFE

The UAE places a high priority on environment conservation. Abu Dhabi's Environment Agency is particularly effective in this regard.

433 species of wild birds have been recorded in the UAE. Of these about 100 breed within the country.

ENVIRONMENT

PROTECTION OF THE UAE'S NATURAL ENVIRONMENT, both on land and offshore, has long been a major focus of government activity, with the first laws to regulate hunting and to protect wildlife having been passed nearly 30 years ago.

REGULATORY BODIES

ENVIRONMENT AGENCY – ABU DHABI

Over the course of the last year, several major new initiatives have been undertaken by the country's leading environmental body, the Environment Agency – Abu Dhabi (EAD). EAD is the authority responsible for all environment and wildlife-related issues in the Emirate of Abu Dhabi. Its tasks include research into and protection of Abu Dhabi's natural habitats and wildlife, the drawing up and implementation of legislation on protecting the environment and wildife, both onshore and offshore and, through its Environment Protection Division (EPD), the issuing of permits for development projects, both governmental and private.

REGULATORY POWERS

This licensing function is of particular importance at a time when Abu Dhabi is engaged in an unprecedented programme of growth. EPD has shown, with some success, that it is not only determined to carry out its mandate but also that it has teeth, in terms of its regulatory powers, that it is ready and willing to use. Somewhat to the surprise of some developers, EPD has laid down strict guidelines on what can, and cannot, be done, requiring plans to be changed, where necessary, and insisting on very detailed baseline studies on the habitat and wildlife of areas destined for development, often also demanding that there is a continuing programme of monitoring and that plans for effective mitigation are drawn up and are put into effect. Only thus, government believes, will it be possible to ensure that the development programme is sustainable in terms of its environmental impact.

EAD's licensing function is of particular importance at a time when Abu Dhabi is engaged in an unprecedented programme of growth.

EAD has led a UAE-wide effort to ensure that the country is properly prepared for the possibility – however unlikely that may be – of the potentially fatal HSN1 strain of bird 'flu arriving in the country.

Another broad programme with which EAD has been actively involved over the last year has been the UAE-wide effort to ensure that the country is properly prepared for the possibility – however unlikely that may be – of the potentially fatal HSN1 strain of bird 'flu arriving in the country. From late 2005, EAD coordinated a regular programme of monitoring key sites for the country's wild bird population, both migrants and residents, working closely with other agencies and with the Emirates Bird Records Committee, a body of researchers in close touch with most of the country's active birdwatchers.

EAD has also acted as the secretariat for a special national emergency committee set up by the Cabinet to plan for any appearance of bird 'flu in the country. The committee brought together representatives from all sectors of government, including the health services, the police, the armed forces, the customs and airports authorities and others, and undertook several successful planning exercises. Fortunately, no cases of bird 'flu were reported, but the UAE now has an effective response system, in place for this, or any similar, environmental emergency.

Part of the process of regulating and protecting the UAE's environment, of course, involves the putting into place of appropriate legislation. Building on the general framework already laid down over the last few years, EAD, which is responsible for over 80 per cent of the land and marine territory of the UAE, has continued to promote the passing of new laws. Law No. 22 for 2005 regulates the hunting of wild animals, including mammals, reptiles and birds, identifying those species that are fully protected, while a by-law issued by the Agency also places tough new controls on grazing of domestic livestock, a step that was urgently required to prevent further degradation of the fragile desert habitat.

Meanwhile the work of the Environmental Agency – Abu Dhabi, in terms of researching and protecting the UAE's wildlife, has continued to yield good results. One major step forward during the year was the declaration of the Yasat Marine Protected Area, a 482-square-kilometre zone in western Abu Dhabi, encompassing four islands and ecologically-significant coral reefs.

Male houbara bustard in display plumage

Avian Research

As part of a programme of research into the country's bird populations, EAD launched in late 2005 a programme to ring and to equip with satellite transmitters some of the greater flamingos found at the EAD-managed Al Wathba Reserve, some 40 kilometres east of Abu Dhabi City. Results from the satellite tracking proved, for the first time, that there is a regular interchange between the flamingo populations found all the way along the UAE's Arabian Gulf coastline, emphasising the necessity for planning for their protection and conservation to adopt a broad approach covering many individual habitats, rather than a site-by-site approach. Two of the flamingos also migrated northwards to breeding sites in north-western Iran and the eastern shores of the Caspian Sea, showing that wildlife protection needs to adopt a regional as well as a national approach.

Results from the satellite tracking proved, for the first time, that there is a regular interchange between the flamingo populations found all the way along the UAE's Arabian Gulf coastline.

Two other bird research programmes have also yielded good results. Significant declines in the population of houbara bustards, the favoured quarry of the UAE's falconers, have been recorded in recent years in their main breeding territories in Central Asia. During 2006 EAD's National Avian Research Centre successfully bred nearly 500 houbara in a captive-breeding programme, and

Dugong feeding on seagrass bed

a release programme is being planned, with the eventual hope that houbara may breed once again in the Emirates. Studies of wild-caught houbara equipped with radio and satellite transmitters have also permitted the movements of the birds to be plotted, both on their wintering grounds in the western deserts of the UAE and also on their migration to and from Central Asia.

And, for the twelfth year, the annual Sheikh Zayed Falcon Release Programme saw saker and peregrine falcons being released back into the wild. The 2006 release programme, in the Chitral district of Pakistan, brought the number of birds released to over 1000, and satellite tracking of some of the birds has provided useful data on their movements and survival rates.

The bird research programmes have implications that stretch far beyond the United Arab Emirates and this was the case, too, with a major international conference organised and hosted by EAD on conservation of populations of dugongs, an endangered marine mammal, throughout the Indian Ocean, the Arabian Gulf and the Red Sea. The UAE has the second largest populations of dugongs in the world, and EAD will now be working with all other countries throughout the range of the species to prepare, and to implement, monitoring and protection programmes.

Coral Reefs

Another major research programme has also involved cross-border collaboration – a joint project undertaken with Qatar's Supreme Council for the Environment and Natural Resources to map and to study the health of the coral reefs in the waters of the UAE and Qatar. Undertaken with support from Abu Dhabi-based Dolphin Energy, which is building a Qatar–UAE gas pipeline, and with involvement both by the WorldWide Fund for Nature and top scientists from around the world, as well as the Emirates Wildlife Society, the programme is of importance because the coral reefs in the Arabian Gulf have suffered from die-backs in recent years that were thought to have been caused by peaks in water temperature, perhaps an effect of global warming. The research has shown, though, that most reefs are in good condition, and are recovering.

Coral grouper with cleaner shrimps

SOE Report

By the end of 2006, EAD expected to have completed and launched the first State of the Environment (SOE) report for the Emirate of Abu Dhabi. Prepared in collaboration with a number of other government and non-governmental bodies, the SOE has been drawn up as part of the Abu Dhabi Global Environmental Data Initiative (AGEDI), which was launched by the UAE Government in 2002 at the World Summit for Sustainable Development in Johannesburg, South Africa.

OTHER ORGANISATIONS

Elsewhere in the country, other work continues to record, identify and protect the UAE's environment and wildlife, both now under pressure, particularly in coastal regions, because of the extensive development programme.

At a federal level, the announcement of the new Cabinet in February 2006 saw the former Ministry of Agriculture and Fisheries being replaced by a new Ministry of Environment and Water, (MEW), bringing management of the UAE's rapidly depleting water resources into the portfolio. MEW has also taken over responsibility for the Federal Environment Agency, previously chaired by the

www.uaeinteract.com/marine

Sand gazelle on Sir Bani Yas island

Minister of Health. The new Ministry is responsible for representing the country internationally in terms of environmental conventions and agreements and for implementing environmental protection legislation at home.

This latter is done in close coordination with local environment departments or agencies in each emirate, these including both autonomous agencies and departments attached to Municipalities, as is, for example, the case in Dubai.

Second only to EAD in terms of the range of its activities, Sharjah's Environment and Protected Areas Authority (EPAA) undertakes a comprehensive and wide-ranging educational programme on environmental issues with local schools, and is also responsible for the Sharjah Desert Park and the adjacent Breeding Centre for Endangered Arabian Wildlife. This Centre houses a unique collection of Arabian mammals and reptiles and is widely recognised internationally as playing a significant role in ensuring the survival of the region's fauna. EPAA also works with other Sharjah government departments to protect key habitats within the emirate.

Sharjah's Environment and Protected Areas Authority (EPAA) undertakes a wide-ranging programme of education on environmental issues with local schools, and is also responsible for the Sharjah Desert Park and the adjacent Breeding Centre for Endangered Arabian Wildlife.

Another emirate to make significant steps recently to enhance the protection of its environment is Ra's al-Khaimah, whose Environmental Protection and Industrial Development Commission (EPIDC) has established a Wildlife and Protected Areas Division. Originally established to monitor the environmental impact of industrial development, EPIDC's new division, headed by a specialist in Arabian mammals who formerly worked on a conservation programme for the endangered Arabian leopard, has been charged with identifying areas of the emirate whose habitat, flora and fauna is suitable for long-term protection.

Dhub lizard in the UAE desert

NATURAL HISTORY

Study of the natural history of the UAE is pursued not only by both resident and visiting professional scientists but, increasingly, by a number of ardent and skilled amateurs, many of whom make important discoveries or observations and proceed to publish their findings. One refereed journal, that of the Emirates Natural History Group, *Tribulus,* published twice yearly, is now in its sixteenth successive year of publication and includes many accounts of this type. Some of the more interesting and surprising finds made over the past year are described here.

PLANTS

In February 2006 a group of birdwatchers looking for migrant birds at the newly-laid golf course at Al Maqam, near Al Ain, suspended their search temporarily when an orchid was found on one of the fairways. The UAE only has one native species of orchid, the helleborine *Epipactis veratrifolia*, but this was clearly different. Nor was it any of the other species known to be present in the rest of Arabia. A stroll around the course soon found there to be many hundreds, if not thousands, of specimens, all most delightfully fragrant. Identification was finally confirmed as being the field zeuxine or soldier's orchid *Zeuxine strateumatica*, a species which originates from Asia and which, over the past 70 years, has colonised various far-flung corners of the globe. While botanists in the UAE are used to finding accidentally introduced species, so-called 'aliens', at least on this occasion it was deemed to be an innocuous one, presumably having come in with imported grass seed.

Desert hyacinth

www.uaeinteract.com/environment

In contrast, and doubtless a natural occurrence, was a new record of a particular species of showy lichen, *Xanthoria parietina*, found growing in the desert near Jebel Ali on dwarf but mature ghaf trees *Prosopis cineraria*. The latter were no more than 1 metre high when over 10 metres is typical and were themselves of special interest.

REPTILES

A large skink, *Mabuya aurata,* new to the UAE, was found, not on the mainland as might have been expected, but on two neighbouring offshore islands, both over 60 kilometres out into the Arabian Gulf, namely Qarnein, better known for its internationally important seabird colonies, and nearby Arzanah. How these individuals colonised is unknown (although *Mabuya* is known to be a competent swimmer), but they are clearly recent arrivals, herpetological surveys having been conducted on Qarnein previously, with no sign of this conspicuous and readily identifiable diurnal species.

At least 54 species of terrestrial reptiles are found in the UAE. Research is continually adding new records to the list.

Another new discovery, albeit of a species that had most probably evaded detection all along, was of Blanford's fringe-toed lizard *Acanthodactylus blanfordii*, the sixth species of this genus known from the UAE. This species has a range across much of south-west Asia, but in Arabia had hitherto only been noted in northern Oman. In December 2005, however, it was recorded and photographed in a small area of sparsely vegetated beach dune at Khor Kalba, Sharjah, on the UAE's East Coast. Measures are to be introduced to conserve this outlying population, so far in its only known locality.

Sharp-eyed observers will notice in future natural history publications that one species has apparently disappeared, with another one appearing in its place. Following critical examination of the scales under the chin of what had been locally recognised as specimens of the highly venomous and typically aggressive species Burton's saw-scaled viper *Echis coloratus* (clearly not an occupation for the novice), the UAE form has been categorised as a separate species, *Echis omanensis*. The type locality for the newly described species is Wadi Siji, near Masafi in the UAE on the west side of the Hajar Mountains and the species is described as a regional endemic. Burton's saw-scaled viper and the new species are geographically isolated, the former being found in southern Arabia south of the Empty Quarter.

MAMMALS

A similar fate has befallen one species of mammal found in the UAE, this being the Libyan jird *Meriones lybicus*. Local specimens are now recognised as being a separate species, Arabian jird *Meriones arimalius*, the former taxon having been perpetuated in the literature as that present in the UAE until the trouble was taken to re-assess thoroughly the morphology and dentition of the animals present in Arabia.

The second item of mammalian interest, a truly noteworthy event in 2005, concerned the discovery of tracks, followed shortly afterwards by the sighting and trapping of a honey badger or ratel *Mellivora capensis* in the extreme west of Abu Dhabi, near Ruwais. At least three individuals were subsequently found to be living in one small area and the UAE's President, HH Sheikh Khalifa bin Zayed Al Nahyan, ordered these animals to receive strict protection. They had long been suspected of occurring, at least intermittently, but the Ruwais discovery constitutes the first confirmed presence of this fearless honey-eating carnivore in the UAE (interestingly, individuals also turned up recently in Qatar). The explorer, Sir Wilfred Thesiger, had reported seeing what he considered to be the species' tracks some 60 years earlier. It was a long wait, but finally worth it.

Turning to marine mammals, ADNOC geologists out on a weekend foray in early 2006 found the skeleton of a whale embedded in sediments some 4000 to 5000 years old, 10 kilometres inland of Abu Dhabi Island, the sediments being marine deposits from when the level of the Gulf was much higher than it is today. Preliminary excavation of the relatively well-preserved bones proved that they belonged to a blue whale Balaenoptera musculus. Detailed analysis, including comparison of the DNA with modern-day blue whales and pygmy blue whales (the form known off southern Arabia today), as well as radiocarbon-dating, is to be undertaken by EAD.

Arabian leopard and cub, born in the UAE

ADNOC geologists out on a weekend foray in early 2006 found the skeleton of a whale embedded in sediments some 4000 to 5000 years old 10 kilometres inland of Abu Dhabi Island.

Flamingos are winter visitors to the UAE that have been encouraged to breed as a result of environmental planning and conservation efforts.

BIRDS

Birds are arguably the best known of the all the animal groups and birdwatching is one of the top attractions for many UAE visitors. Surprises still come along and the UAE's checklist of birds keeps on increasing. Two recent additions, neither predicted nor predictable, were Northern raven *Corvus corax* and fan-tailed raven *Corvus rhipidurus*, taking the national total to 433 species by early 2006. The latter species was recorded by ecologists deep in the Abu Dhabi desert, remarkably some 1500 kilometres from its nearest breeding site in southern Oman; whereas the former, which toured Abu Dhabi City and island for two days, harried by the resident but non-native house crows and parakeets, had only to hop across the Gulf.

The Emirates Bird Records Committee, which maintains the UAE list and adjudicates on all submissions, was also pleased to assist the Environment Agency – Abu Dhabi, (EAD) in the all-important monitoring of waterbirds throughout the country through the year, as part of the national plan to detect rapidly any incidence of bird flu. In the event the UAE remained thankfully clear of any cases.

INSECTS

A detailed scientific study of the Wasit wetland in the city of Sharjah in both 2005 and 2006 also produced interesting results, with the biggest surprise being amongst the insects. Among many new finds were at least four species of soldierfly, representing a family of dipteran fly, Stratiomyidae, that was previously unrecorded in the Emirates.

Serendipity is, of course, always possible, with one find leading to another. Thus one local naturalist, informed of the presence of the new orchid at Al Maqam went there in search of them only to find a new species of damselfly for the UAE, *Ischnura senegalensis*. This delightful little damselfly was predicted as a likely colonist, if indeed not already present somewhere in the country undetected, and many thousand of individuals were estimated as being present around the water hazards on the self-same new golf course. Remarkably, the aquatic holly-leaved naiad, *Najas marina* was also present in abundance in the pond. This freshwater macrophyte appears, at best, to be highly localised in the UAE.

There are probably more than 5000 different species of insects in the UAE.

ECLECTIC MIX

The journal *Tribulus* carries contributions on an eclectic mix of natural history subjects that show the range of expertise amongst both resident and visiting scientists and amateur naturalists. A selection of subjects include description of the first breeding records of purple gallinule *Porphyrio porphyrio*; the occurrence of albino tadpoles of the Arabian toad *Bufo arabicus*; identification of landslide dams in the Hajar Mountains; description of aberrant butterflies; tail-signalling in semaphore geckos; pain-inhibiting pathways in the brain of the camel, and, since being first noticed in 1996, notes on the ecology of the somewhat bizarre Echiuran, or spoonworm, the common name for a little-known phylum of animals.

Even though much scientific research has now been undertaken in the UAE, both amateurs and professionals alike still regularly make valuable discoveries, as the summary above indicates. With phylogenetic analysis, the latest line of biological inquiry, now being applied, it seems probable that a number of new species, of marine gastropods, for example, will shortly be announced to add to the UAE's increasingly recognised and remarkable biodiversity.

INTERNET LINKS

Abu Dhabi Global Environment Initiative:	www.uaeinteract.com/agedi
Biological research:	www.uaeinteract.com/biology
Camel research:	www.uaeinteract.com/camel
CITES:	www.uaeinteract.com/cites
Conservation:	www.uaeinteract.com/conservation
Environment:	www.uaeinteract.com/environment
Geology:	www.uaeinteract.com/geology
Islands:	www.uaeinteract.com/islands
Marine and coastal:	www.uaeinteract.com/marine
Plants:	www.uaeinteract.com/plants
Solar energy:	www.uaeinteract.com/solar
Waste water management:	www.uaeinteract.com/wastewater
Waste:	www.uaeinteract.com/waste
Water:	www.uaeinteract.com/water
Weather:	www.uaeinteract.com/weather
Wildlife:	www.uaeinteract.com/wildlife

The UAE hosts many of the world's major events in a wide range of sports, from horse racing to motor racing, golf, tennis, football, rugby, cricket, sailing, powerboat racing and almost every other competitive sport.

Aside from the international circuit events, the UAE has a healthy indigenous sporting environment with the local community participating in a wide variety of clubs and establishments.

SPORTS

The UAE has already established itself well and truly on the international sporting stage, holding many of the world's major events in a wide range of sports, from horse racing to motor racing, golf, tennis, football, rugby, cricket, sailing, powerboat racing and almost every other competitive sport. These events not only attract large numbers of competing and sports enthusiasts from around the globe, they also see some of the country's own top sportsmen and women in action. Sports play an increasingly important role in the UAE's efforts to develop tourism, and facilities throughout the country are being upgraded or newly constructed. So much so that the country is bidding to host the 2016 Olympic Games and has already been awarded the tenth FINA World Swimming Championships in 2010.

As part of the Dh20.91 billion (US$5.7 billion) Dubailand project, developers are constructing a Dh7.34 billion (US$2 billion) Sports City due to open in 2007. Covering an area of 4.65 million square metres, Sports City will be an integrated purpose-built venue, incorporating a Manchester United soccer school – the first outside Europe – a championship golf course designed by Ernie Els, David Lyons tennis stadium, Butch Harmon golf academy and the International Cricket Council. The City will house four main stadiums with seating capacities ranging from 8000 to 25,000, to host major events in cricket, football, rugby, athletics and field hockey.

Aside from the international circuit events, the UAE has a healthy indigenous sporting environment with the local community participating in a wide variety of clubs and establishments. New sporting councils, such as the Abu Dhabi Sports Council, have been established to coordinate growth and development of local and national sports clubs, and the seven emirates regularly compete in national leagues and cups in a multiplicity of sports that are controlled by specialised governing bodies. Top sporting venues (both indoor and outdoor) and a favourable climate ensure that the activities continue throughout the winter season.

Sports play an increasingly important role in the UAE's efforts to develop tourism, and facilities throughout the country are being upgraded or newly constructed.

Ski-Dubai, situated inside Mall of the Emirates

With the Arabian Gulf on its western shores and the Indian Ocean along its eastern flanks, the UAE is particularly attractive for watersport fans. The emirates on the Gulf coast are blessed with long stretches of sandy beach where residents take part in sports such as sailing, jet-skiing, surfing, swimming and kitesurfing. Snorkelling and diving are hugely popular within the region. Many residents and visitors enjoy the UAE's East Coast, which also provides a wealth of exotic fish and coral. Popular locations for divers include 'Snoopy Island' and the area north of Dibba.

Residents are able to take full advantage of the country's parks and recreational grounds where football, basketball and cricket matches are a favourite pastime, while the desert and mountain areas outside the main cities provide rough, rugged terrain for more adventurous pursuits. It would be extremely difficult to pinpoint a sport that is not enjoyed in the UAE as there are always new centres, clubs and associations being established around the region.

SPORT SPONSORSHIP

Sport sponsorship, considered to be very effective brand advertising, has been used to great effect by UAE companies, led by Emirates airline, which signed its biggest-ever sponsorship deal in 2006. For an agreed investment of US$195 million (Dh716 million), the airline has become FIFA's official partner from 2007 to 2014. The move came on top of an existing 30 million euro (Dh135 million) deal between Emirates and FIFA to act as a sponsor of the 2006 FIFA World Cup. The new deal took Emirates' principal sports sponsorship portfolio to almost Dh1.6 billion.

Sheikh Saeed bin Maktoum bin Rashid Al Maktoum led the UAE team to win the gold medal in the skeet event at the Asian Shooting Championships in September 2006.

The deal is not only the biggest in Emirates' history but also the largest in the history of FIFA. With it Emirates became the sixth and the final FIFA partner, joining Adidas, Hyundai, Coca-Cola, Sony and Visa. It is in the top tier of the world football governing body's new sponsorship programme, which awards six bluechip corporations the highest level of affiliation to FIFA over an eight-year period. Emirates' passengers will also benefit as the airline has the exclusive right to broadcast matches of the 2010 and 2014 FIFA World Cups, either live or delayed, on its in-flight entertainment systems.

Emirates' other key sports sponsorships include the GB£100 million (Dh662.2 million) deal with Arsenal Football Club, which is also one of the biggest club sponsorship deals in English football history. Other smaller sponsorship deals include the Asian Football Confederation, which will run until 2008; a three-year sponsorship for the Franz Beckenbauer Foundation, a charity organisation; a multi-million pounds three-year deal with Referees, the Professional Game Match Official Limited (PGMOL), which Emirates announced in August 2004; and a three-year official partnership deal with Paris Saint Germain, the French football club.

Emirates also signed a multimillion-dollar sponsorship deal with Formula One motor racing team McLaren Mercedes. The metallic grey McLaren cars, sporting Emirates logos on orange backgrounds on the front wings and rear spoiler, have been prominent at Formula One Grand Prix events. Grand prix racing attracts millions of followers around the globe, providing Emirates with a great opportunity to further the airline's brand awareness internationally.

Etihad Airways also supports the promotion of local culture in the UAE and worldwide and from time to time sponsors cultural and sporting events that are consistent with its values of hospitality, team spirit and helping bring cultures together. As a general principle, it only considers projects that have more than a three-month lead time, are televised and involve a series of events. It provides a sponsorship application form on its website.

Arsenal's Thierry Henry chases the ball during their Premiership game against Middlesbrough at Emirates Stadium , in London, 9 September 2006.

Emirates' other key sports sponsorships include the GB£100 million (Dh662.2 million) deal with Arsenal Football Club, which is also one of the biggest club sponsorship deals in English football history.

FOOTBALL

Like any other sporting nation, the UAE has a huge interest in football. The UAE FA was first established in 1971 and since then has devoted its time and effort to promoting the game, organising youth programmes and improving the abilities of not only its players, but of the officials and coaches involved with its regional teams.

Al Ain won the 2006 President's Cup thanks to a goal by Ali Al Wahibi's in the seventy-ninth minute, beating Sharjah 2–1 in a thrilling final.

Beach Soccer's successful journey from the beaches of Brazil to the hearts of millions of fans all over the globe took another big step in May 2006 when one of the fastest growing professional

With sun, sea and sand in abundance, the UAE provides the perfect venue for Beach Soccer, which is now part of the FIFA family.

sports in the world came to UAE shores. Six Asian nations – Bahrain, China PR, Iran, Japan, Philippines and the United Arab Emirates competed at Jumeirah Beach Park for three slots in the FIFA Beach Soccer World Cup 2006 to be held on Copacabana Beach, Rio de Janeiro, from 2 to 12 November 2006. With sun, sea and sand in abundance, the UAE provides the perfect venue for the game, which has become even more popular since 2005, when beach soccer became a part of the FIFA family and the first FIFA Beach Soccer World Cup took place in Copacabana.

Ladies Soccer is also gaining in popularity. The Abu Dhabi Sports Club team represented the UAE in the Arab Ladies Soccer Championship 2006, meeting with early success with a decisive 5–1 win over the Sultanate of Oman team. Ten teams battled it out for a slice of the Dh555,000 (US$151,220) prize on offer in the First Arabian Women's Football Tournament organised by the Abu Dhabi Sports Club (ADSC) in association with the Armed Forces Officers' Club and UAE FA. In the end, Bahrain prevailed. But that didn't happen without the ADSC putting up an impressive fight. The ADSC team was formed in June 2005 and is trained by Egyptian coach Mohammad Al Rasheedi. The 20 girls are aged between 15 and 23 years, and all but two are UAE nationals. While the UAE is still in its teething stage of women's football compared to countries in Europe, the US and Asia who have women's teams, the tournament gives reason to believe that it will grow to international levels.

Martina Hingis of Switzerland returns a shot during her first round match against Sania Mirza of India at the Dubai Women's Championships on 21 February 2006 in Dubai.

CRICKET

The Zayed International Cricket Stadium was opened in April 2006 in Abu Dhabi. The event was marked by a match between India and Pakistan that was held in aid of earthquake victims in Pakistan and India. A total of Dh10 million (US$2.72 million) was handed to the two countries to assist in the humanitarian efforts resulting from the recent earthquake.

TENNIS

Rafael Nadal achieved a stunning come-from-behind victory over World No. 1 Roger Federer in an action-packed Dubai Duty Free Men's Open in March 2006. Federer, a three time winner in Dubai, could hardly have lost with a bigger bang, the eruption being caused by a feisty Nadal who won in three heart-stopping sets 2–6, 6–4, 6–4. About 7000 fans packed the Aviation Club stadium and generated a tremendous atmosphere fitting for the occasion.

Besides denying Federer a record fourth title, Nadal also managed to break the world number one's unbeaten streak of 29 matches in the Middle East. Federer had also gone into the Dubai final with a perfect 16–0 record for 2006, having won the Doha Open in Qatar and the Australian Open already.

Meanwhile Justinc Henin-Hardenne extended her impressive run in Dubai by clinching the third Dubai Duty Free Women's title

@ *www.uaeinteract.com/tennis*

The tennis court was temporarily flooded by unexpected rainfall during the 2006 Dubai Duty Free Open Tennis Tournament.

with an engrossing 7–5, 6–2 win over Maria Sharapova in the final at the Dubai Tennis Stadium in February 2006. Henin-Hardenne raised her game when needed to overcome a stiff challenge from a resurgent Sharapova to claim her second title of the season.

Plans to nurture a UAE champion are being supported by Tennis Emirates, the governing body for the sport in the UAE, which has established training programmes aimed at putting UAE players on the world map. In the next 10 to 15 years, the UAE hopes to develop players of international standard. Al Nasr tennis squad's victory in the International School Championship in France shows that there is real potential in this strategy. The Abu Dhabi International Tennis Complex, which is part of Zayed Sports City, holds an Annual Tennis Championship in March with the aim of seeking out both new and undernourished talent. Men's, women's, mixed and youth tournaments are held with prize money on offer.

CAMEL RACING

The inhabitants of the Gulf states have enjoyed a long and productive relationship with the camel, which is held in great admiration and respect. Formalising camel racing was one way of maintaining its central role in UAE life. The UAE now has no less than 15 race tracks across the seven emirates. Nad Al Sheba, 10 kilometres outside of Dubai, Al Wathba, 30 kilometres south-east of Abu Dhabi, and Al Ain track, which is 20 kilometres west of Al Ain, are all large, well-equipped camel tracks with high-tech facilities. Two smaller tracks are located in Sharjah, one in Ra's al-Khaimah and one in Umm al-Qaiwain. Others are spread throughout the desert areas.

Robot jockeys are controlled by their owners who communicate over a wireless network. Previously, a contesting camel had to carry the jockey, weighing at least 45 kilograms.

Through camel racing, the UAE has been able to maintain the symbolic significance of the camel and, by giving it structure, has developed it into a professional sport with significant prize money. Camel racing is also a big tourist attraction for those people who visit the UAE throughout the winter months. The race season runs from late October to early April with races taking place on Thursdays, Fridays and Saturday at 7.30 a.m., and on national holidays.

Even though camel racing has become a popular pastime in the UAE, it has not been without controversy. Particularly reprehensible were allegations that young expatriate jockeys from south Asia and Africa were being kidnapped or, indeed, sold by their parents, and smuggled into the country. In 2005 the UAE took measures to clarify the prohibition on underage jockeys and improve enforcement of the law. Anyone caught using a jockey under the age of 18 or a jockey that is less than 45 kilograms in weight faces a Dh50,000 (US13,620) fine or a three-year jail sentence, with the penalties being doubled in the case of repeated offences. Prior to the enactment, in a major step to provide protection and support to children involved in camel racing, the UAE Ministry of Interior and UNICEF signed an agreement under which the UAE provided US$2.7 million (Dh9.91 million) to help in the return and re-integration of child camel jockeys into their families and their home communities. In accordance with the agreement, a social support centre was established to provide protection and support for the ex-jockeys and assist in their repatriation.

Electronic, wireless controlled robot 'jockeys' are used in camel races.

The United Arab Emirates has now repatriated over 1000 children to their original countries. The children from Pakistan, Bangladesh, Sudan, Mauritania and Eritrea, returned home after undergoing a rehabilitation programme. Their places were taken by mechanical robo-jockeys that were introduced on a trial basis, bringing considerable weight savings. The robot jockeys are controlled by their owners who communicate over a wireless network. Previously, a contesting camel had to carry a jockey, weighing around 45 kilograms whereas the 4-kilogram robot jockeys enable the camels to achieve their maximum speeds.

The UAE's coordinated programme of banning child jockeys and rehabilitating the children involved drew praise from UNICEF, whose local representative described it as an exemplary model for other GCC states.

MOTORSPORTS

UAE Desert Challenge

This unique event was conceived by Mohammed bin Sulayem, whose motorsport career goes back to the early 1980s. Mohammed, who has a record 14 FIA titles to his name, is well qualified in his role having very considerable experience as a competitor and an

www.uaeinteract.com/camelracing

Seven times Middle East Rally Champion Mohammed bin Sulayem of the UAE celebrates with Michael Schumacher of Germany and Ferrari after winning the pole position in qualifying for the Bahrain Formula One Grand Prix on 11 March 2006.

organiser, together with unparalleled knowledge of the desert, local customs and protocol. The event now spans six days, starting with the Prologue, a spectator 'show' staged in Dubai, which serves as a qualifying stage, establishing the running order for the main event in the desert. It begins with a ceremonial start in Abu Dhabi and heads south into the desert for the first of five hard days of stages. The desert base, the 'Bivouac', is located at Moreeb Hill, the 60 degree slipface of which is used as a hill climb in a unique and rapidly developing niche sport. Although deep in the desert, communications are maintained for the media thanks to the generous support and expertise of Inmarsat.

Stephane Peterhansel and Cyril Despres completed a double French victory in the 2005 UAE Desert Challenge held in November, while Spanish rider Marc Coma was crowned world champion and Yahya Alheli grabbed a well-deserved podium finish for the UAE. At the end of a 2260-kilometre trail, Peterhansel scored his third car victory in the event in four years, reaching the finish in Dubai with his Mitsubishi Pajero/Montero Evolution a huge 3 hours 2 minutes clear of the second-placed BMW X5 of Spain's Jose Luis Monterde.

Again proving himself to be one of the top Arab cross country rallying specialists, Alheli took his ageing Chevrolet Pick-up to a fine third place. While he was 42 minutes further adrift of Monterde, he was almost 11 hours ahead of his nearest Arab challenger, team-mate Ahmed Bin Suqat in seventh place. Dominant again in the battle of the trucks, the Kamaz team celebrated a superb fourth place overall thanks to the combination of Russians Vladmir Chagin, Stanislav Konopko and Eduard Nokolaev.

Securing his fourth Desert Challenge win in four years, Despres won by 11 minutes 20 seconds from a jubilant Coma, who nursed his KTM through the event's final two stages, knowing that a last-day disaster could have seen the world title slip away,

Dubai Autodrome

A Dh16 billion (US$18 billion) development project, the Dubai Autodrome and Business Park is the first motorsports facility in the UAE that meets FIA standards. Situated 25 minutes outside

French driver Stephane Peterhansel is seen in action during the Prologue stage at the start of the UAE Desert Challenge rally for cross country.

of central Dubai, the 700-acre Autodrome offers a range of events, from local to world class. The track is one of the most modern and challenging in the world. At 5.39 kilometres in length, it has six different configurations – the club track, hill handling, international, Grand Prix, national and oval handling, three of which can run simultaneously. Facilities within the grounds are also of world class standard.

The Autodrome also houses a Kartdrome, with a 1.2 kilometre circuit that can be split into two. This has 17 test corners and can accommodate up to 40 cars at one time. The track has over 55 karts made to different specifications, ensuring that karting is on offer to sports fans of all ages. The Autodrome also runs a Race and Driving School for anyone who wishes to develop their driving skills and techniques. The Dubai Autodrome, part of the Dubai Sports City project, staged the LG Super Racing Weekend, which saw the final stages of the FIA GT Championships as well as the FIA European Touring Car Championships and the Formula Renault V Championships. The championships, in their third year, had already attracted a television audience of over 40 million people. The season runs from March to October and before Dubai, races had taken place in Belgium, Italy, France and Germany. The LG Super Racing Weekend at the Dubai Autodrome was the first to take place outside of Europe.

www.uaeinteract.com/motorsports

The FIA European Touring Car Championships, which changed its name to the FIA World Touring Car Championships in 2005, was brought to a close in Dubai. Street cars such as the Honda Civic, Peugeot 307 and Ford Focus, are souped-up and driven on a track. Going into the final round, Dirk Muller had a 12-point lead over Briton Andy Priaulx, with Jorg Muller trailing another five points, but it was Priaulx who somehow managed to bring the race around to his favour. In the FIA GT Championships, competitors took on a three-hour endurance race in road cars that had been adapted for the race circuit. Dubai was not to play host to the grand finale in this event as the season ended in Zhuhai, China. Drivers not only had to compete against each other, there was also the weather to contend with; the heat made for a tough penultimate round.

Formula X

As part of the European Formula X Sport Series, drivers voted to race at the new Dubai Autodrome instead of taking the challenge to Silverstone in the UK. In all, 15 drivers competed, seven of whom entered from the UAE.

Shown as a side event at the LG Super Racing Weekend, Formula X racing recently made its debut in the UAE. Currently big in the States, UK and Australia, Formula X enables amateurs to race competitively. For Dh200,000 (US$54,500) competitors can sign up for an entire season, or a smaller fee for a single race, and everything from the car to the mechanics to the transportation of the vehicle is covered. As part of the European Formula X Sport Series, drivers voted to race at the new Dubai Autodrome instead of taking the challenge to Silverstone in the UK. In all, 15 drivers competed, seven of whom entered from the UAE. In the first heat, Lebanese-born Christophe Hisette, who was competing for the UAE, came third, even though it was his first ever Formula X. In the second heat, another UAE resident, Dutchman Roy van der Weijden, also gained a pole position.

Quad Bike Race

Spirited quad bike riders dashed through the sandy track in Al Sa'ad desert on the first segment of the Red Bull Reach the Top competition. The two-day event was witnessed by hundreds of spectators sitting on the sand dunes surrounding the 140-metre high sandy hill with a 45 degrees face. Some 78 quad bikers were allowed to take part in the competition from the total 147 registered candidates in the four categories of the challenge. The picturesque venue, located some 30 kilometres away from downtown Al Ain in Al Sa'ad district, was glittering with floodlights.

Organised jointly by Red Bull, Abu Dhabi Tourism Authority, and Brown Cruzer3, the contest has two series of contests, including a Quad Bike Race and 4WD Hill Climbing Car Racing Competition. Ahmad Mohammad Al Shamsi was the fastest rider of the first class category at 6.659 seconds. Mohammad Nasser Al Mansouri, with 6.377 seconds, won the race in the open class category. The winner of the second class was Baali Jumah Al Qubaisi, (6.438 seconds) and the winner of the four stroke was Maktoum Salem Al Muhairi (7.869 seconds).

The Red Bull Reach the Top event was witnessed by hundreds of spectators sitting on the sand dunes surrounding a 140-metre high sandy hill with a 45 degrees face.

Other Motorsports

Qatar's Nassir Saleh Al Attiyah won the UAE International Rally 2006 title after a narrow win over UAE's Sheikh Khalid Al Qasimi, who ranked second. The three-day race was organised by the UAE Motor & Tourism Club. The race saw a fierce competition between Al Attiyah and Al Qasimi. The 564-kilometre rally started from the Hilton Al Ain with participants representing the UAE, Oman, Jordan, Britain, Saudi Arabia, USA, Lebanon, Bahrain, Ireland, Qatar and Germany.

GOLF

Immaculate greens, lush fairways, high-tech practice ranges and facility-driven clubhouses make the UAE a world-class destination for golfers (amateur and professional). Innovatively designed clubhouses are outstanding architectural landmarks in their own right, many of the designs being based on traditional aspects of UAE culture. At Abu Dhabi Golf Club, one of the emirate's distinctive golf courses, the clubhouse is in the shape of a falcon swooping down on a golf ball. Emirates Golf Club, although built from thoroughly modern materials such as white concrete and gleaming glass, has managed to create a series of cool, tent-like structures lying low to the ground, redolent of a vanished era. Meanwhile the clubhouse at Dubai Creek Golf and Yacht Club

Abu Dhabi Golf Club

www.uaeinteract.com/golf

The world's number one golfer Tiger Woods and his partner Mark O'Meara take part in the challenge match, two days before the start of the four-day 17th Dubai Desert Classic golf tournament.

evokes the gently billowing sails of a stately dhow and that at Jebel Ali Hotel and Golf Resort the prow of a ship overlooking the Arabian Gulf.

Creation of the Abu Dhabi Golf Championship, one of the most prestigious international sporting events ever staged in Abu Dhabi, constitutes a qualitative step in promoting Abu Dhabi as a top global leisure, business and sporting destination. It is a flagship event in Abu Dhabi's promotional activity and heralds a new era in the emirate's development as a venue for staging world class sports events. Golf tourism continues to grow rapidly around the world and this new event underlines Abu Dhabi's commitment to golf itself. The construction of new courses will be an important element in the emirate's strategy for the development and diversification of its tourism infrastructure in coming years.

The inaugural Abu Dhabi Golf Championship, held in January 2006, was won by 37-year-old American golfer Chris DiMarco, who clinched the US$333,330 first prize (out of a US$2 million prize pot) after a thrilling final day's play at the immaculately presented Abu Dhabi Golf Club. DiMarco carded a final round 67 for a 20 under-par total of 268 and a one-shot victory over the gallant Henrik Stenson, who pushed the American all the way to the final green. The Swede began the day with a one-shot lead, but his closing 69 saw him finish one shot behind the American with a 19 under-par total of 269. Four of the world's top 11 golfers competed at the event, which was watched by over 6000 golf fans. The championship counted for Ryder Cup points and all

The Abu Dhabi Golf Championship is one of the most prestigious international sporting events ever staged in Abu Dhabi.

European Tour members were keen to muster crucial points. It also kick-started what has become known as the 'Desert Swing' taking the players to Abu Dhabi, then Doha and finally back to the UAE for the Dubai Desert Classic.

The 2006 Dubai Desert Classic, now among the world's top events on the global golfing calendar, was fought out in cold, brutal but stirring fashion. But in the end it was Tiger Woods who clinched a thrilling shootout victory over defending champion Ernie Els to win the coveted trophy. Guided by his phenomenal ability and digging deep to find extra reserves of fortitude, Woods prevailed on the first extra hole after Els put his second shot into the lake protecting the eighteenth green. It was a finish that could not have been better scripted for a final day's play.

The playoff was enforced when both players finished on 19 under-par 269, Woods returning a 69 to three-time former champion Els' brilliant final-round 67. For the second tournament in succession in 2006 Woods found himself in a playoff. But just as he had done on at least 11 occasions in the past, he came through with flying colours.

Tiger Woods, Ernie Els, Vijay Singh and Colin Montgomerie are all designing new courses in the UAE.

Ian Poulter and Paul Casey of England, at the launch of their campaigns for inclusion in the Ryder Cup European team, give an impromptu golf lesson to Etihad passenger Khalid Al Shamsi of the UAE. They hit drives from the wing of an Etihad Boeing 767 on the runway at the Abu Dhabi International Airport.

RUGBY

In the UAE, rugby is played by both men and women and by junior age groups, with the majority of teams made up of expatriate players from New Zealand, South Africa, Australia and the UK. However, more and more nationals are coming through at the younger levels, where programmes are in place for the under 14s, 16s and 19s. Governed by the Arabian Gulf Rugby Football Union, teams from Dubai, Abu Dhabi, Sharjah, Ra's al-Khaimah, Bahrain, Muscat, Kuwait, Doha and Saudi Arabia battle it out each season in the hope of winning the Arabian Gulf League and Standard Chartered Arabian Gulf Cup. The Arabian Gulf also competes in international tournaments such as the IRB World 7s Series.

The Dubai Dragons retained their Arabian Gulf League title in 2006, to complete a trophy double after ending the season with a 100 per cent record. Dubai Exiles claimed second place by defeating

The Dubai Dragons retained their Arabian Gulf League title in 2006, to complete a trophy double after ending the season with a 100 per cent record.

Tom Varndell of England scores his second try as England defeats Fiji in the final of the Emirates IRB 7's at the Dubai Exiles Rugby Ground on 2 December 2005.

Abu Dhabi in their final game, finishing a point ahead of rivals Dubai Hurricanes in third position. Meanwhile. the Arabian Gulf Ladies team competed bravely at the Asian Championships in Uzbekistan but returned home without a victory.

The Arabian Gulf team suffered a 20–5 defeat in their Asia region World Cup qualifier against Korea in Al Ain in May 2006. The home side made a slow start against a side 20 places higher in the IRB world rankings, turning around 17 points to 0 down at the break, Korea then extending their lead with a penalty early in the second half. Despite pressure from Arabian Gulf, they only managed one try and it was Korea who were celebrating at the final whistle as they secured their passage to the third and final round of qualifying games for France 2007. The match attracted an estimated crowd of 1200 and was sponsored by the Abu Dhabi Tourism Authority.

WATERSPORTS

Sailing

For both nationals and expatriates, sailing plays a huge part in their weekend activities as excellent facilities in all the emirates, including Abu Dhabi International Marine Club (ADIMC), the Dubai Offshore Sailing Club (DOSC), Dubai International Marine Club (DIMC) and Jebel Ali Sailing Club (JASC), enable enthusiasts to take part in numerous activities and competitions. The UAE is able to offer year-round sailing due to its climate and, for a sport that has only officially been around since 2000, boasts a healthy racing season. Established in 1988, DIMC is the main driving force behind the growth of UAE watersports and was the first Arab organisation to be granted full membership of the *Union Internationale Motonautique* (UIM).

To promote the sport even further, the UAE opened Emirates Sailing School, which is attended by nationals who are eager to meet international standards and represent the UAE. Training covers all water sports but mainly focuses on attaining skills in Optimists, Lasers and Toppers. Currently, the UAE team regularly compete in international competitions in countries such as Bahrain, Qatar, Italy and the UK.

The Dubai Junior Regatta, held in January 2006, attracted 143 Optimist and Laser 4.7 competitors from 18 nations. The Dubai Match Race was launched at the same time as the regatta, which is organised by DIMC in conjunction with the UAE Marine Sports Federation and the ISAF.

Dhow Racing

Al Zeer, skippered by Mohammad Rashid Bin Shaheen, who has often been described as a 'sailor by day and fisherman by night', emerged the overall champion of the traditional dhow (60 feet or 18 metres) 2006 sailing series. *Dahees*, skippered by Khadem Rashid Al Muhairi, won a silver-plated dhow trophy and Dh200,000 (US$54,450) after finishing in second position, while *Gazi*, which had not performed very well through the season's three heats, was third overall. The Sir Bu Nuair races were first held in 1991

The UAE is able to offer year-round sailing due to its climate.

and start from Sir Bu Nuair Island, reliving the historic journey made by the pearl traders of old. Local knowledge and an ability to read the waves and wind shifts are crucial to success.

Jet Skis

A law on the licensing, renting and using of jet skis was issued in Abu Dhabi in early 2006. The law empowered the Transport Administration of the Abu Dhabi Department of Municipalities and Agriculture to coordinate efforts with the Abu Dhabi Tourism Authority to earmark areas allowed for use of jet skis. They are also to monitor the installations that are permitted to rent jet skis. According to the law, the Abu Dhabi Department of Planning and Economy is the sole authority authorised to issue licences to installations that wish to engage in the Jet Ski renting business in the emirate. Jet Ski owners are required to register their jet skis and apply for licences.

Maktoum Offshore Trophy

The 2006 Maktoum Sailing Trophy was collected by Kristian Tzanov, whose K1 Offshore Racing Team, sponsored by Pal Zileri, dominated the series. Tzanov and his crew won each of the three remaining races of the fourth and final round at Dubai International Marine Club to complete the series with a comfortable winning margin over 2005 champions, Horizon FCB. The series is being given a new ten-day format for 2007 in a deliberate move by DIMC to attract more overseas competitors and usher in a new level of competitive fleet racing in the Gulf. Entrants for the event were a mix of racing yachts and cruisers, with a handicap system in place to balance out the individual boat capabilities. Crews of international and national level battled it out over a course of 'around the marks' style short races and the 365-nautical mile Dubai to Muscat race.

Just as dominant in the 2006 Class 2 series, Gill Smith took *Blitzem* to the title for the smaller boats, taking two out of three race wins on the day to complete an almost flawless series.

Competitor in the Offshore Powerboat Challenge

Powerboat Racing

First appearing on the Arabian shores in 1989 when the region's initial race took place off the coast of Mina Seyahi, the UAE has since held the UIM Class 1 World Powerboat Championships a staggering seven times. The UAE powerboat Victory team is classed as the most successful in the history of UIM World Championships, with driving legend Ali Nasser himself picking up 14 world titles in 13 years.

UAE's Rashid Al Merri and co-pilot Salem Al Hamly, on board the boat *Al Masoud*, emerged winners of the first round of the GCC Championship for Offshore Powerboats Class III in the Abu Dhabi Grand Prix in January 2006. The race, organised by the Abu Dhabi International Marine Sports Club (ADIMSC), was delayed for 24 hours because of the strong winds. Al Merri led the race from the start, Amdid was close behind and Al Hamly followed third at the early stage of the competition. Al Hamly overtook Amdid in the third lap of the race, which was held over six laps and represented a stronger challenge to the leaders who were successful to end the race in first place.

The UAE powerboat Victory team is classed as the most successful in the history of UIM World Championships, with driving legend Ali Nasser himself picking up 14 world titles in 13 years.

Success came back to the Victory Team at the closely-contested British Grand Prix, the fifth round of the World Powerboating Championship, at Plymouth in August 2006. Victory 77's first place represented their maiden win of the season, and one that propelled them to the second place in the world championship standings. Victory 77's triumph capped a stunning weekend for the Dubai-based team after Victory 7 took the third spot.

Swimming

Semi-Olympic swimming pools are under construction in four Dubai sports clubs at a cost of Dh47 million (US$12.80 million). The clubs are Al Ahli, Al Wasl, Shabab and Al Nasr and the pools are expected to be ready by August 2007. The project includes a comprehensive swim-training facility in each of the four clubs, comprising a semi-Olympic swimming pool with a total area of 312.5 square-metres, a stadium with a capacity of 340 people, health club, cafeteria, changing rooms, toilets and administrative offices. The buildings are to be centrally air-conditioned and fitted with state-of-the-art water treatment systems and electronic score boards — all in line with international standards set by authorised sports bodies.

These and other initiatives helped Dubai its bid to host the tenth FINA World Swimming Championships in 2010. The 25-metre world championship is held every two years and attracts the world's best swimmers in all disciplines who compete in a ten-lane pool.

EQUESTRIAN SPORTS

Emirates Racing Association is the internationally recognised body overseeing horse racing in the UAE, overlooking rules and regulations, registration of horses and the licensing of trainers, jockeys and officials. Races of thoroughbreds and the legendary purebred Arabians take place in some of the region's top equestrian clubs, including Abu Dhabi Equestrian Club, Ghantoot Racing and Polo Club and Nad Al Sheba. The highlight of the season is the Dubai International Racing Carnival, which is nine weeks of top-class racing concluding with the Dubai World Cup.

Godolphin has been a major contributor to the UAE's racing circuit, offering world-class facilities in Dubai's Al Quoz area. Established by the Maktoum family, Godolphin runs a state-of-the-art operation, having won no less than 117 Group One races in 11

countries. Its headquarters are fully equipped with a private training track, equine pool and a dedicated feed mill in order to regulate and control the diets of the thoroughbreds housed there. Younger horses are broken in to the race season at the specially designed Desert Stables with only the best-bred picked for international competition. Thanks to the UAE's all-year-round sunshine, Godolphin stables provide a perfect winter retreat until the racing calendar gets under way.

Godolphin's *Electrocutionist* came from behind to win the world's richest horse race in a thrilling encounter at the 2006 Dubai World Cup. Ridden by Frankie Dettori and trained by Saeed bin Suroor, *Electrocutionist* was first past the post to take away a cash prize of US$3.6 million.

Dubai World Cup

Godolphin's *Electrocutionist* came from behind to win the world's richest horse race in a thrilling encounter at the 2006 Dubai World Cup. Ridden by Frankie Dettori and trained by Saeed bin Suroor, *Electrocutionist* galloped to take away a cash prize of US$3.6 million. Recognised as the world's richest race, the Dubai World Cup has become the favourite meeting place for the world's racing fraternity.

Endurance Racing

The UAE is classed as one of the forerunners in the development of endurance racing, with its riders and horses currently ranked

Endurance races are gruelling and tough as many exceed the 120 kilometre mark.

amongst some of the world's best. Endurance races are gruelling and tough as many exceed the 120 kilometre mark. Courses are designed to challenge the horses and mid-race veterinary checks ensure that horses are not over-stretched. The UAE can attribute much of its success in this sport to the stamina of the purebred Arabian horse, which is ideally suited to desert terrain, and the passion of its riders.

Abdullah Khamis Ali Saeed and Sheikh Faisal bin Abdullah Al Qasimi did the UAE proud by winning the Senior and Junior rides at the historic Tom Quilty 160-kilometre endurance ride in Australia in June 2006. Abdullah Khamis Ali Saeed from the Al Reef stables rode *Tora Blar-Zay* to victory completing the 160-kilometre distance in a timing of 9 hours 15 minutes. Sheikh Faisal, who won the silver medal at the World Junior Championship held in Bahrain, finished on top in the junior section, riding *Kaysand Farrah* to victory. Sheikh Faisal took 10 hours 39 minutes to win the junior title. The Tom Quilty endurance event is the national endurance riding championship of Australia and is held annually in a different state. The 2006 ride was held in Boonah in south-east Queensland.

UAE Basketball player Jassem Mohammad fights for the ball with Ahmad Mohammad of Bahrain during their basketball third place match for the tenth GCC Basketball Championship for men in Doha, 20 September 2006. UAE won the match 93–71.

POLO

Dubai Polo & Equestrian Club, owned by Emaar Properties, was opened in the spring of 2006. The Club builds on the Middle East's great equestrian tradition and offers luxurious facilities suitable for young and old and people of all abilities. It is a full-service Andalusian-themed equestrian centre themed with a Spanish style clubhouse replete with lounges and dining areas, riding gear and tack shop, spa and a swimming pool. Members of the Club can also watch a polo match on one of two polo fields, test their polo skills on the practice field, or take riding lessons. There's something for every skill level, including show jumping and dressage for advanced riders.

ATHLETICS

The Zayed International Race, dedicated to the memory of the late Sheikh Zayed bin Sultan Al Nahyan, with a prize fund of Dh1 million, took place in April 2006 and was organised by the UAE

Athletics Federation. It attracted over 15,000 runners, of both sexes and varying age groups, together with a huge crowd of spectators. A distinct feature of the 2006 event was the participation of international players for the first time in the history of the race.

Sheikha Maitha bint Mohammed bin Rashid Al Maktoum competes at international level in the martial arts.

RED BULL RACE

The Red Bull World Series Air Race 2006 got under way on 17 March under the auspices of Abu Dhabi Tourism Authority (ADTA). The race includes rounds held in ten cities around the world. American pilot Kirby Chambliss won the Abu Dhabi leg of the 2006 race, pipping his compatriot and 2005 overall winner Mike Mangold. It was a close fight between the two. Mangold had some rough luck, however, as his wing hit an air gate in the last round, pushing him to second position. It was a display of courage, grit and precision. Eleven pilots tested their skills against each

The 2006 World Aerobatics Show, held in Al Ain, attracted competitors from 40 countries, including 83 parachutists and sky divers.

other, each trying to outdo the other in a bid to log the quickest time through the air gates. Spectators watched in awe as the carbon-composite planes twisted, dived and turned, their pilots willing their machines to be the quickest.

Chambliss won the race in a mere 3 minutes 33.37 seconds and Mangold, despite a ten-second penalty, managed to clock 3 minutes 37.94 seconds to take the second position. The winner of the 2005 Abu Dhabi race, Hungarian Peter Besenyei, had to make do with third position in the event with a time of 3 minutes 41.72 seconds.

INTERNET LINKS

Camel racing:	www.uaeinteract.com/camelracing
Cricket:	www.uaeinteract.com/cricket
Endurance racing:	www.uaeinteract.com/endurance
Football:	www.uaeinteract.com/football
Golf:	www.uaeinteract.com/golf
Horse racing:	www.uaeinteract.com/horseracing
Leisure activities:	www.uaeinteract.com/leisure
Motor sports:	www.uaeinteract.com/motorsports
Powerboats:	www.uaeinteract.com/powerboats
Show jumping:	www.uaeinteract.com/showjumping
Sports in Gulf News:	www.uaeinteract.com/sports_gn
Sports in UAE Interact:	www.uaeinteract.com/sports
Tennis:	www.uaeinteract.com/tennis
Watersports:	www.uaeinteract.com/watersports

Purpose-built exhibition centres, modern hotels and conference facilities have attracted major exhibitions and events focusing on the Middle East and Asia.

Throughout the year there are special events designed to improve the quality of life of the UAE's citizens.

EVENTS & EXHIBITIONS

IT IS NOT SURPRISING, CONSIDERING ITS VIBRANT economy and strategic location, that the UAE is the destination of choice for international business meetings, incentive travel, conventions, trade fairs, events and exhibitions. So much so that this area of activity is now a major component of the country's business and tourism expansion plans. With its huge purpose-built exhibition halls and luxury hotels boasting state-of-the-art conference facilities, the UAE provides a unique gateway to the Middle East and Asia. The addition to the equation of a solid infrastructure, a secure environment and diverse leisure opportunities helps to explain why the country attracts major global events.

EXHIBITION CENTRES

ABU DHABI

The exhibition industry in Abu Dhabi is spearheaded by a relatively new organisation, Abu Dhabi National Exhibition Company (ADNEC), a fully independent corporate body that was established by decree in 2005 to organise, promote and participate in exhibitions locally, regionally and internationally. ADNEC replaced the General Exhibition Corporation (GEC).

ADNEC inherited 27,000 square metres indoor and 12,000 square metres of outdoor net exhibition space at the Abu Dhabi International Exhibitions Centre, in which 11 major events are held. These include some of the Gulf's largest and most significant international exhibitions, such as IDEX, a major defence exhibition and conference, and ADIPEC, Abu Dhabi International Petroleum Exhibition & Conference. However, the emirate is in the process of constructing a new world-class exhibition complex to meet the increasing demand from visitors and exhibitors: Abu Dhabi is emerging as a unique market and the massive developments that are planned are attracting a wide range of new exhibitions to its venues.

Some of the Gulf's largest and most significant international exhibitions, such as IDEX, a major defence exhibition and conference, and ADIPEC, Abu Dhabi International Petroleum Exhibition & Conference are held at the Abu Dhabi International Exhibitions Centre.

The new complex will include 57,000 square metres of gross exhibition floor space, a massive 21,000-square-metre visitor concourse and 7500 square metres of multi-purpose halls.

The new complex will include 57,000 square metres of gross exhibition floor space, a massive 21,000-square-metre visitor concourse and 7500 square metres of multi-purpose halls. It will also feature dedicated conference facilities for 1200 people, banqueting areas and more than 30 high-specification meeting rooms.

The first phase of the project is on schedule to host IDEX 2007. Constructed in a classic 'U-shape', the Centre will contain a central landscaped plaza for outdoor events. The focal feature of the complex will be a soaring sea-facing tower. Innovative in its design, the curving tower is a bold architectural statement and will become the brand that promotes the venue and Abu Dhabi to the world.

The location for this Centre has been carefully selected: close to major hotel developments, a short distance from Abu Dhabi Airport and approximately 75 minutes from Jebel Ali, Dubai. The surrounding road network has been planned to allow for easy access and exit to the centre and multi-storey car parks will provide ample capacity for visitor and exhibitors. The area surrounding the new Centre is scheduled for immediate development and will feature hotels, serviced apartments, 17 office towers, a marina development and a retail zone with over 100 outlets. As part of the development, the existing Sheikh Zayed Grandstand will be refurbished and linked to the new halls.

Emirates Palace Hotel

Abu Dhabi also has excellent conference facilities at its many five-star hotels. But the most impressive are to be found at the capital's new seven-star hotel, Emirates Palace. This has a 1200-capacity auditorium, a main ballroom that can accommodate up to 2800 people, 48 meeting rooms, six large function terraces, a media centre and business centre, all built within the heart of a beachfront hotel that stands on 100 hectares of landscaped gardens. The hotel richly deserves its designation as the 'most luxurious and technologically advanced meeting facility in the region'.

DUBAI

At the northern end of Sheikh Zayed Road, the 184-metre Dubai World Trade Centre (DWTC) is the towering figurehead of a large exhibition complex. Built in the 1980s, DWTC was the city's first skyscraper; it remains at the epicentre of Dubai's international trade and business industry having hosted key conferences for 20 years. The six-storey Dubai World Trade Centre Hotel was not so fortunate: on 1 April 2005 it was razed to the ground to make way for the prestigious Hazel Wong-designed World Trade Centre Residence, set to open in December 2007.

In 2003, following an investment of Dh650 million (US$177 million), DWTC launched the adjacent Dubai International Convention and Exhibition Centre (DIEC). During the IMF and World Bank meetings held there in 2003, the complex attracted 15,340 delegates to its various exhibition halls spread across 8100 square metres, with the auditorium alone hosting up to 6500 persons at any one time.

With the DWTC and DIEC working successfully in tandem, the Dubai Airport Expo Centre completes the trio. An international conventions facility also managed by DWTC, the Expo Centre is a convenient five-minute drive from the Dubai International Airport (hence the name).

Dubai World Trade Centre hosted a record 92 exhibitions in 2006, making it officially the busiest year-to-date. Events such as GITEX, Arab Health, Gulfood and the Middle East International Motor Show have become firm dates in the region's diary, attracting many local, regional and international visitors. Major growth areas for the Middle East economies – such as real estate and hospitality – are also served by international trade shows, alongside more niche areas, such as coating products and equipment for horses, creating economic opportunities for a wide variety of local and international companies.

Longer term, the Dubai government is building Dubai Exhibition City at Jebel Ali Airport City. This Dh8 billion (US$2.17 billion) project was launched in 2005 on a 3-million-square-metre site comprising not just the world's largest display space but offices, halls, restaurants, hotels, residential apartments and parking space for more than 20,000 cars. It is expected that the completed 'City' will be ready for the Dubai Air Show 2009.

Many of Dubai's luxury hotels also boast conference facilities, but arguably the most notable is at the Madinat Jumeirah. This has five

Dubai World Trade Centre hosted a record 92 exhibitions in 2006, making it officially the busiest year-to-date. Events such as GITEX, Arab Health, Gulfood and the Middle East International Motor Show have become firm dates in the region's diary, attracting many local, regional and international visitors.

inter-connected meeting rooms, a 3600-square-metre conference hall, an outdoor function area called Fort Island, a 1000-capacity amphitheatre, a 424-seated indoor theatre and a multi-purpose venue. The modern facilities have been used for events such as the Dubai International Film Festival and Vienna Opera Ball.

SHARJAH

Sharjah pioneered the region's exhibition industry in 1977 when it opened an exhibition complex in the emirate. Twenty-five years later, with an investment of Dh183.5 million (US$50 million), the Expocentre Sharjah was inaugurated as the centrepiece of a larger 'Expo City'. Managed by Sharjah Chamber of Commerce and Industry (SCCI), the Expocentre currently comprises four large exhibition halls spread across 20,000 square metres in which 20 exhibitions were staged in 2006 with over half a million visitors. Now further expansion is required and SCCI will spend Dh200 million (US54.50 million) extending the exhibition facilities by 50,000 square metres and building a 300-room hotel that will give exhibitors and foreign delegates easy access to the venue.

Sharjah pioneered the region's exhibition industry in 1977 when it opened an exhibition complex in the emirate. Twenty-five years later, with an investment of Dh183.5 million (US$50 million), the Expocentre Sharjah was inaugurated as the centrepiece of a larger 'Expo City'.

The Centre hosts regular specialised trade fairs, including TEXPO, an annual international trade exhibition for garment machinery, textiles and accessories, the National Careers Exhibition aimed at UAE nationals in the banking and finance sectors; the biannual Mideast Watch and Jewellery Spring and Autumn Shows; Arab Asia Trade Fair, showcasing everything from DIY products to flora and fauna, and the Sharjah World Book Fair. The Expocentre Sharjah is bordered by Sharjah's Al Khalid Lagoon, making it an attractive option for marine events such as the highly successful Gulf Maritime Exhibition.

AJMAN

Ajman International Exhibition Centre, occupying an area of 22,000 square metres, is designed to carry out complementary activities to those conducted by the other UAE exhibition centres, further supporting rapid economic development in the country and creating facilities for promoting local industries worldwide.

RA'S AL-KHAIMAH

The Ra's al-Khaimah Exhibition Centre is a 37,400-square-metre complex located in the Al Nakheel area close to the active business centre. Inaugurated in 1996, it has a major exhibition hall of 2100 square metres and 3000 square metres of exterior space for local fairs. Its calendar for 2006 and 2007 includes the Families Exhibition, Drinks & Food Stuffs Fair; Career & Training Fair, Ramadan Festival and Egyptian Products Exhibition.

FUJAIRAH

The Fujairah Exhibition Centre (FEC) on the East Coast covers 1080 square metres of indoor floor space, an outdoor display area, exhibition halls, management offices and service utilities, and is centrally located between both the International Airport and Fujairah Trade Centre on one side and the seaport and free zone on the other. A number of internationally important exhibitions have been held at the Centre since its establishment, such as Buildex, the Motor Show, the Fujairah International Agricultural Exhibition, and Fujairah International Education & Training Exhibition. It also hosts seasonal fairs for the general public.

Ajman, Ra's al-Khaimah and Fujairah each have their own exhibition centres hosting both local and international exhibitions.

EVENTS

The following is a small representative selection of the many exhibitions, conventions, conferences and other events that take place every year in the UAE.

ABU DHABI INTERNATIONAL HUNTING & EQUESTRIAN EXHIBITION (ADIHEX)

More than 525 companies from over 42 countries participated in the Abu Dhabi International Hunting and Equestrian Exhibition (ADIHEX), the four-day annual platform for the hunting and equine industries held from 11 to 15 September 2006. As well as bringing together the best names in the hunting equipment industry and devotees to deep-rooted Arabian pursuits, this event also has a unique cultural and social slant, featuring popular

ADIHEX is a major hunting and equestrian exhibition held in Abu Dhabi.

competitions for hybrid falcons, Nabati poetry, painting and photography, all focusing on falconry and other heritage sports. In 2006, a 'Arabian Saluki Beauty' competition and a 'Lure Coursing Show' were held for the first time.

ABU DHABI INTERNATIONAL BOOK FAIR

The sixteenth Abu Dhabi International Book Fair, held in the grounds of the Cultural Foundation in Abu Dhabi from 29 March to 7 April 2006, welcomed 315 participating publishing houses from 20 countries: the bustling crowds were able to peruse and purchase 275,000 Arab and 115,000 non-Arab book titles and electronic publications on topics such as culture, literature, science, languages, and heritage.

ABU DHABI INTERNATIONAL JEWELLERY AND WATCH SHOW

ADIJEX, one of the foremost international exhibitions of jewellery, gemstones, watches, gold, silver, and manufacturing equipment in the region, is held annually at ADIEC, with the 2006 event being scheduled for 15 to 19 November. ADIJEX provides manufacturers, craftsmen, designers and suppliers with an unbeatable opportunity to present their luxury wares to an expanding market.

ABU DHABI INTERNATIONAL PETROLEUM EXHIBITION AND CONFERENCE

Two-thirds of the world's known oil reserves are concentrated in the region and Abu Dhabi plays a vital role in shaping the industry's development, accounting for 95 per cent of the UAE's actual oil output. Over the next five years, an estimated investment of US$5 billion is planned for new gas infrastructure. It is not surprising, therefore, that Abu Dhabi hosts one of the most prestigious of the industry's exhibitions and conferences.

Progressing phenomenally since it began in 1984, the sector's major showcase ADIPEC is supported by key industry players such as ADNOC (Abu Dhabi National Oil Company) and SPE (the Society of Petroleum Engineers). A biennial event, ADIPEC was acquired by dmg world media early in 2006. The twelfth ADIPEC, hosted at ADIEC from 5 to 8 November 2006, attracted over 1000 leading oil and gas companies from more than 50 countries, together with high-profile decision-makers from the global oil and gas industry.

ABU DHABI WORLD LEADERSHIP SUMMIT 2006

The first Abu Dhabi World Leadership Summit, which was held in November 2005 at the Emirates Palace Hotel, was a resounding success, bringing together some of the world's most influential and persuasive speakers. These world leaders shared strategies for excellence in leadership and international business development with corporate delegates.

Speakers included Bill Clinton, 42nd President of the United States; Sir Richard Branson, CEO Virgin Group; Sheikh Nahyan bin Mubarak Al Nahyan, UAE Minister of Higher Education; Benazir Bhutto, the first female Prime Minister of Pakistan; John Edwards, 2004 US Democratic Vice-Presidential candidate; and Mohamed Ali Alabbar, Chairman of Emaar Properties.

The line-up of speakers for the 2006 event, which will also be held at the Emirates Palace Hotel, is no less prestigious and includes George Bush Senior, 41st President of the US, Sheikha Lubna Al Qasimi, UAE Minister of Economy; Gerhard Schröeder, former German Chancellor; Khaldoon Khalifa Al Mubarak, Chairman of Abu Dhabi Executive Affairs Authority; and Lee Kuan Yew, Minister Mentor – Singapore.

The Abu Dhabi World Leadership Summit was attended by ex US President, Bill Clinton.

AL AIN AEROBATIC AIRSHOW

Al Ain Aerobatic Show incorporating the twenty-third FAI World Grand Prix, exceeded all expectations. Worldwide participation involving 40 countries, massive crowds (in excess of 120,000), and top-level organisation ensured that the show was a great success. Because it coincided with the Eid Al Adha holiday (from 11 to 16 January 2006), it was also a family affair with cultural, social, recreational and heritage-related activities to suit all tastes. Night air shows were performed for the first time in the Middle East, and there were spectacular aerial acrobatics, 'wing-walking' displays, precision parachuting and attempts to break many

Over 40 countries participated in the 2005 Al Ain Aerobatic Show.

Guinness world records, such as the jump performed by Nasr Al Nayadi, UAE champion skydiver, carrying the world's largest flag. The UAE input in 'Al Ain 2006' was much greater than in previous shows as it included an F-16 display, the stunning solo Apache display, and the participation of the Armed Forces Technical Studies Institute, the Emirates Aviation Society, and the UAE Jet Team.

But the huge international contribution also ensured an extremely thrilling show, including the breathtaking displays. One of the most impressive was the world's largest free-fly formation by 54 skydivers from the world free-fly team. This latter event was organised by Nadia H. Adam Ali, the UAE's first woman skydiver.

AL AIN CLASSICAL MUSICAL FESTIVAL

A yearly event featuring classical music concerts of a high artistic standard, the sixth Al Ain Classical Music Festival from 8 to 12 March 2006, was organised by the Abu Dhabi concert committee, with the assistance of the Austrian Embassy and the Intercontinental Resort, amongst others. This classical music festival, which is based in the 'cultural capital' Al Ain, has managed to attract consistently larger crowds and 2006 was no exception. To the delight of music lovers, the inaugural ceremony and the gala concert were held at the historic Al Jahili Fort, the theme being 'Mozart in the Oasis', featuring musical tributes by the Vienna Chamber Orchestra to the world-renowned composer.

Arab Health has an impressive history spanning 31 years, offering companies the chance to showcase their products and services in one of the fastest growing and most lucrative healthcare markets in the world.

ARAB HEALTH

Arab Health has an impressive history spanning 31 years, offering companies the opportunity to showcase their products and services in one of the fastest growing and most lucrative healthcare markets in the world. Hosted at DIEC, the annual event caters for a wide range of medical, pharmaceutical, surgical and dental specialisations. There has been unprecedented growth in exhibition space since 2001 with a steady increase of 25 per cent year-on-year. Firmly established as the leading healthcare exhibition in the Middle East, Arab Health attracts senior decision-makers from the regions healthcare sector.

The thirty-second Arab Health exhibition will be held from 29 January to 1 February 2007. The Arab Health Congress, which is held in conjunction with the exhibition, is celebrating 28 years of bringing world-class healthcare education programmes to the Middle East. The conferences are accredited with the American Academy of Continuing Medical Education (AACME).

ARABIAN TRAVEL MARKET

The Arabian Travel Market (ATM) is universally recognised as the leading travel industry event for the Middle East and pan-Arab region, another rapidly expanding economic sector. In 2006, the four-day annual event, from 1 to 4 May, brought together over 1750 exhibitors from 59 countries, making it the biggest ATM since it was launched in 1994. The prestigious travel and trade show was judged a 'resounding success.'

HH Sheikh Mohammed bin Rashid Al Maktoum reviews a stand at the Arabian Travel Market.

CABLE, SATELLITE, BROADCAST & COMMUNICATIONS EXHIBITION

This major communication technologies platform was launched in February 1994 to accommodate the region's boom in electronic media. With the support of the Arab State Broadcasting Union, Asia Pacific Broadcasting Union, International Association of Broadcasting Manufacturers and Global Satellite Forum, the exhibition provides solutions to buyers in the local market. CABSAT2006, held at DIEC from 7 to 9 March, had a gross exhibition space of 13,680 square metres (15 per cent up on the previous year) with 439 companies participating from more than 45 countries, 350 (80 per cent) of whom were international companies. Also on offer was a comprehensive programme of industry-related conferences and seminars to further facilitate the information flow between trade visitors and industry experts.

Contracts worth US$27.2 billion were signed at Dubai's ninth International Aerospace Exhibition in November 2005.

DUBAI AIRSHOW

Dubai's ninth International Aerospace Exhibition, Dubai 2005, held in November 2005 at Dubai Airport Expo Centre, once again set new records not only in the number of exhibitors (726 in 15 national pavilions) and visitors (over 35,000) but also in the volume of contracts signed, estimated to have crossed the Dh100 billion (US$27.2 billion mark), the highest in the history of the biennial event. More than 100 planes were on display, indicating the importance of the aviation industry in the region. The aerospace extravaganza also includes the Dubai Aviation Forum, second Middle East Air Chief's Conference, Middle East Aviation Information Technology Manufacturing Forum and the fifth Middle East Aviation Financial Conference. Dubai 2007 will be held from 11 to 15 November 2007.

DUBAI INTERNATIONAL ARABIAN HORSE CHAMPIONSHIP

The Dubai International Horse Fair caters to the equine industry, from traders to consumers.

This four-day beauty pageant for the equine world, first held in 2004, has since spawned the Dubai International Horse Fair (DIHF), which caters to the equine industry, from traders to consumers. However, the main thrust of the event is the showcase of purebred Arabian horses, judged before a panel for their looks, agility and lineage, culminating in the Championship on the final day. The 2006 event was a huge success with 295 horses entered from 14 countries, competing for prizes valued at US$600,000. Held at the DIEC, the 2007 Championship will be run from 26 to 28 March 2007. This will have the added excitement of the final round of the Dubai Gold Cup – International Series. Final points awarded in Dubai will be double for any other show in the series, so competition will be at its best. DIHF will open on 25 March 2007, one day earlier than the Championship, and run through to the 28 March 2007.

DUBAI INTERNATIONAL BOAT SHOW

Dubai International Boat Show (DIBS) 2006, held from 14 to 18 March 2006 at the Dubai International Marine Club at Mina Seyahi, attracted more than 25,000 visitors. DIBS 2006 occupied an exhibition space of 14,791 square metres, an increase of 51 per cent in net space, making it the region's largest gathering of leisure craft, equipment and associated services. On display were 123 yachts (up by 56 per cent), powerboats and motor boats, including 'super yachts' – measuring over 24 metres in length. Over 427 companies (an increase of 7 per cent) recorded US$100 million in sales involving 140 boats, including at least 25 luxury yachts. Sales of marine equipment, fishing gear and accessories were also significant. The show's growth is a reflection of the region's flourishing multi-million dollar marine industry and the massive boom in marina-based property development projects.

DUBAI INTERNATIONAL HUMANITARIAN AID & REDEVELOPMENT CONFERENCE & EXHIBITION

With the United Nations (UN) as one of its major sponsors, DIHAD marks an important annual event for international humanitarian assistance organisations. Representatives of the UN Office for the Coordination of Humanitarian Affairs (OCHA), key UAE leaders and 200 humanitarian relief organisations from 30 countries attended the 2006 meeting from 10 to 12 April. Jan Egeland, Under-Secretary-General for Humanitarian Affairs & Emergency Relief Coordinator, Head of OCHA, made the opening address to delegates and Sir Bob Geldof, rock star and poverty campaigner, concluded proceedings with an address on the final day. DIHAD 2007 will take place from 1 to 3 April 2007.

V1 Yachts are manufactured in Dubai and are forming a new class especially suited to match racing.

ENVIRONMENTAL CONFERENCE & EXHIBITION 2007

Environment 2007 the fourth edition of the Middle East North Africa (MENA) region's leading environmental exhibition, will be held from 28 to 31 January 2007 at the Abu Dhabi International Exhibition & Conference Centre. The event, organised in conjunction with the Environment Agency – Abu Dhabi, focuses on energy, water, waste, air and land management issues.

This is a particularly hot topic at present as MENA countries are expected to invest Dh16.5 to Dh22 billion (US$4.5–US$6 billion) annually on freshwater projects over the next ten years. According to the World Bank, the UAE will invest at least Dh168 billion (US$46 billion) over the next decade in environmental and pollution control projects. In addition, the UAE's estimated outlay for solid waste management is Dh451 million (US$123 million), Dh198 million (US$54 million) for wastewater treatment, and Dh110 million (US$30 million) for medical waste disposal.

Environment 2007 Exhibition & Conference, the fourth in the series since the event was first initiated in 2001, will target over

Land-management issues are a major focus of environmental conferences and exhibitions in Abu Dhabi.

GITEX is the region's most important telecoms show. Over 127,000 trade visitors attended the 2005 exhibition.

375 exhibitors from around the world, building on previous successes: over 10,000 visitors came to the 2005 event with the conference sessions attended by more than 1000 delegates. The event also saw the signing of the 'Abu Dhabi Declaration on Sustainable Transportation' by more than 20 Environment Ministers from the Arab region.

GULF INFORMATION TECHNOLOGY EXHIBITION (GITEX)

GITEX celebrated its twenty-fifth anniversary in September 2005, confirming its status as the region's most important telecommunications exhibition. Trade visitors, at 127,724, were up 9.77 per cent on the previous year. There was also a surge in exhibitors from Saudi Arabia, with 1200 square metres of floor space booked by KSA companies – a 20 per cent increase on 2004, reflecting the growth of the region's information technology industry. The event also serves as a launch pad for many new products and services from the different sectors, with GITEX Shopper showcasing the latest in games, audio and digital technology.

The 'Global ICT Leaders @ GITEX 2005' was also held from 24 to 29 September at DWTC, with discussions on the vision required to be a successful ICT leader in the twenty-first century. The event focuses on strategic use of best practices and real world leadership experiences from IT and business executives.

In addition, the fifteenth edition of GITEX Shopper took place at the Airport Expo in October 2005, immediately after the GITEX exhibition. The seven-day IT retail extravaganza proved to be a big draw for consumers attracted by promotions and cash prizes, including 1-kilogram-of-gold-a-day offers, with retailers reporting sales in excess of Dh76 million, marking a 36 per cent increase in transactions.

GULFOOD

The Middle East's biggest trade event within the food sector showcases the latest innovations in the hospitality trade, from food and beverage to catering equipment and packaging. Attendees include international, regional and local manufacturers, buyers, chefs and hoteliers. The tenth biennial Gulfood conference in 2005

was so successful that the event is now being held annually. Gulfood 2006 recorded an all-time high in the level of transactions and business activity, confirming the region's reputation as a gourmet's paradise. Gulfood 2007 will take place from 19 to 22 February 2007 at DIEC.

Waste management is a high priority in the UAE's development planning.

INTERNATIONAL AUTUMN TRADE FAIR

Dubai International Autumn Trade Fair (IATF), held at the end of every year, is a launch pad for the international business community to access the MENA market. The 2005 DWTC event was its nineteenth, attracting visitors from a wide range of trade sectors, including home wares, timepieces, handicrafts, cosmetics, DIY tools and ceramics. The five-day fair concludes with an open day for the general public. IATF06 is being held from 17 to 20 December 2006.

INTERNATIONAL DEFENCE EXHIBITION & CONFERENCE (IDEX)

Officially supported by the UAE Government and coordinated with the active assistance of the Armed Forces, IDEX is the world's largest tri-service defence exhibition incorporating land, sea and

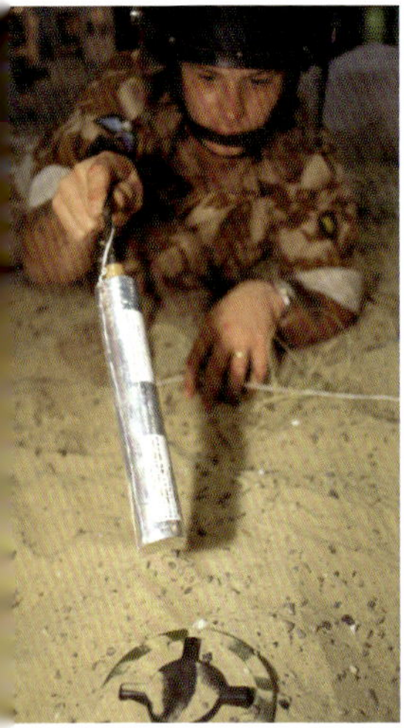

IDEX is the world's largest tri-service defence exhibition.

air operations. Held biennially at ADIEC in Abu Dhabi, the eighth IDEX will take place from 18 to 22 February 2007, providing the ideal venue for the defence industry to display new equipment to prospective buyers from the growing defence market in the Middle East Asia and Far East. In 2005 more than 900 companies from 50 countries exhibited the latest technologies on over 25,000 square metres of indoor and outdoor space, clinching deals totalling Dh6.8 billion (US$1.85 billion). Key decision-makers, defence ministers, senior army, air and naval officers, equipment manufacturers and system solutions providers, all with a shared interest in armament acquisition and integration, are present under one roof during the five-day arms extravaganza. IDEX also incorporates a day-long conference, which is regarded in international academic and military circles as a top forum on defence strategies and technologies.

INTERNATIONAL JEWELLERY & ACCESSORIES FAIR

The International Jewellery & Accessories Fair (IJAF) takes place concurrently with the International Watches & Clocks Fair at DIEC. The venue hosts a varied array of wholesalers, manufacturers, distributors and marketers of the latest in jewellery and timepieces, including gems, pearls, beads, gold, silver and platinum, along with the instruments and equipment that make them. IJAF 2007 will take place from 20 to 22 February.

There are a number of fairs and exhibitions in the UAE devoted to jewellery, watches and accessories.

WATCH & JEWELLERY DUBAI

Trade and top-end consumers attend this successful exhibition of jewellery, loose stones and timepieces, which was renamed and moved in 2005 to Dubai Airport Expo in recognition of its expanded profile. Recent innovations include 'Diamond Day', a two-day session dedicated to the precious gem organised by the London-based Diamond Trading Group, part of De Beers. WJD 2006 will take place from 11 to 15 December at DIEC.

LEADERS IN DUBAI

'Leaders in Dubai' is a high profile forum on the international business calendar. The line-up of guest speakers for the 2006 event, held on 28 and 29 November, included former US Secretary of State Colin Powell, lecturing on the topic of taking charge; former Disney CEO Michael Eisner speaking on growth through innovation; ex-IBM Chairman Louis V. Gerstner Jr on leading change'; H.M Queen Noor of Jordan on leadership and public service; Professor C.K. Prahalad, one of the business world's most influential consultants, on corporate strategy; bestselling financial author Harry S. Dent Jr, on predicting the economic future; and lateral-thinker Edward de Bono, on creative thinking.

MIDDLE EAST INTERNATIONAL MOTOR SHOW

The biennial Middle East International Motor Show at DIEC is the biggest event of its kind in the region targeting the buoyant automobile market. The show's eighth outing, from 12 to 16 December 2005, was attended by hordes of automobile enthusiasts and prospective buyers, whilst 90 international vehicle manufactures displayed their wares in ten exhibition halls, including fleets of off-road vehicles, concept cars, high-performance sports cars, custom-built automobiles and motorcycles. Manufacturers participating included BMW, Mercedes-Benz, Volkswagen, Lamborghini, Jaguar, Rolls-Royce, Suzuki and Land Rover, to name but a few.

The biennial Middle East International Motor Show at DIEC is the biggest event of its kind in the region.

MOTOR TUNING SHOW (MTS 2006)

At least 80 of the world's leading automobile makers and car-tuning companies participated in the debut Motor Tuning Show (MTS 2006) held in Abu Dhabi from 23 to 26 April 2006. Over 70,000 visitors to the 15,000-square-metre venue were able to view the latest sports and high performance cars, four-wheel drives and motorcycles: power, precision and glamour rolled into one.

POWER-GEN MIDDLE EAST

The fourth POWER-GEN Middle East was held from 30 January to 1 February 2006 at ADIEC in Abu Dhabi with the participation of 200 international and regional companies from the power generation, transmission, distribution and desalination sectors. Strong demand growth coupled with significant structural changes within the electricity sector ensure that the UAE remains a key market in the Middle East. Further afield, the entire Middle East and North Africa (MENA) region will require more than 74 GW of additional capacity by 2010.

ROADEX had 180 exhibitors from 35 countries taking part, occupying an exhibit space of 14,000 square metres.

ROADEX

ROADEX 2006 exhibition and conference, the Middle East's premier event for the road industry, was held at ADIEC from 12 to 15 March 2006. ROADEX had 180 exhibitors from 35 countries, occupying an exhibit space of 14,000 square metres. The exhibition encompassed all elements of road transportation including design, construction, operation, maintenance and engineering management, and proved to be a highly productive meeting ground for all industry players.

ROADEX also featured a conference on Road Safety organised by the International Road Federation. Over 35 international speakers spoke at the conference sessions and addressed the topic of road safety and intelligent traffic systems.

SECURITY AND SAFETY EXHIBITION AND CONFERENCE

The second biennial Security and Safety Exhibition and Conference (Middle East 2005) was held at ADIEC over a four-day period in November 2005. Organised by ADNEC/GEC in conjunction with the Ministry of Interior and the German Essen Corporation, the event attracted 243 exhibitors from 37 countries showcasing the latest technology in security and safety equipment. More than 11,650 visitors, including key decision-makers, were received over the four days of the exhibition. A 'live' demonstration of equipment helped visitors gauge the capabilities of the goods on display. The exhibition hopes to provide technical and technological solutions towards making the world a safer place, despite growing security challenges.

The crux of the Fair's manifesto is to encourage reading habits whatever the age, nationality and culture, and to make quality books both accessible and affordable to all.

SHARJAH WORLD BOOK FAIR

Sharjah World Book Fair is a ten-day annual event usually held during the first half of December (the twenty-fifth session was from 5 to 15 December 2006) at the Sharjah Expocentre. The crux of the Fair's manifesto is to encourage reading habits whatever the age, nationality and culture, and to make quality books both accessible and affordable to all. Participants and visitors include worldwide publishing houses, agents, research centres, colleges, universities, educational aid manufacturers and the media. Each year, a 'Publishers Prize' and 'UAE Book Prizes' are awarded.

WOIBEX FORUM

National Women's Day is held on 8 March each year, and to coincide with this date the annual Global Woibex Forum is organised by Datamatix and usually held at the Burj Al Arab hotel. The convention, attended by international and local women leaders and businesswomen, was created in 1999 to help empower women in the workplace, encourage entrepreneurship and share leadership skills and experiences. The event also incorporates the Middle East Women's Achievement Awards, which was introduced in 2001 to give recognition to key players in the region.

DUBAI SHOPPING FESTIVAL (DSF)

It has been said that the UAE has three national sports – camel racing, horse racing and shopping! Certainly, for 45 days during January and February, devoted shoppers revel in the Dubai Shopping Festival enthusiastically searching for bargains in malls, street markets, heritage fairs, coinciding sports events and the Global Village. DSF began in 1996 as a retail showcase to raise Dubai's tourist profile – and it worked, with many shop outlets reporting a 600 per cent increase in sales and hotels 100 per cent occupancy. DSF generated revenues of Dh6.67 billion (US$1.82 billion) in 2005. About 25 sponsors contributed up to Dh25 million (US$6.81 billion) in sponsorship fees to the Dh85 million (US$23.16 billion) budget earmarked for the eleventh edition of the DSF in January 2006. Unfortunately, owing to the death of the Ruler of Dubai and UAE Prime Minister, HH Sheikh Maktoum bin Rashid Al Maktoum, the event had to be cancelled and was re-scheduled for 20 Dec 2006 to 2 February 2007.

Each year during the Festival, the emirate's many malls hold major sales and feature children's entertainment, tombolas, weekly car draws, lucky dips and raffles giving away everything from Rolls Royces to gold bullion. Global Village is the Festival's 1.6 million-square-metres centrepiece with a host of pavilions from around the world selling gifts, handicrafts, furniture, clothing and ethnic food every day from 4 p.m. Other attractions are the usual nightly entertainment, such as fireworks, performances at the 6000-capacity amphitheatre, a funfair boasting the region's tallest Ferris

For 45 days during January and February, devoted shoppers revel in the Dubai Shopping Festival enthusiastically searching for bargains in malls, street markets, heritage fairs, coinciding sports events and the Global Village.

Dubai Summer Surprises is a source of entertainment for the children during the hot summer months.

wheel, and the popular DiggerLand. In 2005 Global Village moved from its former location at Dubai Festival City to the Dubailand site.

Amidst the bustle and excitement is Dubai Heritage & Diving Village, which hosts a Bedouin Festival with live music, dancing, arts and crafts. The House of Talents at DWTC is a showcase of locally made handicrafts, while the Carpet Oasis at Airport Expo Dubai is a favourite hunting ground for the house proud. Entertainment extravaganzas, street performances, laser shows and contemporary cultural events complete the picture.

DUBAI SUMMER SURPRISES (DSS)

Modhesh, a yellow, spiky-haired fellow with an accordion-like torso, is the mascot for the second annual shopping event of the year's calendar. He is literally the beaming face of a four-month festival that largely keeps the kids entertained while school is out for summer. Child-friendly exhibitions, music shows, theatrical performances, competitions, light shows and educational workshops are held in malls and parks across Dubai with themes such as Flower Surprises, Ice Surprises, Sweet Surprises, Art Surprises, Colour Surprises and Adventure Surprises, plus the pinnacle of fun houses, Modhesh Village at DWTC. Summer festival sales were in the region of Dh2 billion (US$545 million) in 2006 compared to Dh1.72 billion (US$468 million) in 2005.

INTERNET LINKS

Abu Dhabi Chamber of Commerce and Industry:	www.uaeinteract.com/adcci
Abu Dhabi International Book Fair:	www.uaeinteract.com/adibf
Abu Dhabi International Hunting and Equestrian Exhibition (ADIHEX):	www.uaeinteract.com/adihex
Abu Dhabi National Exhibition Company:	www.uaeinteract.com/adnec
Abu Dhabi World Leadership Summit:	www.uaeinteract.com/adwls
Abu Dhabi International Jewellery Exhibition (ADIJEX):	www.uaeinteract.com/adijex
Abu Dhabi International Petroleum Exhibition (ADIPEC):	www.uaeinteract.com/adipec
Ajman Chamber of Commerce and Industry:	www.uaeinteract.com/ajcci

The UAE has worked hard to make shopping a pleasant and rewarding experience. Events such as Dubai Shopping Festival create unique opportunities for shoppers.

INTERNET LINKS

Al Ain Aerobatic Show:	www.uaeinteract.com/aaaerobatics
Arab Health:	www.uaeinteract.com/arabhealth
Cable, Satellite, Broadcast & Communications Exhibition:	www.uaeinteract.com/cabsat
Dubai International Humanitarian & Redevelopment Conf. & Exib. (DIHAD):	www.uaeinteract.com/dihad
Dubai Airshow:	www.uaeinteract.com/dubaiairshow
Dubai Chamber of Commerce and Industry:	www.uaeinteract.com/dcci
Dubai International Arabian Horse Championship:	www.uaeinteract.com/diahc
Dubai International Autumn Trade Fair (IATF):	www.uaeinteract.com/iatf
Dubai International Boat Show (DIBS) 2006:	www.uaeinteract.com/dibs
Dubai Jewellery Show:	www.uaeinteract.com/djs
Dubai Shopping Festival:	www.uaeinteract.com/mydsf
Dubai World Trade Centre (DWTC):	www.uaeinteract.com/dwtc
Environment 2007:	www.uaeinteract.com/environment2007
Expocentre Sharjah:	www.uaeinteract.com/expocentre
Fujairah Chamber of Commerce and Industry:	www.uaeinteract.com/fujairahchamber
GITEX:	www.uaeinteract.com/gitex
Global Woibex Forum:	www.uaeinteract.com/woibex
Gulfood:	www.uaeinteract.com/gulfood
IDEX:	www.uaeinteract.com/idex
Leaders in Dubai:	www.uaeinteract.com/leaders
Middle East International Motor Show at DIEC:	www.uaeinteract.com/dubaimotorshow
Motor Tuning Show (MTS 2006):	www.uaeinteract.com/mtsad
Ra's al-Khaimah Chamber of Commerce:	www.uaeinteract.com/rakchamber
Ra's al-Khaimah Exhibition Centre:	www.uaeinteract.com/rakexpo
ROADEX:	www.uaeinteract.com/roadex
Security and Safety Exhibition and Conference (Middle East 2005):	www.uaeinteract.com/securitysafety
Sharjah Chamber of Commerce and Industry:	www.uaeinteract.com/scci
Sharjah International Book Fair:	www.uaeinteract.com/sibf
The Arabian Travel Market (ATM):	www.uaeinteract.com/atm
The Fujairah Exhibition Centre (FEC):	www.uaeinteract.com/fec
The International Jewellery & Accessories Fair (IJAF):	www.uaeinteract.com/ijaf